Trying to Make Law Matter

Trying to Make Law Matter

Legal Reform and Labor Law in the Soviet Union

Kathryn Hendley

Ann Arbor
THE UNIVERSITY OF MICHIGAN PRESS

Published in the United States of America by
The University of Michigan Press
Manufactured in the United States of America
♾ Printed on acid-free paper

1999 1998 1997 1996 4 3 2 1

A CIP catalog record for this book is available from the British Library.

Hendley, Kathryn.
Trying to make law matter : legal reform and labor law in the Soviet Union / Kathryn Hendley.
p. cm.
Includes bibliographical references and index.
ISBN 0-472-10605-8 (hardcover : alk. paper)
1. Employees—Dismissal of—Law and legislation—Soviet Union. 2. Employees—Transfer—Law and legislation—Soviet Union. 3. Law and socialism. 4. Employees—Dismissal of—Soviet Union—Moscow—History. 5. Employees—Transfer—Soviet Union—Moscow—History. 6. Rule of law—Russia (Federation). 7. Effectiveness and validity of law—Russia (Federation) I. Title.
KLA1304.H46 1996
344.47'012596—dc20
[344.70412596] 95-52805
CIP

Contents

Acknowledgments

This book represents the culmination of a journey, both literally and figuratively. I am fortunate to have had many people who helped keep me going and contributed to my intellectual development, though the ultimate responsibility for the views expressed is mine alone.

I am indebted to a number of institutions for financial support. Research for this book was supported in part by a grant from the International Research and Exchanges Board (IREX), with funds provided by the National Endowment for the Humanities and the United States Information Agency. The United States Department of Education Fulbright-Hays Doctoral Dissertation Abroad Program provided additional funding for the field research in 1989–90. Funding for subsequent trips to Russia and support during the writing of the book was provided by the Social Science Research Council, the Berkeley–Stanford Program for Soviet and Post-Soviet Studies, the Center for German and European Studies at the University of California, Berkeley, and the Center for International Security and Arms Control at Stanford University.

On a more personal note, I am grateful to Gail Lapidus for encouraging me to pursue a topic that pushed beyond the then traditional boundaries of Sovietology. George Breslauer has also been steadfast in his support, both moral and intellectual. He did not hesitate to use his influence to help me gain access to Soviet industrial enterprises. Peter Maggs provided detailed comments on all of the chapters, often by return mail. Many hours of conversation with Dick Buxbaum have been critical in shaping my theoretical perspective on law. Finally, my deepest thanks go to Bob Kagan, who consistently pushed me to tackle the difficult questions and who provided much needed moral support during the many months of field research in Moscow and whose extensive, incisive, and timely comments on numerous drafts improved the book immeasurably.

Many others helped at various stages. Conversations with Peter Hauslohner, Jerry Hough, Mary McAuley, Bob Sharlet, Louise Shelley, Peter Solomon and Ger van den Berg, among others, helped sharpen the inquiry as I embarked on the research. Don Barry invited me to present my ideas at an early stage at the Conference on the Law-Governed State at Lehigh University in May 1991. Greg Grossman, Herb Jacobs, Sandy Muir, Martin Shapiro, and Brian Silver gave me valuable criticisms on parts of the book. Marina Lipelis provided editorial assistance.

The research for the case study that lies at the heart of the book was carried out in Moscow during the 1989–90 academic year, with briefer return trips in 1991, 1992, 1993, and 1994. Peter Hauslohner, Gianmaria Ajani, and Louise Shelley, among others, generously shared the names and coordinates of Soviet scholars, which was a tremendous help in getting started. In some ways, my life in Moscow was rather intellectually isolated, and I benefited greatly from conversations with more senior Western scholars who passed through during my year in Moscow, including Donna Bahry, Michael Burawoy, Jeff Hahn, Peter Juviler, Nancy Lubin, and Michael Swafford.

Organizing the research in Moscow proved to be a constant uphill battle. Unable to gain access to enterprises or trial courts through official channels, I was forced to rely on Soviet friends and colleagues, and I am particularly indebted to L. L. Grigoryan, E. L. Makeeva, M. N. Marchenko, M. Matskovskii, M. N. Nochevnik, Iu. I. Permiakov, A. A. Shugaev, A. A. Zverev, and the many managers who patiently answered my endless questions. Special thanks are due to M. I. Vinr, the general director of a Moscow factory, who opened my eyes to how Soviet enterprises really worked. R. Z. Livshits guided me through the intricacies of Soviet labor law. On a personal level, Marina Glukhovskaia and her family opened their home to me and made it mine as well.

I would also like to thank the Centre for Socialist Law at the Faculty of Law of the University of London (William E. Butler, Director) and the Documentation Office for East European Law of the University of Leiden (F. J. M. Feldbrugge, Director). I took advantage of the splendid library facilities of these two centers during the fall of 1990 after leaving Moscow.

I have also been fortunate to be surrounded by a group of supportive friends who made the researching and writing of the book more pleasant. Particular thanks are due to Jane Dawson, Jehanne Gheith, Kelly Smith, Tanya Smith, Jay Tobin, and Glennys Young.

My most profound thanks go to my father and my sister, who have been unflinching in their support for me throughout all of my career permutations. They provided encouragement at every step and a welcome refuge whenever it was needed.

Part 1
Statement of the Problem

CHAPTER 1

Introduction

What does it mean to say that law "matters"? How do we determine whether law "matters" in a given society? At a minimal level, we can say that law, defined as a body of formally articulated rules that are enforced by specially authorized officials,[1] matters when it affects attitudes and behavior of the rulers and the ruled within society. But this definition of law and its societal relevance is not satisfactorily subtle, for it leads to the conclusion that law matters in all societies. After all, conceiving of a society in which law is entirely absent is virtually impossible.[2] Even the most extreme authoritarian regimes have legal rules by which society is ordered, both publicly and privately.[3] Despite the oppressive content and often capricious enforcement of these rules, people nonetheless make some effort to adapt their behavior to them.

While the importance of law under such conditions cannot be denied, my interest goes beyond the capacity of law to impose basic social order in a *coercive* fashion. More interesting is the capacity of law to serve as a means of constraining official power, vindicating citizens' grievances, and facilitating private transactions. That is, we can speak of "law" mattering in a consciously *reciprocal* sense that acknowledges the existence of both state and society as participants in the creation and maintenance of a legal regime. Seen from this vantage point, law comes to matter reciprocally within a society when it is valued by political elites and by significant portions of the citizenry, and when it is generally embraced by both as a mechanism for remedying wrongs and advancing interests.

This study is concerned with the social and political forces and factors that promote (or impede) the realization, in varying degrees, of a legal order in which law can be said to matter in this reciprocal sense. More specifically, it is a study of the effort to institutionalize the rule of law in the Soviet Union—to make law matter in a reciprocal rather than a coercive sense—and the attendent obstacles. The Soviet context raises the question of whether the rule of law can become an institutionalized part of social inter-

action in a regime that lacks, for the most part, private property and free economic markets and in which multiparty democracy is absent or fragile.

The implicit distinction between ideal-typical societies in which (1) law matters coercively and (2) law matters reciprocally is grounded in the basic conceptualization of law and the role of law in society. At its most extreme, the coercive vision of law mattering is based on the positivist view of law as a mere projection of state authority. This top-down view leaves little room for society; citizens' only function is to obey the law generated from above without question. The emphasis is on law as a tool of social control rather than on law as a force that binds society together by promoting social cohesion and stability.

In contrast, the notion of law mattering reciprocally reflects a vision of law as a means of structuring society based on broadly shared values.[4] The defining elements of law that matters reciprocally are legitimacy, accessibility, and efficacy. Most critical in fleshing out this ideal type is the institutionalization of universality in law; that is, that law binds the rulers and the ruled in like fashion. Universality also implies that people can rely on law as a predictable force within society. The underlying rules are relatively stable and generally perceived as fair. Concretizing law in this way arguably legitimizes law and generates trust for law.

No society can live up to an ideal type. But Soviet law was almost the mirror image of law that matters reciprocally. Throughout the history of the Soviet Union, law was generally viewed as a coercive and effective instrument of the state for imposing its policy goals on an often reluctant but necessarily politically passive citizenry. Law had no autonomy within society.[5]

In the hands of the Party elite, law became a flexible tool. This state of affairs had a corrosive effect on the role of law in Soviet society. Law proved incapable of restraining the powerful. Years of watching law and legal institutions being manipulated by the Party tainted them in the eyes of the public. Ordinary citizens grew skeptical of the ability of courts, for example, to act impartially and so shied away from using courts to resolve disputes. Even the powerful shied away from law, for power is rarely absolute. Once stripped of its capacity to serve as a relatively neutral language of mediation in disputes, the political elite was subject to having its interests trumped in favor of those with more power. For all, the legal process was regarded as best avoided—the idea of using it to further or to protect individual interests would have been rejected as ludicrous. Thus, to the extent that law mattered in the Soviet Union, it mattered coercively rather than reciprocally.

With the accession to power in 1985 of M. S. Gorbachev came a rethinking of the role of law.[6] He and his supporters often spoke of the need to create a socialist law-based state *(sotsialisticheskoe pravovoe gosudarstvo)* in the Soviet Union.[7] The goal was a state in which law represented a stable force that established the ground rules for all strata of society—a shift toward law mattering reciprocally. In other words, the Gorbachev regime sought to move away from the coercive image of law as a sword of Damocles always hanging over the public toward a more inviting image of law as an expression of community norms that would be enforced in an evenhanded manner by legal institutions.

The Scholarly Context

The questions raised by this study have not been widely addressed by scholars of Soviet law. As might be expected from the positivist conceptualization of law that held sway during the Soviet period, Soviet scholars tended to limit themselves to studying statutory law.[8] Even in the late 1980s, when I was carrying out my field research in Moscow, the idea of studying the law in action, for example, examining the implementation of the law governing dismissals and transfers of Soviet workers, struck most scholars I interviewed as bizarre and somehow unscholarly. Although there were some who studied the "effectiveness" of various aspects of law,[9] they were the exceptions. As a general matter, Soviet scholars did not allow themselves to question publicly whether the law was actually being implemented at the grassroots level.

Western scholars were able to be more forthright about Soviet law. They understood that much of the written law never made the transition from rhetoric to reality and that it was subject to being countermanded by Party officials (whether pursuing their own agendas or following orders from Moscow).[10] The documentation of this gap between the law on the books and as implemented came primarily through firsthand accounts written by emigre Soviet legal scholars and practitioners.[11] While providing valuable information, these accounts lack the objectivity and intellectual rigor that a less testimonial approach might provide. For most of the Soviet period, however, Western scholars were unable to gain the access necessary for detailed empirical research. The decades of autarky created a distrust of foreigners—a legacy that is now only slowly being dissipated.[12]

Western scholars had no choice but to make do with what they could learn from written sources and from the few Soviet legal scholars willing to take a chance by consorting with foreigners. As a result, the Western scholarship on the Soviet legal system focuses principally on written law. Detailed analyses of statutory law exist for almost every substantive area of law.[13] These studies do not merely duplicate the efforts of Soviet scholars but complement them in that the Western scholars bring different methodological approaches to the enterprise. At the same time, while exhaustively documenting the twists and turns of the written law, these studies devote little attention to implementation. As a body of work, they provide an impressive overview of the formal legal structure of the Soviet Union but little insight into how law functioned within Soviet society.

Some Western scholars managed to break out of the constraints typically imposed by Soviet authorities. During the 1960s, Mary McAuley gained access to several Leningrad factories and studied relations between workers and management.[14] She demonstrated that notwithstanding the collectivist ideology of Leninism individual conflicts continued to arise, and she documented how they were resolved. Her interest in the role of law within the enterprise, however, was peripheral. Her work is helpful in understanding the realities of labor relations in the Soviet context, and it provided a kind of baseline for my research.[15]

Several decades later, Nicholas Lampert returned to the issue of Soviet labor relations, with a particular focus on attitudes toward whistle-blowers.[16] Refused access to enterprises and workers in the Soviet Union, he interviewed Soviet emigres in Israel. This methodology, while yielding information unavailable elsewhere, is problematic in that it relies on informants who demonstrated their alienation from the Soviet system by leaving at a time when this could not be done casually.[17] He concludes that the law did not act as a meaningful constraint on enterprise management in its dealings with whistle-blowers. Notwithstanding the letter of the law, which prohibited retaliatory dismissals, ways were found to get rid of perceived troublemakers. Lampert then extends this conclusion to Soviet law in general, which represents quite a leap of faith.[18] Even if Lampert's conclusion that law was irrelevant in the Soviet workplace is accepted at face value, his study fails to address the broader theoretical issues that motivate my own study; namely, why law became so marginalized and what obstacles exist to the evolution of a new role for law in post-Soviet Russian society.

In addition to these monographs, there are two studies of the Soviet court system that draw on extensive field research in Moscow. One was completed in the ideological "thaw" of the Khrushchev period,[19] and the other was written in the more recent Gorbachev era of *glasnost'*.[20] Both are primarily factual in nature, providing a glimpse into the day-to-day routine of Soviet courts and thereby a frame of reference for my observations. Neither makes any effort to develop a theoretical explanation of the role of courts during the Soviet period or to place the Soviet experience in comparative context.

My work represents a new direction in scholarship on Soviet law from both substantive and methodological points of view. My theoretical arguments are based on a detailed case study of the implementation of the law governing the dismissal and transfer of Soviet workers during the 1980s. Although I reviewed relevant published materials, I did not rely on them exclusively. My research also included fieldwork in Moscow factories and trial courts, thereby allowing me a firsthand view of how law worked. Only by understanding the specific characteristics of the gap between the written law and the law as implemented in the Soviet context can a realistic evaluation be made of the obstacles to the realization of a legal order in which law matters not coercively but reciprocally.

Moreover, the questions with which I am concerned go beyond narrow doctrinal issues to the very heart of the role played by law in society. I have been fortunate in the timing of my work. During the course of researching and writing this book, the Soviet Union unraveled, as did the structure and ideological hold of the Communist Party on Soviet society, which had previously seemed so invincible.[21]

While more than seven decades of Leninism leave behind a legacy that must be taken into account,[22] the end of Party domination gave me the freedom to explore issues of tremendous theoretical significance. These include such fundamental questions as the conceptualization of law, the relationship between democracy, markets, and the rule of law and the reshaping of legal culture, all of which contribute to the central theoretical concern of this study: how to make law matter in a reciprocal fashion. Western legal theorists have long debated the process by which the rule of law became institutionalized in the West and have developed competing models.[23] Of course, these theories were premised on the transition from feudalism to liberal capitalism.[24] Scholars who studied the Soviet Union assumed the underlying models to be irrelevant, largely due to the specificity of the Soviet experience and the presumption of continued dominance of the Party over political life.[25] Comparativists interested more broadly in the transitions from various forms of authoritarianism (including Leninism) to democracy have generally ignored law and the importance of making a transition in the legal system simultaneously with reforms in the political and economic systems.[26] Thus, my work represents one of the first systematic efforts to address the necessary prerequisites for the evolution of an autonomous legal system from Leninism.

The book is organized into four parts. In part 1, the role played by law in the advanced industrialized democracies is compared with its role under state socialism. Law under liberal democracy has become an interactive process in which state and society participate in shaping the legal order on a relatively equal footing. In contrast, Leninism subordinated law to politics, creating a legal order in which law mattered coercively.

Part 2 is a case study of the implementation of a specific law in the Soviet Union during the 1980s. The case study is designed to illustrate the obstacles to the institutionalization of the rule of law and to bring into sharper focus the contours of the gap between Soviet law in theory and in practice. Under scrutiny is the law governing dismissals and transfers of workers at the initiative of management. I chose this law in large part because the published materials (including concrete case decisions) suggested that the law, in fact, protected workers' rights and constrained managerial arbitrariness. In other words, the law in question appeared to be one of a very few Soviet laws that actually worked or "mattered" in a reciprocal sense, that is, it was regularly invoked by ordinary citizens and operated to restrain official arbitrariness.

Chapter 3 outlines the relevant statutory law on dismissals and transfers of Soviet workers and reviews how this law had been interpreted in the published case decisions. A careful reading of these materials suggests that the law favored workers over management. This inference is drawn not from the fact that workers usually prevailed in the published cases—though they did—but from the way in which they prevailed. The courts consistently held management to a higher burden of proof on the critical issue of whether the workers' rights had been violated. While mere oral allegations by workers could shift the burden of proof to management, the courts required management to provide conclusive documentary evidence in order to rebut these unsubstantiated charges. The courts seemed to be bending over backward to ensure that workers' rights were vigorously protected—that the letter and the spirit of the law were strictly enforced. Thus, based on the published materials, we might well conclude that Soviet workers regarded their rights as meaningful and trusted the courts to protect them.

In chapter 4, this hypothesis is tested by bringing in the evidence gathered during my fieldwork. While in Moscow during 1989–90, I studied eight industrial enterprises and reviewed the records of two Moscow trial courts for the 1980s. What I discovered was a pattern of perfunctory behavior. At every stage of the legal process, beginning with the hearing of the factory trade union committee and continuing through the trial court proceedings, those charged with implementing the law went through the motions of obeying the statutory law, but their behavior was largely devoid of substance. Put simply, while judges and managers obeyed the letter of the law, they ignored the spirit of the law. Thus, the published materials gave rise to a misleading image of law and legal institutions. By digging deeper, I came away with a more realistic image of law that serves the interests of the powerful—the managers—rather than an image of law that protects those incapable of protecting themselves—the workers.

In part 3, I look beyond the existence of a gap between law in theory and in practice in the Soviet Union to examine why it exists and persists and what it suggests about the obstacles to the institutionalization of the rule of law in post-Soviet Russia.

Chapter 5 focuses on the courts. My fieldwork revealed a general lack of impartiality on the part of lower court Soviet judges. This prompts an inquiry into the preconditions for creating an impartial judiciary. As a threshold matter, the concept of impartiality is broken down into its institutional and individual components, each of which is necessary but not sufficient on its own. Consequently, merely removing the corrosive influence of the Communist Party is not sufficient to revitalize the judicial system. Instead, much deeper structural and cultural changes are needed. During the Soviet period, a culture of dependency evolved within the judicial corps that has outlived the Soviet Union and from which judges must be weaned.

Chapter 6 looks at the Soviet workplace. The evidence strongly suggests that law failed to constrain management. Indeed, by all accounts, Soviet managers became expert at meeting the technical requirements imposed by the law while ignoring the deeper purposes of the law within society.

The roots of the perfunctory attitude toward law, which was exhibited not just by managers but also by trade union activists and workers, lies in the underlying economic incentive system, which provided no deterrent against legal evasion and often even encouraged such behavior. The disciplining force of the market was absent in the Soviet context. The administrative-command system was rigidly hierarchical; the managers' superiors in the industrial ministries and the planning apparatus were solely concerned with whether the enterprise had fulfilled the economic plan. No one cared much how this was accomplished or how many legal corners were cut along the way. By the same token, there was no real pressure on managers from below to comply with the law. The cooptation of Soviet trade unions by management was well known to all. Workers assumed that the influence of enterprise management extended to the courts as well. As a result, they became deeply skeptical of the legal process and saw no point in mobilizing the law to protect themselves.

In part 4, the disparate threads are woven together into an argument concerning the necessary prerequisites for the evolution toward a post-Leninist legal order in which law matters reciprocally. These include a number of structural changes, particularly in the organization of the judiciary and of economic relations. But more critical is a change in the way people from all political strata think about law. The prevailing contempt for law must be replaced by a respect for law and a willingness to obey and use it when appropriate.

This argument stresses the critical importance of market forces in making law matter reciprocally. As managers are no longer able to rely on administrative levers to enforce contractual obligations, a need (and, consequently, a demand) for a common language for arbitrating among competing forces within society will arise.[27] Law can serve as this common language. In theory, the introduction of freer markets for labor, capital, and commodities brings societal pressure to conform with legal standards, at least when those standards conform to generally accepted community practices.

This brings home the importance of the "supply side" of the equation for institutionalizing the rule of law. Demand is not enough. If demands for law are not met, then there is a real danger that contempt for law will grow deeper. The primary "supplier" of law is the state. At a minimum, the state must (1) provide legislation or administrative regulations that are comprehensible and accessible, (2) provide a neutral forum for adjudication and enforce its decisions (even when they go against the interests of the state), and (3) continue to maintain law and order.

This raises the question of what the future holds for Russia. At this point, definitive predictions about the future seem rather foolish. Democracy in any form is certainly not a foregone conclusion, nor is it necessarily a precondition for the institutionalization of the rule of law. In the final chapter, several possible paths of development are explored, and what each might portend for the role of law within society is analyzed.

CHAPTER 2

Law under Capitalism and Leninism: A Comparative Analysis

Introduction

During the late 1980s, a new element crept into the political rhetoric of the Soviet Union: the demand for legality. The Polish legal theorist, Adam Czarnota, argues that the revival of the *idea* of law was one of the primary features of the revolutionary changes that swept the formerly Leninist bloc.[1] The rhetoric reflected a desire for a fundamental change in the role played by law in these societies—a desire for law to matter in a reciprocal sense.

Leninism gave rise to a legal system under which the powerful were able to manipulate the law to serve their own institutional and individual interests. The courts lacked the authority to reign in the "new class" *nomenklatura* of Party officials.[2] Indeed, judges' continued tenure in office and their retention in the lower rank of that caste depended on staying in the former's good graces.[3] The absence of a consistently apolitical and neutral judiciary contributed to the development of a legal culture in which people were highly cynical about the law and continue to be skeptical about the capacity of the legal system to be reformed in a meaningful way.

Law under Capitalism

Given that the participants in this reform process are looking to the Western industrialized democracies for guidance as they endeavor to reshape the Soviet legal system, a brief review of the key functions of law in these societies is in order.[4] Generalizing about the role played by law in the Western industrialized democracies is not an easy task.[5] Continental Europe is dominated by a civil law legal tradition and an inquisitorial legal system, whereas England and the United States share a common law legal tradition and an adversarial legal system.[6] Even countries that share the same legal tradition often diverge on specific procedural and substantive issues. Indeed, viewed from the perspective of the practitioner or the citizen, the differences often seem to outweigh the similarities. However, if the inquiry is raised to a higher level of abstraction, the commonalities rise to the surface, thereby allowing the development of an ideal type of a state in which law matters reciprocally.

Although Western industrialized democracies uniformly claim the rule of law as one of their formative and guiding principles, the extent to which they are true to its ideals varies greatly, both among and within these countries.[7] As Selznick has noted, "the rule of law . . . refers to aspirations that distinguish a developed legal order from a system of subordination to naked power."[8] Thus, the presence or absence of the rule of law in a society is not an either/or proposition but rather a more/less proposition.[9]

In addition, ideas of the rule of law vary, from a "minimalist" version, in which the state is constrained to some degree by formally stated legal rules, to a "maximalist" version, in which there are strong constitutional protections for individual rights, juridical decisions trump ordinary legislation[10] and rules themselves must be justified "in depth" in terms of principles of justice.[11] Thus, societies can be conceptualized as existing on a spectrum, with placement of a given society being a matter of constant reevaluation.[12]

One measure of the rule of law as a living phenomenon is the degree to which law, in fact, fulfills certain social functions. In contrast to the peripheral role played by law under Leninism, liberal capitalism has fostered legal systems in which law acts to assure the stability of expectations of rulers and ruled alike in both public and private transactions and relationships. What does this mean in practice?[13] In the public realm, law (1) serves as a *legitimating force,* both in terms of preserving the existing system and in terms of maintaining an acceptable level of public order and (2) acts to *restrain* the power of officialdom and to *regulate* the pursuit and transfer of political power.

In the private realm, the multifarious roles played by law can be summed up by three general categories. First, it *encourages economic efficiency* by guaranteeing and facilitating the fair operation of markets. This is accomplished by a variety of means, including legislation (and enforcement mechanisms) to protect a reasonable degree of freedom of contract, to prevent fraud and anticompetitive behavior, and to compensate for "market failures," such as pollution and compensation for workers injured on the job. Second, law endeavors to *prevent harm* through regulations on such matters as product safety, environmental pollution, workplace safety, and civil rights and provides redress when harm does occur. Third, law provides a workable mechanism for *resolving disputes.*

Underlying these basic roles played by law in Western societies is the common dynamic of law not only as *legitimator* and *regulator,* but also as *facilitator.* Ideally, law serves as a means (both substantively and procedurally) for citizens to fulfill their goals and redress their grievances in accordance with socially sanctioned expectations. The fact that, in practice, the legal systems of the Western industrial democracies often fall short of these lofty goals is not terribly important.[14] More relevant is their common vision of law as important and relevant not only to society as a whole but also to individual citizens.

From a comparative perspective, this raises the question of why law has come to play these roles in the Western context. Put more graphically, under what conditions does law come to matter in more than a coercive sense? Legal theorists in Western societies, where law *does* matter reciprocally, have scarcely begun to address this issue. Speculatively, however, I would suggest that there are five critical preconditions: (1) conceptualization of law as a reciprocal process, (2) procedural regularity, (3) substantive legitimacy of law, (4) efficacy of law, and (5) an accessible system for resolving disputes.

Conception of Law: Reciprocity

While acting to legitimize the existing social and political order, law in democratic Western societies is not viewed as coterminous with the state. The positivistic notion of law as a one-way projection of authority from the state has been thoroughly rejected.[15] More satisfying to democratic societies is Fuller's definition of law as "the enterprise of subjecting human conduct to the governance of rules."[16] This notion of law as an enterprise suggests that law is a collaborative process in which both state and society participate. Citizens believe that law should and to an extent does reflect their interests, not just the interests of the politically or economically powerful.[17] This belief buttresses the legitimacy of law and fosters a willingness to obey and use the law.[18] Over time, these beliefs deepen into a sense of trust in the system.

The hallmark of this process is reciprocity.[19] This reciprocity lessens the likelihood of law stagnating and becoming unresponsive to the needs of society, which, in turn, tends to undermine its legitimacy. Although the law's central purpose is to stabilize and fulfill societal expectations, the nature of these expectations is constantly changing. Sometimes the dynamic is circular, as the law itself becomes the driving force behind these attitudinal changes.[20]

Procedural Regularity

The legal order that emerges coincidentally with this conceptualization of law as a reciprocal force is characterized by the rule of law. The rule of law has meant somewhat different things to different people over time and has often taken on considerable ideological baggage.[21] I understand the term, and in this study will use it, as a procedural concept.[22] It sets the rules of the game for the struggle over power and, in so doing, endeavors to establish a level playing field. Selznick is helpful in this regard. He points out that the rule of law "has to do mainly with *how* policies and rules are made and applied rather than with their content."[23]

The core element of the rule of law is that law applies in equal measure to the powerful and the nonpowerful and that legal institutions have sufficient authority and independence to make meaningful the remedies imposed against the powerful. The rule of law dictates that law limits the freedom of action of political authorities and legislators as well as citizens.[24] If those who make the rules fail to obey them, they breach the bond of reciprocity with the citizenry and seriously undermine their authority and the legitimacy of the law itself.[25]

The critical institutional component of the rule of law is an independent judicial system.[26] The duties of judges, administrators, and legislators are compartmentalized. Judges stand apart from the political fray, leaving them free to enforce and interpret the law with no danger of interference from those in power. At the same time, they take care not to overstep their authority by interfering in substantive policy issues.[27] According to Nonet and Selznick, "Legal institutions purchase procedural autonomy at the price of substantive subordination."[28] Their authority stems largely from their perceived political neutrality. Consequently, judicial decisions, to the extent possible, should be tied to positive law or precedent; judges should "make law" only when statutes are unclear or incomplete.[29]

The goal of equal justice for all that underlies the rule of law is further buttressed by a series of lower level procedural guarantees. Law is openly promulgated and available to all at a minimum of effort and expense. The substance of a given law is not subject to constant alterations. The level of vagueness and internal contradictions of positive law is kept to an absolute minimum. Finally, law does not impose duties on individuals or entities that are impossible to fulfill. Fuller argues that the presence of these procedural guarantees imbues law with an "inner morality."[30]

For me, the rule of law refers to procedural regularity within the legal system. Because of the tendency to overintellectualize what is meant by the rule of law, I do not use it in the remainder of this book. Instead, I use the less ideologically loaded phrase, "procedural regularity." Procedural regularity is, of course, merely one of the prerequisites for a legal system in which law matters reciprocally.

Substantive Legitimacy

Procedural regularity can, however, be a rather hollow concept. It makes no demands on the content of the law; it requires only that the law be promulgated and implemented in a given manner.[31] Yet more is needed if law is to become relevant to people's lives. If law is to come to matter, people must find the substance of the law to be basically just. In Weberian terms, formal rationality, that is, procedural regularity, must come to be augmented by substantive rationality.[32]

Defining substantive legitimacy in terms of justice, while intuitively appealing, is not particularly helpful because of the elusive nature of justice. Attempts to define the latter lead us back to the endless and often tiresome debate between theories of natural law and positivism. On the other hand, attempts to define justice within specific societies reveal its inevitable cultural relativism. Cahn states the problem cogently: "The lofty abstract concept lurks somewhere beyond our discernment; it offers no incarnation which may be trusted as quite unmixed and pure."[33]

Although the knowledge of what constitutes perfect justice may well be beyond us, what is knowable and *does* serve as a powerful motivating force is the sense of injustice.[34] Indeed, Cahn suggests justice should be understood as "the *active process* of remedying or preventing what would arouse the sense of injustice."[35] The sense of injustice is a more culturally neutral, less elusive concept than justice. Shklar describes it as "the betrayal that we experience when others disappoint expectations that they have created in us."[36] It can be provoked by situations in which human dignity is not respected, where the punishment is out of proportion to the crime (or, in the civil context, where the remedy does not fit the wrong), where agreements are not kept or where hard-won property or earnings are arbitrarily taken away, or where people are treated differently for no apparent reason, even if "reason" here is to a degree culturally determined. The list is endless, but the common theme is the perception of being treated unfairly.

This sense that the law ought to be basically fair, despite being difficult to capture in words, underpins the legal systems of the Western liberal democracies. This is not to say that all laws enjoy universal respect. After all, no heterogeneous society can possibly have a body of laws that all citizens consider just. As a general matter, however, the underlying trust of most citizens has given rise to legal cultures in which, for the most part, the law is respected and obeyed.

Efficacy of Law

Western legal systems are also characterized by a relatively high rate of mobilization of the law. People tend to make use of the law when they feel their rights have been violated. Certainly, trust in the basic fairness of the law is important in encouraging this. Just as important, however, is a belief that the remedies provided by law are meaningful in a practical sense.

Mobilizing one's rights via the legal system is rarely the easy way out. Even under the best of circumstances, considerable time and money are expended.[37] In order to make this worthwhile, the wronged party must believe that it will get its just deserts or, at the very least, that it can recover its losses. When there is a misfit between the harm suffered and the remedy provided for by law, people tend to bypass the legal system and pursue other means for recovering their losses.[38]

Accessible Legal System

Whether people mobilize their rights when violated is not just a function of the appeal of the remedies provided by law but also of the accessibility of legal institutions themselves. What does it mean to say that a legal system is accessible? Basically, it means that a person is able to get a dispute resolved by a legal institution without undue delay or expense. Also relevant, however, is the complexity of the system, that is, whether a relatively well-educated person can file a complaint without help from a legally trained professional. If some type of assistance is required, it does not necessarily follow that the system is inaccessible. Instead, the inquiry shifts to whether such assistance is available at a reasonable cost.

Indeed, the legal systems of most Western liberal democracies are characterized by a high level of complexity. To some extent, the existence of an independent legal profession compensates for this—but not completely. Lawyers and other legal professionals can act not only as facilitators but also as gatekeepers. Access to the legal system can be effectively denied to those who cannot afford their services and to those whose legal claims are considered weak.[39]

Conclusion

Within this ideal-typical legal system developed under liberal capitalism, law matters in a reciprocal sense. Law is generated through a process in which both state and society participate, and disputes are resolved by politically neutral judges. Citizens view law as a tool of liberation and protection rather than oppression. They trust the system and are willing to use it when warranted in order to vindicate their rights.

Law under Leninism: 1917–85

A very different picture emerges when examining the role played by law under Leninism. Before turning to that question, however, two points need to be made about Leninism and Leninist legal systems. The first is the obvious point that Leninism no longer exists as a potent political force. During the research and writing of this book, the Communist regimes of Eastern Europe and the Soviet Union collapsed.[40] Leninism has thus become a historical phenomenon. As a result, this book is about what was rather than what is. As so often is the case, however, what was is having a profound influence on what is and what will be. Leninism is deeply rooted in the fiber of these societies, and its legacy will live on for generations.[41] This is particularly true for the Soviet Union, which lived with Leninism for almost three-quarters of a century.[42]

The second threshold issue is more a point of clarification. In discussing Leninist legal systems, I am drawing almost exclusively on the Soviet experience. This is appropriate because the Soviet Union consistently held itself out as a model to be copied religiously.[43] Furthermore, only in the Soviet case can the full developmental arc be seen. Following the October Revolution, the Bolsheviks were faced with a basically European legal system, which they set out to transform. They ultimately created the system of socialist law that, despite having roots in the civil law tradition, is typically recognized as being distinct from it.[44] Understanding the twists and turns of this developmental process is essential if the final product is to be comprehended fully. Yet these permutations took place only in the Soviet context. By the time Stalin moved to impose Leninism on Eastern Europe in the wake of World War II, the legal system had gelled and so was imported and imposed with little regard for local customs and norms.

Soviet law presents an almost classic example of what Nonet and Selznick have characterized as "repressive law."[45] Law mattered coercively. In the public realm, law acted to maintain the existing political system and to forestall social unrest. In the private realm, law's basic functions were threefold. First, law endeavored to further the economic goals of the regime.[46] Second, it reinforced the basic social values espoused by the regime, while attempting to extirpate competing values.[47] Finally, law provided a mechanism for enforcing norms and resolving disputes.

As in Western liberal democracies, law under Leninism served as a legitimating form for governmental policies. There was, however, a qualitative difference in the nature of the legitimation process. In the West, the law serves to enforce ideals that large segments of society have come to agree upon through democratic processes. Open to debate is whether the widespread Western belief in the "basically fair" nature of the legal system is warranted, that is, whether those in power create a false consciousness among the masses.[48] For my purposes, it is enough that people by and large have come to trust the law and the legal system to uphold their rights and interests.

In contrast, law under Leninism was used in such a blatantly instrumental manner that no pretense could be made that it expressed the interests of the people. Instead, the masses viewed law as a sword to be wielded at the pleasure of the regime rather than as a shield to protect them from abuses of power by the regime. Despite the existence of an ostensibly practicable system for resolving disputes, it was bypassed both for disputes among individuals and for disputes between an individual and the state. The legal system was considered an appendage of the regime to be avoided whenever possible.

What are the conditions under which law becomes so thoroughly marginalized? Why didn't law matter in the Soviet Union? A reexamination of the general avenues of inquiry that helped clarify why the legal systems of the Western liberal democracies have taken on such a distinctive shape will bring into focus the reasons for the general irrelevance of law under Leninism.

Conception of Law: Political Instrumentalism

Perhaps most important, law never became an autonomous force in Soviet society. Instead, law was always closely identified with the state (and the state with the Communist Party) and subordinated to the state's desire for self-perpetuation. Law was viewed not as an interactive process that took account of societal interests but as a one-way projection of authority that reflected only the interests of those in power. The masses had no role to play in the law-making process. Their only contribution was to obey the law unquestioningly once promulgated.

The highly instrumental nature of law followed logically from the political structure that Lenin created. He argued that the reins of power should be placed in the hands of the proletariat. Like Marx, however, he believed that the false consciousness created among the masses by the oppressive forces of capitalism had rendered them incapable of acting in their best interests. As a result, Lenin developed the notion of the vanguard party, whose function was to propel society forward, to act in the best interests of the proletariat until it had developed the necessary consciousness to act on its own. A pattern was created. Officials of the Communist Party became accustomed to presenting the Party's interests (and sometimes their own personal interests) as those of society.[49] The development of the policy of democratic centralism and the consequent stifling of debate within the Party well before Lenin's death in 1924 dashed any hope that as society became better educated the masses would find (and could express) their voice.[50]

While instrumentalism was the defining feature of Soviet law, the precise nature of this instrumentalism changed over time. And the extent to which the law was openly coercive made it particularly susceptible to such change. As Nonet and Selznick suggest, the need for overt coercion recedes over time. The society becomes worn down and takes on what John Austin called "the general habit of obedience."[51]

Law under Lenin. Despite Lenin's formal legal training, law was not central role to his theoretical writings.[52] Like Marx, he viewed law as just one of many means used by the ruling class to oppress the workers. When the Bolsheviks came to power, they set about to reverse the process.[53] To this end, they quickly dismantled the tsarist judicial structure, replacing it with local people's courts and revolutionary tribunals.[54] More important, however, was their skepticism about the existing written law. These newly created legal institutions were instructed to disregard such law whenever it contravened the spirit of the revolution. Just what this actually meant was left to be determined on a case-by-case basis. This legal nihilism rendered law inherently unstable.[55]

The practice of defining law in terms of revolutionary justice made it flexible and opened the door to its becoming coercive and arbitrary. Law became a tool for maintaining social order and consolidating political power, to be used at the discretion of the Bolsheviks. Not surprisingly, the Bolsheviks used law (or the color of law) to justify the elimination of their perceived political rivals and to legitimate their assumption of control in the far-flung regions of the former Russian Empire.[56]

In the first years after the October Revolution, this vision of law was justified in pragmatic terms. Arguments would occasionally be advanced that framed the rejection of tsarist law in terms of the "withering away of law" predicted by Marx, but they lacked theoretical rigor. The theoretical underpinnings came later with the "commodity exchange theory of law" articulated by E. B. Pashukanis and his followers during the mid-1920s and early 1930s, the period of the New Economic Policy.[57]

As the name given to his theory suggests, Pashukanis saw all legal relationships, both public and private, as based on the exchange of commodities. In bourgeois capitalist societies, laws and legal institutions had been created and were necessary to police these exchanges. In his view, the elimination of capitalism would likewise eliminate the need for law. Thus, capitalist law was not to be replaced by socialist law but rather by no law. Sharlet comments that "Pashukanis predicted that law (that is, private law and the legal state) would gradually begin to 'wither away,' as soon as its economic prerequisites of private property and commodity exchange were replaced by a public property economy based on the principle of economic planning."[58]

Pashukanis's ideas enjoyed great influence in the late 1920s. Indeed, as Sharlet has noted, his theory was "accorded the status of *the* Marxist theory of law."[59] Initially, it dovetailed nicely with the interests of those in power. Pashukanis argued that law was a necessary but temporary expedient for a revolutionary state. Thus, the promulgation of statutory codes and the reconstitution of legal institutions beginning in 1918 were not necessarily inconsistent with his theory. Had Pashukanis's approach prevailed, these laws would have been gradually phased out with the transition to communism. Events dictated otherwise. Neither Pashukanis nor his ideas were to survive Stalinism.[60]

Law under Stalin. The "commodity exchange theory of law" was fundamentally inconsistent with Stalinism. As the so-called Stalin Constitution of 1936 vividly demonstrates, Stalin had no intention of allowing the state to wither away. Just the opposite: he wanted a strong state, the prerogatives of which would be protected by a variety of stable institutions, including law.[61] As this suggests, the concept of law that emerged under Stalinism was highly positivistic, that is, law was the command of the sovereign, not some body of higher or fixed principles that could constrain the ruler's discretion. Yet the legal utopianism (or perhaps nihilism) of the immediate postrevolutionary period was not completely abandoned in that "revolutionary justice" continued to be prominent among the stated purposes to be served by law.

This bizarre combination of positivism and ideological fervor laid the groundwork for the emergence of a legal culture that Sharlet aptly characterizes as "a dual system of law and terror."[62] The use by Stalin and his henchmen of law (or color of law) as a means of sanitizing the massive purges of supposed "enemies of the people" has been well documented by memoirists and historians.[63] At the same time, however, legal institutions operated in a fairly normal fashion when confronted with cases that lacked political significance. Yet one could never be sure that law would operate with regularity and, for the average citizen, law inevitably became tainted by its use as a tool of repression.

Even in its most politically neutral form, law under Stalinism was very much a top-down phenomenon.[64] Law was conceptualized as a set of norms emanating from and enforced by the state with no meaningful role for the masses. The efforts by Soviet theorists of the period to prove that law reflected the will of the people by arguing that they had voted unanimously for the legislators who passed the laws represented a gross perversion of the logic of representative democracy. After all, elections in the Soviet Union involved only one candidate from the ruling Communist Party and were compulsory affairs. People obeyed the law not because they believed it reflected their interests but because they feared the consequences of not obeying. In other words, law mattered coercively.

Law under Stalin's Successors. Although the death of Stalin in 1953 brought an abrupt end to the reign of political terror and thus radically diminished the coercive element of Soviet law, it effected little change in the underlying definition of law. Law continued to be viewed as a one-way projection of authority from the state. None of the Soviet leaders from Khrushchev to Chernenko made any real effort to recast law as an interactive process that depended on achieving a consensus among the rulers and the ruled. Yet the decrease in the level of coercion brought a corresponding decrease in the level of fear. Consequently, the willingness to obey the law (which had never been grounded in a sense of reciprocity or voluntarism) also decreased precipitously. This is not to say that chaos ensued but that over time people became more and more willing to skirt the law.

Procedural Regularity

Accountability of Officialdom. Nonet and Selznick suggest that the absence of procedural regularity is a hallmark of "repressive law," and the Soviet case provides ample support. Critical in this regard is that the law did not apply equally to everyone. Instead, political criteria, including Communist Party membership, were relevant and often decisive in determining the applicability of the law. While legal institutions consistently took extralegal factors into account, the probative value of various factors changed over time in response to the prevailing political conditions.

Immediately after the October Revolution, class origins were most important. As Hazard notes, "there was agreement that until society was no longer divided into classes, the new court must be a class court defending the interests of the toiling elements of the population."[65] This utopian notion of courts as "proletarian class courts" is consistent with, and perhaps necessary for, the equally utopian notion of "revolutionary justice."[66]

As the revolutionary fervor died down and society began to normalize in the early 1920s, class origins took a backseat to Communist Party affiliation. In theory, Party membership was relevant because members were supposed to serve as examples to the masses and, arguably, were to be punished more harshly when they stepped out of line. In practice, however, just the opposite was true. With the development of patron-client networks in Soviet society, judges were often told how to decide cases involving fellow Party members. Such orders typically came via telephone from someone above them in the Party hierarchy, thus giving rise to what became known as "telephone law." As a result, where one came from became less important than who one knew.

Another aspect of procedural regularity notable for its absence in the Soviet context is accountability of officialdom. There was no legal mechanism by which an official (whether governmental or Party-affiliated) could be held responsible for violations of the law committed while carrying out his official duties, even when such violations had an adverse impact on the rights of citizens.[67] The notion of governmental tort liability was virtually nonexistent.[68] Not surprisingly, abuse of office was most widespread and morally reprehensible under Stalin, but it continued to exist after his death, albeit in different forms and with different goals. But the impunity with which officials acted was consistent; they did not fear legal repercussions.[69]

Independence of Judiciary. The Soviet Union also lacked the institutional component of procedural regularity, namely, an independent judiciary.[70] This is not surprising given Lenin's view of courts as organs of state power.[71] In practical terms, the Party controlled the judiciary. As with so many other governmental sectors, control was achieved through a combination of structural changes and cadre policy.[72]

Upon taking power, the Bolsheviks immediately overhauled the courts by introducing people's courts and revolutionary tribunals in place of the tsarist courts. The goal was not to create an independent judicial system but to simplify the existing system and ensure its ideological purity. As Hazard convincingly demonstrates, the attempt to create a legal system in which disputes could be decided without a great deal of rigmarole was largely a failure. By the early 1920s, the courts' practice was once again being governed by detailed civil and criminal procedure codes.[73]

Although the Bolsheviks' efforts at structural transformation failed, their personnel policy succeeded in transforming the system ideologically. Most tsarist judges were fired. These judges, despite (or perhaps because of) their education and experience, were ideologically suspect. Revolutionary justice, after all, did not require that decision makers be steeped in the technicalities of law. Political reliability was more important and was guaranteed in several ways. The selection criteria set forth in the July 1918 regulations made participation in so-called proletarian organizations (including the Communist Party) as important as prior legal education.[74]

Judges did not have lifetime tenure but fixed terms (the number of years depended on the level of the court). Who became a judge and whether he or she was permitted to continue in that post were firmly controlled by the Party. Under these conditions, the susceptibility of Soviet judges to pressure from Party apparatchiks is hardly surprising. Furthermore, this system of selecting judges underwent only incremental changes in the years preceding Gorbachev's accession to power.

The trials of "enemies of the people" began in the late 1920s and continued until Stalin's death in 1953, reaching a frenzied peak with the purge trials of 1937–8. They demonstrated graphically the extent to which the Party had "captured" the legal (and quasi-legal) institutions.[75] The vast majority of these cases were heard not by duly constituted courts but by extralegal tribunals specially created for this purpose.[76] Whether ordinary citizens appreciated such niceties is open to question. What is clear is that all institutions that participated in the Stalinist purges acted under the color of law. Indeed, they demonstrated a remarkable ability to go through the motions of obeying the law scrupulously, while all the time subverting the goal of justice. The decision makers were typically satisfied by confessions (as were most Western observers),[77] knowing better than to depart from the script to question whether such confessions had been given freely. Defense counsel were not permitted to do so either.[78] Indeed, non-high-profile trials lasted, on average, only 20 minutes, indicating that the outcome was a foregone conclusion, that the accused's guilt had been settled long before the trial began.[79]

Although the patently unfair nature of these proceedings may be obvious today and, indeed, was apparent to many at the time, it is important to remember that many Soviet citizens believed that those sent away to the gulags were guilty. Stalin had convinced the masses of the threat posed by the capitalist encirclement of the Soviet Union and the consequent need to industrialize rapidly and rid society of those "wreckers" and "enemies of the people" who allegedly sought to impede the country's progress.[80] This paranoia permeated Soviet society. To question governmental or Party policy marked one as a potential traitor.[81] Thus, the fact that so few allowed themselves to recognize, whether openly or privately, the "cookie-cutter" character of the justice of the purge trials is hardly surprising.

Khrushchev's "secret speech" to the Twentieth Party Congress in 1956, in which he revealed the scope of the repression countenanced by Stalin and denounced his "cult of personality," began the process of officially opening people's eyes to what had gone on in their country under Stalin.[82] Khrushchev spoke of the baseless persecution of millions of individuals and entire ethnic groups, and under his leadership the process of rehabilitating the victims of the purges was begun. As the survivors of the gulags rejoined society, many felt the need to write about their experiences. Their stories had a chilling sameness. Among other things, they revealed the courts' collaborative role, that is, their consistent willingness to rubber-stamp the verdicts and sentences demanded by the political authorities. The unjust nature of the proceedings described was apparent to all. Indeed, these revelations only further eroded the already minimal trust placed in the legal system by the citizenry at large.

In the years following Stalin's death, efforts were made to ensure that the horror of the mass purges would never be repeated. Berman lists ten critical changes that he contends restored procedural due process in political cases. Chief among these were the elimination of special tribunals, which had enjoyed unlimited jurisdiction, and the reintroduction of the principle of presumption of innocence and the rule that confessions had to supported by other corroborating evidence. Writing in the 1960s, Berman concludes that "[t]he Soviet citizen is now protected against police terror, false charges and faked trials to a far greater extent than ever before in Soviet history."[83]

Yet the post-Stalin changes did not go far enough. Had the judges tainted by their involvement in the purges been prosecuted or even replaced and the system revamped to eliminate (or at least minimize) the influence of the Party, higher levels of trust in the system might well have been generated among the masses.[84] Instead, no meaningful structural changes were introduced. The Communist Party continued to control the selection and retention of judges and, consequently, "telephone law" continued to flourish in the post-Stalin era.[85] As always, the courts seemed to be motivated more by political expediency than by fundamental fairness.

At the same time, it is important to recognize that the marginal impact of de-Stalinization on the legal system more generally was not unique. The point of the "secret speech" and the entire de-Stalinization process was not to indict the system but to demythologize the figure of Stalin and ensure the end of state-sponsored terror. Khrushchev and his cohort were committed Leninists and, as such, remained true to the ideals of the vanguard party and democratic centralism. They had no intention of disengaging the Party from the key levers of power. The basic concept of law as an instrument of the regime remained unchanged, and it was expected that the Party would continue to control the judiciary.

What this all meant in practice was that while in the post-Stalin era the courts (and other quasi-legal institutions) no longer acted as a conveyor belt of repression on a mass scale, they were more than capable of doing so on an individual basis. That the courts did so in fact has been well documented by the participants in the major dissident trials of the

Brezhnev period as well as by Western scholars of that period.[86] The defendants in these trials were treated differently than those in other nonpolitical trials. For example, their right to counsel was limited to lawyers sanctioned by the KGB, and these Party-approved lawyers were often unwilling to do anything more than enter a guilty plea.[87] In addition, their punishment was typically wildly out of proportion to their crime.

One can argue that politically charged cases are a special category from which general conclusions about the nature of the system should not be drawn. However, that argument is flawed on two grounds. First, the very existence of these cases, in which the outcome was dictated from above, demonstrated that the Communist Party had permeated the judiciary. This, of course, has profound implications for the trustworthiness of the legal system itself. Furthermore, the argument implies that the number of political cases is relatively small and that their character as such is immediately apparent to all. In fact, the definition of a "political" case was far from clear. In a country like the Soviet Union, riddled with patron-client networks, a judge could never be sure whether a case would bring a telephone call from a superior ordering a particular outcome.[88] This was true in both civil and criminal cases.

This is not to say that the Party micromanaged every trial. Indeed, the Party took no interest in most trials. Yet the specter of interference always hung over a trial. As a result, the dual legal culture that developed under Stalin persisted under his successors. In other words, legal institutions operated normally much of the time, but they were willing to abandon the rules without regard to the interests of justice when so ordered.

The upshot was a legal system that was held in low esteem by the masses. They did not believe that they would get a fair hearing and so avoided the courts whenever possible. This lack of trust in the law cannot be attributed to any single factor but developed gradually over the course of Soviet history as a result of various manifestations of the subordination of law to politics.

Accessibility of Law. Soviet citizens could not rely upon the basic procedural guarantees that, according to Fuller, constitute the "inner morality of the law." For one thing, the law was not published in any systematic fashion and so non-specialists often found it very difficult to locate relevant law.[89] Furthermore, the common practice of amending law through administrative regulations rather than through legislation frequently stymied even the specialists. Such regulations often went published, but nonpublication was not considered a bar to their use by those fortunate enough to be aware of them. Although other European countries also struggled with how best to consolidate statutory law, the Soviet Union lagged far behind.[90]

Stability of Law. Closely related to the question of accessibility is that of stability. In a system with a high degree of procedural regularity, people have a reasonable level of assurance that the law will not be changed under their feet. Fuller cogently remarks that "[a] law that changes every day is worse than no law at all."[91] The Soviet record in this regard is mixed. At first glance, the basic statutory codes appear quite stable. They remained in use for relatively long periods, for example, the 1924 Civil Code was replaced only in 1964.[92] However, the practice of amending these codes through administrative regulations (*podzakonnie akty*) meant that they were, in fact, changing all the time and that it was almost impossible to keep track of their substance.[93]

Another source of instability stemmed from the adaptability of law to the political needs of the powerful. This instrumental view of law first came to the fore with "revolutionary justice," through which courts were instructed to be guided "exclusively by the circumstances of the case and by revolutionary conscience."[94] As Soviet society became gripped by political terror, this tendency to regard law as a means to an end only intensified. A. Ia. Vyshinsky, the chief prosecutor for many of the high-profile purge trials, writing in 1937, put it quite bluntly: "One has to remember Comrade Stalin's instructions that there are sometimes periods . . . when the laws prove obsolete and have to be set aside."[95] This set in motion a seemingly never-ending search for law that served the economic and political goals of the regime. As his biographer reminds us, Vyshinsky's unique talent lay not only in justifying this perpetual instability but in convincing people that it represented a triumph of lawfulness.[96]

The death of Stalin brought an end, for the most part, to state-sponsored political terror and so a decrease in the incidence of laws being set aside for reasons of political expediency. Yet the basic concept of law remained unchanged. Building a stability of expectations among the masses never became a primary function of law.

Examples of law being ignored under Stalin's successors abound. Trials of political dissidents continued, albeit with less frequency, and they were typically replete with examples of laws being studiously ignored. The case of A. D. Sakharov represents a nadir in that he was ordered into internal exile without even the pretense of a trial.[97] One may argue that the treatment of dissidents was not representative of the system and should not be used to indict it. On the other hand, it is often through the "hard cases" that a system reveals itself and proves its mettle. Certainly, that is true for the Soviet Union.

Vagueness and Inconsistencies within the Law. The largely ad hoc nature of the changes in the law arising from administrative regulations and decrees inevitably gave rise to internal inconsistencies. The jurisdiction of the ministries often overlapped, and no one kept tabs on the regulations being issued. Instead, they were simply churned out in response to discrete problems, with little thought given to whether they were compatible with one another. The frequent lack of precision in the statutory language only compounded the problem and further undermined procedural regularity. The declaratory and programmatic language favored by those who drafted legislation provided little guidance for those charged with implementing these laws.

Vagueness and internal inconsistencies in the law are, to some extent, inescapable. Western experience demonstrates that legislators can never foresee every situation; some room for maneuver must be left.[98] Much of the vagueness and inconsistency in Soviet law could be categorized as inadvertent and unavoidable. A good example of this is the law governing internal transfers of Soviet workers, which distinguished between a "transfer" *(perevod)* and a "shift" *(peremeshchenie)*. Although the statute listed objective criteria to be used in making this distinction, practice revealed the futility of general rules. Each situation was different and so could only be resolved on a case-by-case basis.[99] A similar pattern can also be observed in cases alleging personal injury or negligence.[100]

More problematic is the deliberate vagueness found in much of Soviet law. Once again, the source can be found in the Bolsheviks' distrust of written law. The revolutionary tribunals founded soon after the October Revolution used ideological rather than legal yardsticks to judge conduct. When the relegalization of society began in the early 1920s, many statutes were drafted so as to maximize judges' discretion (thereby minimizing the level of predictability of the law). Perhaps the best example of this was the law permitting local authorities to seize the property of rich peasants or kulaks. Just who was or was not a kulak was not clear from the law.[101] As Stalin's policy of eliminating the kulaks as a class picked up steam in the late 1920s and early 1930s, this lack of clarity in the statutory language gave officials the latitude to categorize (and punish accordingly) as a kulak anyone who opposed the collectivization of agriculture. As Lewin notes, under such conditions "legality is purely mythical."[102] Similar tactics were used to neutralize the political enemies of the regime. As Solzhenitsyn and Western historians of the purge period have documented, the statutory language was sufficiently vague that any person could be convicted at any time.[103]

Even outside these highly politicized areas of legal practice, judges often found themselves reasoning backward, that is, starting with the result desired by their superiors in the party hierarchy and then having to find the necessary facts to give such holdings the color of law. The lack of clarity in the underlying statutory law facilitated these activities.

The post-Stalin criminal code (1960) retained the crimes of anti-Soviet activities. The dissident trials of the Brezhnev period demonstrated the malleability of the statutory language. Any activity, regardless of how benign it might appear taken in the abstract, could be construed as anti-Soviet and punished accordingly. Certainly, the sheer numbers of people affected decreased dramatically with the demise of Stalinism, but the fact remains that the practice of allowing crimes that existed not in any absolute sense but only in the eye of the beholder continued and flourished.

Feasibility of Law. Another feature of the Soviet legal system that undermined procedural regularity was the tendency to enact laws requiring the impossible. In Fuller's words: "[t]o command what cannot be done is not to make law; it is to unmake law, for a command that cannot be obeyed serves no end but confusion, fear and chaos."[104] The Soviet case illustrates his point well, particularly in the realm of economic law.

The annual and five-year plans for the national economy had the status of law. Underneath the plans a unique brand of contract law developed that was designed to facilitate plan fulfillment.[105] Yet the goals set by Soviet planners consistently outstripped the physical capacities of the economy. In the late 1920s, Stalin set the country on a course of rapid industrialization, memorialized in the first five-year plan (1929), which called for a doubling of the fixed capital stock and a 70 percent expansion of light industry.[106] Subsequent five-year plans were equally unrealistic. However, the cycle continued because the extent to which the plans were unfulfilled remained largely unexposed. Over the years, the practice of lying about economic performance and thus going through the motions of obeying the law while, in fact, disregarding its substance became institutionalized on every level of the economy.

At first, this attitude toward the plan and the network of contractual and other economic-legal relations underlying it was prompted by a well-justified sense of fear. Impossibility of performance was not an acceptable excuse for not fulfilling the plan, and the consequences of nonfulfillment for those held responsible were quite serious.[107] Under Stalin, for example, the penalties ranged from being dismissed and losing one's Party membership to being tried for sabotage (or, in the vernacular of the period, "wrecking").[108] Sabotage was one of those crimes that was loosely defined, and consequently most of those accused were convicted. The punishment meted out was typically harsh; oftentimes convicted saboteurs were sentenced to years at hard labor, and in a number of high-profile cases they were even executed. Under these conditions, it is hardly surprising that lying to one's superior about output and fulfillment of the plan became commonplace.

With the demise of Stalinism, this behavior could no longer be justified on the grounds of fear for one's personal safety. Under Stalin's successors, the typical penalty for nonfulfillment of the plan became dismissal, not death. Notwithstanding this, misrepresentations continued, and they continued to be prompted by fear, albeit of a qualitatively different nature. Managers and planners feared losing their positions of privilege as members of the *nomenklatura* and so continued to build up this economic house of cards, which collapsed in relatively short order when exposed to meaningful public scrutiny in the late 1980s.[109]

The point to be made is that when law demands that which is impossible it ceases to be taken seriously. People merely go through the motions, and when they find that no one notices, such behavior becomes ever more widespread until this kind of pro forma attitude becomes the rule rather than the exception. In the Soviet case, this not only undermined procedural regularity but fostered an overall sense of contempt for the law within society. Indeed, Fuller might have underestimated the corrosive effect on society of laws that demand the impossible. He predicted chaos, but what came to pass in the Soviet Union was perhaps even more devastating for the country in the long run—a society in which law lost all credibility, a society in which law ceased to matter.

Conclusion. The argument in the Soviet case is not that procedural regularity was entirely lacking but that the "dual legal culture" resulted in its being absent often enough such that a reasonable person could not depend on its presence. The absence of an independent judiciary combined with the fact that statutes were often vague, internally contradictory, and subject to constant change gave rise to a legal culture in which law was not respected but merely tolerated.

Substantive Legitimacy

Although certainly important, the relative lack of procedural regularity was not the sole cause of the marginalization of law in the Soviet context. Other factors contributed, principal among them being the frequent absence of substantive legitimacy or, to put it more bluntly, an all-too-common lack of trust in the basic fairness of the law.

Revolutionary Justice. This skepticism toward law was well grounded. The revolutionary tribunals established after the October Revolution did not follow universalistic norms but rather judged those brought before them by whether they had lived up to the ideals of the revolution as well as by their political beliefs and affiliations. Predictability gave way to the goals of those holding political power.

Substantive Injustice under Stalin. The relegalization of Soviet society that began in the early 1920s brought the return of statutory codes and with them the reintroduction of what appeared to be objective standards. However, the appearance of objectivity was all too often illusory. The vagueness of the statutory language and the politicization of the judicial process rendered the law highly unpredictable and thereby undermined societal respect for it. In other cases, the language was unambiguous but was patently unfair as judged by then prevailing community standards. Typically, the unfairness stemmed from the unduly repressive nature of the penalties imposed for noncompliance. Predictability was achieved, but it was often predictable injustice, enforced by Stalin's terror machine.

The question of the fairness of law is always knotty.[110] Determining community standards at a given point in time is difficult, particularly for an outsider. It is further complicated when the society in question is in turmoil, as the Soviet Union was for much of the 1920s and early 1930s. Stalin and his cohort were determined to remake society. This entailed industrialization of the economy, collectivization of agriculture, and russification of the population at large.[111] The turmoil arose not just from the ambitiousness of the planned transformation but also from Stalin's determination to have it carried out at breakneck speed. The process was very much a revolution from above, and the extent to which its various manifestations enjoyed the support of the masses is much debated among historians of the period.[112]

Notwithstanding these difficulties, there are certain laws from the Stalin period that stand out as particularly unfair. The agricultural policy of the late 1920s, culminating in the decision to organize the peasants into collective farms, provides numerous examples.[113] Although grain had been confiscated from the peasants to feed the cities during the Civil War, relations normalized in the years that followed. The authorities imposed a tax-in-kind of a given percentage on the peasants and permitted them to sell the remainder on the market. In 1928, Stalin became convinced that the peasants were hoarding grain and was determined to bring them to heel. He ordered that they be prosecuted under an article of the criminal code that had previously been used for speculators and which provided for prison terms of up to five years with confiscation of property. That this contravened community standards is evident from the reluctance of local Communist Party functionaries (including judges) to follow through on his instructions. Compliance was forthcoming only when it became clear that failure to prosecute would result in being branded as a collaborator.[114]

This procurement crisis was initially blamed on the rich peasants (kulaks), even though the authorities were well aware that the middle peasants *(seredniaks)* were just as culpable. The kulaks were a convenient and ideologically appealing scapegoat. Similarly, when Stalin resolved to collectivize agriculture on a grand scale, the kulaks became the first victims. Once again, the policy was actualized through legislation.[115] The law prohibited the leasing of land to kulaks and also empowered the local authorities to confiscate land whenever they deemed such action necessary. By 1930, deportation was legally sanctioned as the liquidation of the kulaks as a class became coterminous with collectivization.[116] Lewin stresses the implicit danger of these measures in that "every one of them was in fact a double-edged weapon, since it constituted a permanent threat to the other peasants."[117] His point is well taken. The policy of dekulakization soon extended beyond just the rich peasants to encompass anyone who opposed collectivization. The use of law in such a crudely instrumental fashion, over the protests of the masses, could not help but subvert its authority.

One of the consequences of collectivization was a large-scale migration of peasants into the cities to work in the factories. Transforming them into the sort of highly disciplined workforce needed was an arduous task. Efforts made to encourage discipline through workplace stimulants (both negative and positive) failed to produce the desired results.[118]

In 1940, the regime responded by enacting what Nove charitably describes as "draconian legislation,"[119] under which workers were prohibited from leaving their jobs without permission and criminal sanctions were imposed for attempting to do so. Along similar lines, absenteeism was criminalized and redefined to include being more than 20 minutes late for work. As with the laws relating to grain procurement, the disjuncture between these laws and the community standards is clear from the fact that prosecutors and judges pursued cases involving violations of labor discipline only after the Party made clear that failure to do so would be prosecuted.[120] In relatively short order, these cases were being pursued with great gusto, perhaps reflecting the atmosphere of terror that still gripped Soviet society.

Other examples of Stalin-era laws that seem unfair on their face are not difficult to find. One particularly troubling category is legislation that, in essence, outlawed the traditional cultures of the various republics. Russian was imposed as the lingua franca. Organized religon of all persuasions was repressed. Indeed, an effort was made to secularize family life by mandating civil ceremonies for marriage and other rites of passage. Massell has documented how the Soviet authorities used law to impose the "new revolutionary morality," including the emancipation of women, on Central Asian society.[121]

The pattern common to the Soviet period is for law to be used as a means of achieving political goals. Certainly this is not unique to the Soviet case. Weber convincingly demonstrated the interrelationship between the rise of capitalism and the development of what he called a rational-legal order in Western Europe. This was, however, a gradual process marked by reciprocity between state and society. What was distinctive about Stalinism was the determination of those in power to push forward with their ambitious plans for social and economic engineering without waiting for society to catch up with them and their willingness as well to use political terror to force compliance with their plans. This attitude followed from the notion of the vanguard party and the view of law as an exclusively top-down process. The urgency was a natural outgrowth of the desperate desire of Stalin and his cohort to catch up with the already industrialized West.

Substantive Injustice under Stalin's Successors. A necessary precondition for the use of law as a sledgehammer is the willingness of those with political power to back up law with terror. After Stalin's death, Khrushchev and the rest of the party leadership agreed on the need to halt state-sponsored terror. Unfortunately, however, the Stalinist legacy was not entirely disowned. To be sure, agriculture had long been collectivized, and it had been years since anyone had been accused of being a kulak, much less jailed or deported on such grounds. By the same token, the harsh labor laws of 1940, while not repealed until 1956, fell into disuse in the early 1950s. Yet the laws suppressing traditional culture remained in force. At the same time, judging the extent to which the masses considered these laws unfair was complicated by their inability to express themselves freely. Certainly the dissident literature of the time reflected a deep-seated resentment of them. The widespread nature of these feelings was confirmed when the masses were finally "demuzzled" in the late 1980s.

Although the incidence of patently unjust laws diminished in the post-Stalin period, examples are still readily available. One such law is the so-called antiparasite law, enacted in many of the republics in 1957, in which those who failed to engage in "socially useful labor" were subject to criminal sanctions. The constitutional duty to work provided the theoretical justification for this law.[122]

The low esteem in which law was held under Khrushchev and Brezhnev stemmed not so much from the obvious unfairness of the law but rather from its perceived hollowness. The 1977 Soviet Constitution illustrates this point well. Under its terms, citizens were guaranteed broad social and political rights, and much was made of the fact that these rights were now to be meaningful (in contrast to the 1936 Constitution, which all recognized as a sham).[123] However, when activists attempted to exercise these rights, they quickly learned that they existed only on paper.[124] This gap between the letter and spirit of the law was endemic to the post-Stalin era. Repression was replaced by a hypocrisy of aspirations. Implicit in this was a recognition of the nonautonomous nature of law, that is, that it was inevitably defined by the political elite. Regardless of what the law actually said, this elite had no intention of allowing law to be transformed from its sword into a shield that could be used to defend societal interests and perhaps even to limit the prerogatives of power.[125]

Efficacy of Law

The low level of trust in the basic fairness of law (both substantively and procedurally) gave rise to a reluctance on the part of Soviet citizens to turn to the legal system for vindication when their rights were violated. Also contributing to their reticence, particularly in the civil context, was the inadequacy of the remedies available. All too often, Soviet law failed to make those legally wronged whole again.

Soviet contract law illustrates the basic problem well. Within the confines of the economic plan, factories entered into contracts with one another to supply various goods. When one party to such a contract reneged the other party was obligated under law to go to a special economic court *(arbitrazh)* and seek damages for the breach.[126] Yet the money damages available were meaningless in this context. The damaged party could not obtain the needed materials elsewhere because no market existed. What the damaged party really needed was an injunction directing the party who had breached to perform. Yet *arbitrazh* lacked the power to order specific performance.[127] Even if such remedies had been within its arsenal, they would have been meaningless in practice. In most cases, contractual breaches resulted from bottlenecks further down the line, making performance literally impossible. As a result, managers learned to bypass the legal system in favor of appeals to ministerial or Party officials who had the power (though not the legal right) to compel performance.

Similar patterns can be observed in other substantive areas of the law. Remedies that appear rational when taken in the abstract are meaningless when observed through the prism of Soviet conditions. As a result, people had little reason to turn to the law when their rights had been violated.

Accessible Legal System

In the West, mobilization rates have been linked with the accessibility of the legal institutions. When the barriers to getting into court are unreasonably high, people tended to be discouraged from making the effort, or so the argument goes. Yet the Soviet case suggests that the argument is not terribly convincing when reversed.

In the Soviet Union, getting a dispute heard by the court was relatively easy. The courts routinely accepted handwritten complaints of one or two lines that alleged wrongdoing but did not make out a clear legal cause of action. No elaborate legal arguments had to be advanced. Cases were rarely dismissed for failure to state a cause of action. More often, the petitioner was given the opportunity to explain at trial rather than having his or her case thrown out on the basis of the pleadings. The assistance of legal counsel was, therefore, not necessary in order to get before a judge. Cases were typically heard within one or two weeks of filing. Delays occurred, but these were more often due to the nonappearance of one of the parties than to an overcrowded court calendar.

The ease of entry did not prompt a rush to the courthouse. Thus, accessibility, while necessary, is not sufficient. It can be undermined by a lack of respect for legal institutions and an absence of meaningful remedies.

Conclusion

This brief overview of Soviet history reveals that the people did not trust or respect law and so avoided it. At the root of this crisis of confidence in the legal system stood the consistently prevailing view of law as an instrument to be used by the regime in order to further its political goals. From this conceptualization stemmed the patron-client relationship between the Party and the judiciary that, in turn, facilitated the relative absence of procedural regularity. Similarly, the subordination of law to politics encouraged the promulgation of laws that were vague, so those charged with implementing them would have the greatest possible latitude. While this coercive vision of law may have been expedient for the regime in the short run, it only served to undermine the legitimacy of the legal system over the long run.

Law under Leninism: 1985–91

Beginning with his accession to power in April 1985 and culminating with the disintegration of the Soviet Union in December 1991, Gorbachev attempted to reform the Soviet system, both politically and economically, without abandoning the central tenets of Leninism. Tracing the course of this reform effort is not my goal here. Others have documented Gorbachev's ultimately futile struggle to steer a safe course between the conservatives, who wanted to maintain the Brezhnev status quo, and the liberals, who advocated the dismantling of the old system and the introduction of market capitalism.[128] By the same token, I am not attempting to trace in any detail the much-ballyhooed plan to introduce a "law-based state" *(pravovoe gosudarstvo)* in the Soviet Union or to assess its likelihood for success in the long run. Other scholars, both Soviet and Western, have undertaken that task.[129]

My purpose in this section is to explore in a tentative and general way the effect (if any) of these efforts at political and economic transformation on the role played by law in Soviet society. A careful reexamination of the key features of the legal system reveals numerous structural changes that would seem to portend a reinvigoration of the system. Yet all indications are that attitudes failed to keep pace with these structural changes, that is, that people continued to be highly skeptical of the law, both procedurally and substantively.

Conception of Law: Modified Instrumentalism

From an official standpoint, the definition of law remained largely unchanged during the Gorbachev era. Law continued to be closely identified with the party-state and, as the state and the Party began to crumble in the late 1980s, with the personalities of those holding power. Instrumentalism endured. The view persisted of law as a one-way projection of authority rather than as an interactive process in which state and society participated on a relatively equal basis. Within these confines, however, there were some interesting and important shifts in the ways officialdom thought about the law. When Gorbachev first came to power, he had a very idealistic notion of the power of law. He seemed to view it as a magic wand that only had to be waved over society in order to eliminate problems. Indeed, his first major policy initiative, the antialcohol campaign, reflected this attitude. The approach was very much top-down and included legalistic solutions, such as cracking down on public drunkenness and restricting the hours during which alcohol could be sold. Similarly, his initial plans for restructuring the economy put great weight on the curative power of law. He consistently railed against the petty tutelage of the ministries and blamed the rigid administrative-command system for the low productivity of Soviet industry. His answer was to grant enterprises their independence legislatively.[130] In both cases (and countless others), it quickly became evident that merely passing laws was not sufficient to change behavior in a society that had become accustomed to maneuvering around the law.

Gorbachev was clearly frustrated by the failure of his legislative initiatives to effect meaningful change. He and his advisors bemoaned the masses' disregard for these new laws. Yet the fact that their exhortations fell on deaf ears did not lead to a reappraisal of their basic approach but only hardened their commitment to reform initiated from above. Indeed,

Gorbachev seemed to lose patience with the endless debates of the legislature (now that it no longer simply rubber-stamped party resolutions) and sought to bypass it by having his executive powers increased dramatically. By late 1990, presidential decrees were being churned out on what at times seemed like a daily basis in a desperate attempt to hold the country together politically and economically.

These decrees were no more successful in effecting the desired changes in behavior than had been the bona fide legislation. The reasons are many, but one critical factor was the lack of legitimacy of law or anything that smacked of law. The political elite refused to accept the Fuller notion of law as a collaborative enterprise, clinging instead to its conceptualization of law as a one-way projection of state authority. At the same time, the political will to force compliance with the law through repression was long gone. Absent force and authority, neither average citizens nor bureaucratic elites had any compelling reason for compliance.

Discouraging though this official view of law during the Gorbachev years may be, reasons for optimism can be found if we dig a bit deeper. Perhaps most encouraging is a series of law review articles in which Soviet legal scholars appeared to distance themselves from positivism by arguing that law should be true to some underlying sense of moral rightness, that is, that promulgation by a duly constituted legislature was not sufficient. These scholars seemed to be moving toward a kind of natural law jurisprudence in which the ultimate source is not the word of God but the universally accepted norms of human rights.[131] While still identifying law with the state, they recognized the importance of society in the legitimation process. This represents a first step toward the Weberian notion that authority is built through a reciprocal process.

In several instances, this new society-driven vision of law has made the jump from words to action. For example, the law guaranteeing freedom of the press was drafted not by the Party-controlled legislature but by an independent group of experts who were dissatisfied with the official draft of the bill. On the level of high politics, Gorbachev and his cohort were initially opposed to amending the Soviet Constitution to remove all references to the leading role of the Communist Party. Only through public pressure (including mass political rallies and other such tactics) were they convinced to change their position.[132] In these examples, a nascent trend toward society involving itself in the legal process can be observed.

Procedural Regularity

The Gorbachev years brought many changes that, in theory, would seem to militate in favor of an increase in procedural regularity. Change is, of course, an inherently relative concept. Thus, while great strides have been made since the days of lawful repression under Stalin, both the remnants of the Soviet system and the new Russian system have a long way to go before it can attain the kind of "normality" so envied in the legal systems of the Western industrialized democracies.[133]

Accountability of Officialdom. One of the key components of a law-based state is that the law should bind everyone equally. Though Gorbachev frequently espoused the rhetoric of the law-based state, he was reluctant to force Party members to give up their long-standing privileges. Others were prepared to end the *nomenklatura* system. As Sobchak argues, "[t]he nomenklatura parasitized our society. Its strength lay in a collective freedom from accountability."[134] Others joined with Sobchak in denouncing the double standard of justice that for so long had inured to the benefit of Party members.[135] During the Gorbachev years, this sort of rhetoric took on substance through legislative and executive action.

Legislatively, the first attempt to introduce governmental tort liability came under Gorbachev. In the past, average citizens whose rights had been violated by officials had been limited to administrative remedies. The absence of independent oversight made in-house review of officials' actions largely meaningless. Hopes were raised by article 58 of the 1977 Soviet Constitution, which purported to give citizens the right to sue when harmed by the illegal actions of officialdom, but the failure to pass enabling legislation rendered this guarantee illusory. In 1987, however, a statute was enacted that permitted citizens to pursue claims of official misconduct in court. Although the statute was seriously flawed in that it made actionable only individual actions when most official decisions were made collectively, it nonetheless represented an important first step. The law was amended in 1989 to remedy some of these shortcomings, but it remains far from ideal. As a result, while the introduction of governmental tort liability is important from the standpoint of symbolic politics, the flood of complaints that some Western and Soviet commentators had predicted failed to materialize.[136]

The prosecution of high-level governmental and party officials represented yet another step forward. In some cases, such as the prosecutions of the former first party secretary of Uzbekistan and his cronies for corruption, these actions were clearly motivated by a desire to clean house politically.[137] However, the public nature of these prosecutions and the simultaneous freeing of many of the restrictions on the press meant that the process quickly spun out of the control of the Kremlin. By the spring of 1990, there was the incredible spectacle of then Prime Minister N. I. Ryzhkov being accused of self-dealing through his alleged involvement in a scheme to export Soviet tanks. In a highly emotional defense, he expressed astonishment at the very fact that his credibility was being assailed on national television.[138]

This is not to say that the goal of equal justice for all was achieved through the Gorbachev reforms. Patron-client networks were deeply embedded in the Soviet system, both structurally and psychologically, and remain a defining element of the post-Soviet Russian system. Eliminating them requires more than superficial changes in the law and token prosecutions.

Independence of Judiciary. Critical structural reforms designed to increase the independence of the Soviet judiciary were also undertaken under Gorbachev. In 1989, the articles of the Soviet Constitution dealing with the judicial branch were amended in an effort to mitigate party and other outside influence. Judges began to be selected by the legislature (the level of the legislative body doing the selecting depends on the place of the court in the judicial hierarchy), and their terms of office were elongated. Criteria for selection were established whose intent was the emphasizing of competence over political reliability. In addition, the constitution was amended in 1988 to create the Commission for Constitutional Supervision, a new quasi-appellate organ with limited powers of judicial review. This action perhaps indicated a willingness on the part of those creating the new order in the Soviet Union to make the judicial branch truly a coequal partner.[139]

Upon closer examination, these structural changes turned out to be largely symbolic. Turnover was minimal. For the most part, judges continued to be Party members. The reasons for the low turnover are discussed in more detail in chapter 5, but two reasons can be suggested here. First, not many people wanted to become judges. As a profession, the judiciary was held in low esteem by society in general and was poorly recompensed. Second, all too often the legislative bodies that selected the judges continued to be dominated by the Communist Party. Where they were not, the legislators have proved to be just as willing to bring extralegal pressure to bear on judges as Party apparatchiks were in years past. "Telephone law" lived on.[140]

As a result, the structural changes and the accompanying rhetoric on the part of Gorbachev and his close associates about the need for an independent judiciary did not have the desired effect of legitimizing the legal system.[141] Only time will tell, but initial impressions suggest that promising so much and delivering so little only deepened the public's cynicism about the system's capacity for change.

Accessibility of Law. As to the procedural guarantees that comprise the "inner morality of the law," first impressions again prove somewhat deceiving. For example, law would appear to have been extremely accessible during the Gorbachev years. Indeed, the full text of many laws (in both draft and final versions) were printed in mass circulation newspapers, often on the front page. In addition, the systematization of statutory law had largely been completed under Gorbachev. The official law collection *(Svod zakonov SSSR)* contained the major pieces of legislation and, because it was in loose-leaf form, was easily updated.

On the other hand, the practice of amending legislation in an ad hoc fashion through administrative regulations continued.[142] The usual difficulties in keeping abreast of such changes was further complicated by a paper shortage that resulted in many regulations never being published or being published in insufficient quantities. In a May 1990 interview, the Soviet Minister of Justice, V. F. Yakovlev, revealed that even he was hard-pressed to keep up with the changes. One can only imagine how intimidating it must have been for a layperson.

Stability of Law. The Gorbachev years were marked by political and economic turmoil. Although the perestroika process began as an effort to reform the existing system, it gave rise to a reevaluation (and ultimately a rejection) of many of Leninism's basic precepts. As private property, political pluralism, and other concepts previously unthinkable in the Soviet Union became realities, they required a legal foundation. New legislation, such as the land and property laws, that introduced fundamental changes in the state-society relationship was being churned out at a dizzying pace. There was hardly time to absorb one law before being confronted by another.

Vagueness and Inconsistencies within the Law. The poor quality of many of these statutes from a technical standpoint only compounded the problem of instability. They were often riddled with vague language and internal inconsistencies. A good example is the 1987 enterprise law, which attempted to introduce worker participation in management. However, the ambiguity of the language resulted in the rights ostensibly granted to workers' councils *(sovet trudovogo kollektiva* or *STK)* being largely meaningless. Also compromising the effort was the continued statutory allegiance to the principles of one-man management, which, of course, is fundamentally incompatible with worker participation.[143] Subsequent laws were similarly flawed. The ownership of security interests in enterprises was legalized by the 1990 laws on property and on joint-stock companies, but the rights of stockholders (particularly to buy and sell shares) were obscured by the language of both of these laws.[144] In addition to these internal tensions, the fast pace of legislative reform led to numerous cases of inconsistency between laws.

The so-called "war of laws," which broke out in the late 1980s as the republics began to assert their independence vis-à-vis the central government, provided yet another source of inconsistency in the law.[145] In the past, a law would be passed by the USSR Supreme Soviet and, in short order, a virtually identical version would be enacted by all of the republics' legislatures. This all changed as the republics came to understand that their interests were not necessarily coterminous with those of Moscow.[146] The result was a virtual smorgasbord of laws. People reacted accordingly, picking and choosing among the laws and obeying those that were most convenient for them. Likewise, factory directors studied these new laws in an effort to determine whether they should switch from All-Union to republican jurisdiction (or vice versa).[147] The differences between the USSR and Russian enterprise laws, for example, were not cosmetic by any means, but had a major impact on the relative rights of the director and the labor collective.

On the positive side, the Gorbachev years saw the elimination of many of the Stalinist vestiges of purposeful vagueness. In particular, the articles of the criminal code dealing with anti-Soviet behavior, under which many dissidents were jailed under Brezhnev, were amended in 1989 and were made less malleable. A graphic reflection of this changed atmosphere was the return of Sakharov from internal exile and his election to the legislature (along with many other former political prisoners).[148]

In contrast to the situation that existed for much of Soviet history, the vagueness of the perestroika-era legislation was not entirely intentional but was a consequence of the relative inexperience of the legislators. These lawmakers had no training in how to draft a workable statute or how to maneuver it through a faction-ridden legislative body.[149] As one of these new legislators notes, "[w]e were parliamentary pioneers, lacking aides, technical support, money—and, more critically—lacking experience. . . . None of us had the faintest idea how to organize the workday."[150] To further complicate matters, these legislators were trying to create—almost overnight—institutions that for the most part had never existed in the Soviet Union. In their eagerness to get something down on paper quickly, they often seized on foreign examples and passed them into law without stopping to consider their applicability to Soviet circumstances. This is not uncommon among countries attempting rapid transformations.

While lack of professionalism makes the prevalence of vague and contradictory legislative language understandable, the promulgation of such patently flawed laws could not help but undermine any effort to build legitimacy for law and the legal system. Predictability still gave way to political goals. The only difference was that under Gorbachev the goal was not personal aggrandizement but the creation of market socialism.

Feasibility of Law. This subordination of law to politics was likewise reflected in the tendency, which continued under Gorbachev, for the law to demand the impossible. Once again, this was most obvious in the realm of the economy. As the administrative-command system broke down, Gorbachev stepped in with a series of presidential decrees in an effort to forestall chaos. For example, in the fall of 1990, he ordered that all inter-enterprise contractual ties that had existed for more than two years were to be maintained, irrespective of the wishes of the parties.[151] However, events had moved beyond this, and the decree proved to be impossible to implement.

In reviewing perestroika-era law, Fuller's comment that legislators often cast themselves in the role of teachers—demanding more of their students than the students think possible in order to stretch their capacities—is instructive.[152] In the Soviet case, the teacher-policymakers expected too much. As a result, law became not something to shoot for but something to be gotten around. This tended to dilute the already tenuous respect for law.

Conclusion. Two tentative and somewhat contradictory conclusions can be drawn from this brief review of the various indicators of procedural regularity under Gorbachev. On the one hand, progress was clearly made. The reform of the system for selecting judges, the efforts to make the political elite answerable to the masses, and other structural changes lend credence to the conclusion that there was rather more procedural regularity in 1991 than there had been in 1985. On the other hand, the movement along this continuum during this period fell far short of what had been promised and hoped for. The profound distrust of the system that had grown up in the years since the October Revolution could not be wiped out with reforms that, as of 1991, existed largely on paper.

Substantive Legitimacy

A similarly mixed picture emerges when we turn to the issue of substantive legitimacy. Clearly, the Gorbachev years witnessed movement in the direction of more (rather than less) substantive legitimacy for the law and the legal system. Many of the laws regarded as unfair on their face were rescinded. The cultural hegemony of Russians was no longer enforced by law. Instead, legislation mandating tolerance of traditional culture and language was enacted. Even more remarkable was the open discussion of the desire of many of the republics to leave the Soviet Union, culminating in the passage of a statute setting forth a procedure for secession. Although important on the level of symbolic politics, as a practical matter these statutes did little to prevent the explosion of ethnic tensions throughout the Soviet Union.

Other presumptively unjust laws fell into disuse. The antiparasite law is a good example. Although it remained on the books, its force was largely vitiated by an official recognition that unemployment was unavoidable and that those who found themselves unemployed were not moral degenerates. Indeed, coincident with perestroika, Soviet economists predicted massive unemployment, and efforts were made during the Gorbachev years to provide some level of social guarantees for those displaced by the reforms.[153]

Despite these changes, the sense that law was not to be trusted persisted. While the relative absence of procedural regularity played a role, the distrust went deeper. People could no longer point to specific statutes that shocked the conscience, but they continued to distrust law as a general matter. Perhaps systemic changes outpaced attitudinal changes. Trust in the law may grow as these systemic changes become institutionalized. Certainly the disjuncture between structural and cultural change is relevant, but the lack of substantive legitimacy is not a problem that will cure itself if given sufficient time.

The root of the problem instead lies in the law's lack of autonomy. Soviet law consistently served as the handmaiden of the powerful. The masses have watched as institutional structures, grounded in legislation, have been created that purport to give them much-desired economic and political rights, only to have them abandoned once they no longer served the interests of the political elite. For example, Lenin's New Economic Policy encouraged the development of a capitalistic sector at the same time that major industries were being nationalized.[154] However, those who believed this reform was genuine later had their property and profits summarily confiscated and were persecuted for having trusted in the state and its laws. Similarly, the so-called "thaw" period of the late 1950s and early 1960s saw a flowering of political rights and burgeoning economic reforms that promised greater independence for enterprise management but which were discarded along with Khrushchev.

Given their history, citizens' failure to immediately embrace the new institutions created under Gorbachev is hardly surprising. They feared that the changes were only temporary. Consequently, most adopted a wait-and-see attitude. Those who did jump on the bandwagon were typically looking for short-term profits rather than investing for the long haul. To be fair, the instability of the fiscal and legal structure of society during the Gorbachev years made long-term investment virtually impossible. One might argue that if this structure stabilizes investors will come around. I disagree. More important than structural constancy is a belief that it exists independent of the whims of the powerful. Only when autonomy of law is achieved will substantive legitimacy follow.

Efficacy of Law

The progress made during the Gorbachev years to increase the level of procedural regularity and substantive legitimacy of the legal system did not give rise to a big jump in the rate at which people who believed they had been wronged mobilized their rights (whether newly created or longstanding). The marginal nature of the changes and the unwillingness of the masses to trust that they would not be arbitrarily rescinded certainly played a role in this reticence. More directly relevant, however, were the continuing inadequacies of the remedial structure. The Soviet case illustrates the self-evident proposition that people will not make use of the law if it does not hold out the promise of giving them what they want or believe they deserve.

A pattern can be observed in which citizens being given long-desired rights discover that the law fails to make them actionable in any meaningful way. For example, the fact that only individual decisions by officials were made actionable (in a system in which most decision making is done collectively) greatly diminished the impact of the law that purported to make officials accountable for their actions. The widely predicted flood of litigation failed to materialize.

The 1987 Law on State Enterprises provides yet another example.[155] One of its stated purposes was to free enterprises from the petty tutelage of the ministries. To this end, the law granted enterprises the right to challenge ministry orders by petitioning *arbitrazh* for injunctive relief when an order would cause them irreparable harm. Indeed, Pomorski describes this section as the only true innovation of the law.[156] In practice, however, enterprises failed to avail themselves of this right. The reason was simple. They depended on these ministries for raw materials and other supplies and could not risk raising their ire by suing them. As Clark and Wildavsky note in their work on Poland, "what rational manager would take his supplier to court for nondelivery, even if the manager has an excellent chance of winning? Nothing could better ensure never receiving a delivery from this supplier in the future."[157] Yet the fact that parties who have a continuing business (or other) relationship tend to resort to legal action only as a last resort, while well known to Western legal scholars,[158] was apparently not taken into consideration by those who drafted the 1987 enterprise law.

Examples abound of perestroika-era laws that fail to provide meaningful remedies. While the inexperience of the legislators makes these sorts of flaws understandable, it does not lessen their corrosive impact on society. The efforts of the regime to build up the legitimacy of law through strong political rhetoric and structural reforms were undermined by the persistent enactment of laws that so clearly fell short of their goals.

Accessible Legal System

Making the existing legal institutions more accessible was not a high priority for the architects of perestroika. One possible reason for this was that the courts had long been relatively accessible, at least when compared to Western practice.

The reform of the bar *(advokatura),* while not undertaken with the express goal of making legal institutions more or less accessible, may well have a profound impact on accessibility over the long run.[159] In the past, trial lawyers who engaged in defense work *(advokaty)* had had very little freedom of action. They were required to work in "legal consultation" offices *(iuridicheskaia konsul'tatsiia)* and to accept any case they were assigned. Fees, whether for office consultations or court work, were set from above by the College of Advocates, a kind of bar association, to which a percentage of all fees was paid. To refuse to go along was to risk disbarment.

All of this changed under Gorbachev. While the College of Advocates still existed, it no longer exercised such stringent control over the activities of its members. Lawyers were set free to set their own fees and to work independently of the "legal consultation" offices. This newly found freedom may prove to be a double-edged sword for the average citizen. On the one hand, if the citizen's complaint promises to be lucrative for the lawyer, he or she will undoubtedly accept it and pursue it with more vigor than he or she might have under the old system in which lawyers' remuneration was limited. One indication of this is the eagerness with which Soviet lawyers pursued participants in joint ventures who would be willing to pay them in convertible currency. On the other hand, lawyers may well shy away from routine matters that would consume considerable time but yield only a small fee, such as divorces or housing disputes. Thus, whether the freeing of trial lawyers from their bureaucratic shackles will cause them to become more aggressive in pursuing clients and pressing their legal claims remains to be seen.

As of December 1991, little had changed with regard to accessibility. Legal institutions were highly accessible, but this accessibility was largely irrelevant because people tended not to take advantage of it. The lingering distrust of the legal system and those who administered it, combined with the inadequacies of the remedial structure, led the average citizen to pursue grievances through extralegal channels rather than by appealing to the court.

The ultimate impact of perestroika on the role played by law in Soviet society remains unclear. I have outlined the many changes introduced under Gorbachev both in the structure of legal institutions and in legislation. At the same time, I have been careful to note that most of these changes have yet to make the leap from paper to practice. In some societies, this transition might be taken for granted, but in the Soviet Union where the gap between what the law says and what it means has been so profound and enduring, such an assumption is unwarranted. This skepticism about the meaningfulness of the reforms undertaken thus far is only deepened by the persistence of the societal distrust of the legal system. As Black has argued, "the demise of law is more likely to result from citizens who fail to mobilize courts. . . . One by one, citizens may lose interest in a law and, in private, the law may die a slow death."[160] In the Soviet case, this indifference will result not in death, for law is already largely moribund, but in nonresurrection.

Conclusion

My analysis of the role played by law under democratic capitalism and Leninism demonstrates the importance of the ways in which law is conceptualized. In the Western industrialized democracies, law is seen to be a reciprocal process in which state and society participate and for which they share responsibility. This gives rise to a basic trust in the law itself and in the legal institutions that administer it that, in turn, permits the development of procedural regularity and substantive legitimacy.

Under Leninism, in contrast, law was considered a one-way projection of state authority. Given that the state was so closely identified with the Communist Party, in practice the political elite were able to manipulate law to serve its personal interests. The precise nature of these interests has changed over time—from Lenin's desire to consolidate the Bolsheviks' hold on power to Stalin's determination to industrialize and arm the country, to Gorbachev's dream of making the Soviet Union competitive on the world market. The pattern, however, is the same—the autonomy of law consistently gave way to political exigencies. Each of these leaders imposed his vision on society and used law and legal institutions to force-feed the desired changes. Never did they allow society to participate in the process. Its only role was rather to obey the laws once they were passed down. To make matters worse, the law often did not even mean what it said. As a result, people became accustomed to merely paying lip service to the law and, not surprisingly, had little faith in legal institutions. The gap between what the law said and what it meant became virtually institutionalized and, consequently, law never came to matter in anything but a coercive sense.

Part 2
The Case Study

CHAPTER 3

The Law on the Books: Soviet Labor Law through the Prism of Published Materials

Introduction

The highly instrumental view of law that held sway in the Soviet Union from the days of the October Revolution through its demise in December 1991 had a debilitating effect on the value of law in society. Law served the interests of those in power and was one of many means used to impose their vision of society on the masses. This subordination of law to politics undermined its capacity to serve as a societal touchstone. Because people felt no kinship to the goals promoted by law, going through the motions of obeying the law became commonplace.

Coexisting with this ritualistic legalism was a tendency to skirt the law. Avoidance of the law required considerable political savvy; one had to learn to discriminate between "show" law and "real" law. The distinction, while not apparent to outsiders, was obvious to factory managers and other insiders accustomed to reading between the lines of Soviet politics. Guessing wrong was dangerous, particularly during the Stalinist repressions. Thereafter, miscalculations might bring dismissal, but rarely criminal prosecution for anti-Soviet activities.

The existence of a gap between the law in theory and practice was hardly unique to the Soviet Union. To some extent, such gaps exist in all societies, including those in which law matters reciprocally.[1] Sometimes this gap is even purposeful. Legislatures may pass a law for symbolic reasons or as a societal stimulus, knowing full well that it will lie dormant. More often, however, such gaps are unintended consequences. Bona fide efforts to implement a law often fall short of aspirations, whether due to a lack of political will, financial wherewithal, or other reasons.

In the Soviet context, however, the gap between the official "truth" and the unofficial reality was different from that found in the West, not only in degree but in kind.[2] It was not simply an unintended consequence.

An appreciation of the magnitude of the gap and why it persisted is critical to understanding the role of law in Soviet society as well as its capacity for change.

In this chapter, I outline the law as it existed on the books and as it appeared to be implemented based on published sources.[3] In the next chapter, I expand the analysis to include my field research. This two-pronged approach will highlight the stark contrast between the rigorous attitude toward compliance with the law reflected in the published materials and the pro forma attitude observed and documented in practice.

Labor Law as a Case Study

Labor law was one of only a few areas of Soviet law in which Soviet citizens had the right not only to question the legality of actions taken by those in positions of authority but also to obtain ostensibly meaningful remedies.[4] Since the late 1950s, a Soviet worker who believed that management had failed to comply with the dictates of the law had the right to challenge his or her dismissal or transfer. If the worker prevailed, he or she had the right to be reinstated to his or her prior position. Indeed, as this chapter will demonstrate, the statutory law and the published case decisions seem to indicate that workers' rights in this regard were vigorously defended by the courts, and they seem to suggest as well that this law actually mattered in more than a coercive sense.

The focus of my case study is on the law governing dismissals and transfers of Soviet workers at the initiative of management. The period covered by the study is 1980–91, although I make some use of pre-1980 materials in order to explain more fully how the legal regime of the 1980s developed.

The political and economic crises that characterized the Gorbachev period make the law governing dismissals and transfers particularly appropriate for in-depth study. The success of the economic reforms depended largely on increasing labor productivity. The Gorbachev regime planned to achieve this increase by reducing the featherbedding endemic to Soviet industry. This rationalization of the Soviet workforce was to be accomplished through dismissals of redundant workers. Estimates of the number of workers to be affected by the turn of the century ranged as high as 40 million.[5] Massive unemployment was predicted.

These conditions should have exerted pressure on the legal system. On the one hand, both management and the courts might have been tempted and perhaps pressured from above to ignore the legal niceties in order to meet Moscow's goal of increased labor productivity. On the other hand, judicial protection of workers' rights might have helped to legitimate the push for greater efficiency.

Sources of the Law on the Books

There are three basic sources of Soviet law: statutory law, Supreme Court interpretations, and case law.[6]

Statutes. The first and most important source of law is statutory. Labor relations in the Soviet Union were governed by the Fundamental Labor Legislation of the USSR and the Union Republics (the Fundamentals), adopted in 1970,[7] and the labor codes of the union republics, most of which were adopted in 1971.[8] As the name suggests, the Fundamentals set forth the basic principles of labor law and served as the basis for the more detailed union republic codes.[9] The codes did not vary widely among republics. For the sake of convenience and because my research was based in Moscow, I have relied on the labor code of the Russian Republic (the RSFSR Labor Code).[10]

Supreme Court Interpretations. The "guiding explanations" *(rukovodiashchoe raz"iasnenie)*[11] and decrees *(postanovlenie)* issued periodically by plenary sessions of the Supreme Courts of the USSR and the RSFSR are the second source of Soviet law.[12] The USSR and RSFSR Supreme Courts each issued a series of decrees interpreting various aspects of Soviet labor law.[13] Their purpose is to instruct the lower courts as to how to resolve commonly encountered issues.[14]

Case Law. Finally, I have relied on the published decisions of Soviet courts of various levels in cases of dismissals and internal transfers. Objections to using case law in order to understand Soviet law can and have been raised on two grounds. First, some have argued that the cases reported are too few in number to permit general conclusions to be drawn.[15] Decisions are reported in the *Bulletin of the Supreme Court of the USSR* and the *Bulletin of the Supreme Court of the RSFSR.* Because these are bimonthly and monthly publications, respectively, the number of published cases dealing with dismissals, internal transfers, or other labor law issues is relatively small. However, keeping in mind that the cases published were carefully selected and were intended to have instructional value for the lower courts, the decisions represent an important indicator of what the law was intended to be.[16]

I have supplemented these decisions with references to other cases described in scholarly articles. Sometimes these articles are written by judges who report on what is going on in their courts,[17] and sometimes they are written by scholars who enjoy unusual access to court records.[18]

In all cases, they provide insights otherwise unavailable to outsiders. Again, this evidence cannot be accepted unquestioningly, but can be helpful in providing confirmation of trends in court behavior.

The value of case law has also been questioned on the grounds that the Soviet Union's civil law legal tradition means that judges cannot make law. The implication is that, in contrast to countries with common law tradition, precedent carries little weight in civil law countries.[19] The first problem with this argument is its assumption that the Soviet Union was a "civil law" country. Certainly, for many years this was the conventional wisdom. However, as the dissimilarities between the Soviet legal system and the traditional "civil law" systems of Europe became more apparent, an ever increasing number of Western scholars of Soviet law argued that a new designation was needed for the Soviet legal system and its progeny. They argue that these countries should be regarded as having a "socialist law" tradition.[20] Others continued to hold to the characterization of the Soviet Union as a "civil law" country.[21]

Regardless of whether the Soviet Union is categorized as a "civil law" or "socialist law" country, the unimportance of judicial decisions should not be taken for granted. While on a formal level, both "civil law" and "socialist law" theory admonishes that the decision of a court is binding only on the parties and has no precedential value, in practice, reliance by other judges and litigants on prior decisions is commonplace.[22] The truth of this in the Soviet context is apparent from the *Kommentarii k zakonodatel'stvu o trude* (the *Kommentarii*), the official commentary to the Fundamentals and the RSFSR Labor Code.[23] The commentators consistently refer to previous court decisions in support of their interpretations.[24]

The Law Governing Dismissals

Parameters of the Law

Soviet labor law was highly prescriptive and forbade dismissal of workers unless management could show that its decision was motivated by one of the statutorily sanctioned causes. Both the Fundamentals and the RSFSR Labor Code contained identical and exhaustive lists of reasons justifying dismissal.[25] Traditionally, the exhaustive nature of this list was much praised by Soviet labor law specialists as "an important legal guarantee of the [constitutionally guaranteed] right to work."[26] The argument was that by restricting the flexibility of management, Soviet workers would be protected from the unpredictability of at-will employment.[27]

The economic reforms of the Gorbachev years caused some of these specialists to rethink their position. As situations arose that had not been contemplated by the 1970 law, the prior practice of simply adding new bases for dismissal to the statute was quickly becoming unwieldy. The specialists argued that the law should be restructured to provide more general guidelines for management behavior, leaving the specifics (including the permissible reasons for a worker's dismissal) to be worked out at the enterprise level through the collective bargaining process. Notwithstanding the scholarly consensus, this aspect of the law was left untouched when the Fundamentals were amended in May 1991.[28] The detailed, specific labor law of 1970 remained in effect for the remaining years of the Soviet Union.[29]

When originally enacted, the Fundamentals and the RSFSR Labor Code contained six statutorily sanctioned reasons for the dismissal of a worker at the initiative of management. By 1991, the list had been expanded to include nine. As a general matter, these nine can be separated into two groups: disciplinary and non-disciplinary reasons. My primary focus is on the latter category and, more particularly, on dismissals prompted by a "reduction in staff" *(sokrashchenie shtata)*.[30] The clarity and objective nature of the legal standards for layoffs made these dismissals more appealing as a case study of implementation than disciplinary dismissals in which the worker's behavior was inevitably the central issue, leaving considerable room for subjectivity. Moreover, dismissals for redundancy related most closely to the supposed push for greater efficiency within Soviet industry that was the sine qua non of perestroika.

Workers who were laid off (or dismissed on other grounds) had the right under the law to challenge this action in court if they believed management had acted illegally. The basic remedy was reinstatement. When discussing this remedy, however, it is important to recognize that, regardless of the egregiousness of management's conduct, the remedy was not self-enforcing but required workers to mobilize the law on their own behalf.[31] Furthermore, the court was empowered only to reinstate workers to their prior position and the court order had to be specific. In a 1990 case, the RSFSR Supreme Court sent the case of a truck driver back to the trial court for clarification because the decision had not specified what kind of vehicle he was to drive upon reinstatement.[32] On the other hand, if the petitioner's job had been eliminated, the court could not force management to find other work for him.[33] When dismissing a worker on grounds of redundancy, management had to follow the procedure outlined in the statute. The law required management to offer the worker another job at the same enterprise if an appropriate vacancy existed. It further required the enterprise trade union committee *(profkom)* to review management's decision and give its consent to the layoff.

Failure on the part of management to respect these procedural guarantees of workers' rights constituted grounds for reinstatement. As I will discuss below in more detail, assessing whether management complied with its labor placement duties was often difficult for the court, requiring it to make subtle determinations as to whether sufficient effort was expended and whether any of the posted vacancies could be filled by the petitioner. In contrast, the question of *profkom* consent was more straightforward. The statute specifically required that the consent be preliminary *(predvaritel'no),* which was consistently interpreted to mean that management had to have it in hand before the order *(prikaz)* relating to the dismissal could be issued. If management failed to comply (either by not requesting *profkom* consent or by doing so in a nontimely fashion), laid-off workers who challenged their dismissal would automatically be reinstated by the courts.

Profkom consent as a precondition for a dismissal was introduced in 1958 and was heralded as an important legal guarantee of the right to work. Indeed, the limited statistical data indicate that a lack of *profkom* consent prompted the vast majority of court-ordered reinstatements. Over time, however, it began to be seen less as a protection of the right to work and more as a formalistic limitation on management discretion. Management came to see the reinstatement of workers due to a lack of consent as a distasteful technicality.

The February 1988 amendments to the Fundamentals and the RSFSR Labor Code attempted to remedy this shortcoming by eliminating the requirement that the consent be preliminary. As one Soviet labor law specialist noted, "the principle of intolerance of dismissal of workers without *profkom* consent has been retained, but the element of formalism has been excluded from it."[34] Under the new law, when faced with a reinstatement petition from a worker whose dismissal had not been sanctioned by the *profkom,* the court simply sent the case back to the enterprise in order to allow deliberation on that point. Consideration of the case on its merits proceeded only if *profkom* consent was forthcoming. Otherwise, the lack of consent would serve as sufficient grounds for reinstatement without the need for further action by the court.[35] Thus, the *profkom* retained veto power, but the political costs to the *profkom* (both for the members and the institution) of exercising it were greatly increased, given that it occurred so late in the process.[36]

In May 1991, the changes in the law were rescinded. Once again, preliminary consent of the *profkom* to any dismissal at the initiative of management was obligatory and, in its absence, the worker had to be reinstated.[37] In the next chapter, I examine the practical significance of these flip-flops in statutory language.

The February 1988 amendments introduced an additional procedural protection for workers dismissed on grounds of redundancy. The law was amended to require management to notify such workers two months before any proposed layoff. Whether the failure to do so constituted grounds for automatic reinstatement was not entirely clear. Neither the USSR nor the RSFSR Supreme Court ever addressed the question. The lower courts, however, did and, while finding the lack of notice to be prejudicial to management's case, they refrained from reinstating workers on that basis alone.[38]

Once the court got past these initial procedural inquiries, three additional questions became relevant when considering a reinstatement petition from a laid-off worker. First, did a layoff actually take place? Second, did management take all legally required measures to find the worker another job? Third, did management respect the worker's preferential rights, if any, to remain on the job?[39] If the answer to any one of these questions was "no," then the court had to reinstate the petitioner.[40]

Proving a Layoff Occurred

Whether the dismissal was really a redundancy-based layoff *(sokrashchenie shtata)* was a threshold question. Because the proof demanded to justify a layoff was impersonal, management sometimes used this rubric to get rid of particularly contentious workers, even when management was convinced that the workers' behavior warranted dismissal on disciplinary grounds.[41] The appeal of doing so was that it eliminated the need to assail publicly the dismissed worker's job performance and his or her personal character. Consequently, the court had to verify that the layoff was bona fide, that is, that it occurred for economic reasons and that management was not carrying out a personal vendetta against a particular worker. In pursuing this line of inquiry, the court was not allowed to question the advisability or business sense of the layoff.[42]

Management had the burden of proving that the dismissal was a layoff; the dismissed worker was not required to prove that it did not take place. The *Kommentarii* to the labor code contained a list of the sorts of evidence considered probative. This list did not change materially during the period under study and was comprised solely of documentary evidence.[43] Of these documents, the personnel schedule *(shtatnoe raspisanie)* was undoubtedly the most important. Examining the before and after versions of this document allowed the court to determine whether the laid-off worker's position had been eliminated. If the position continued to exist and a new person had been hired to fill it, this served as potent evidence of a sham layoff. Failure to provide the court with the relevant personnel schedules could, on its own, serve as grounds for sending a case back to the trial court for a new hearing, as is illustrated by the decision of the RSFSR Supreme Court in a 1986 case involving an allegedly laid-off secretary.[44]

Taken as a whole, the published cases indicate that this requirement that a "layoff" be proved by documentary evidence was strictly enforced by the courts. Oral representations by management were consistently held to be insufficient.[45] This is well illustrated by a 1985 case in which the RSFSR Supreme Court reinstated a worker because the date of his dismissal preceded the date on which the personnel schedule that put the layoff into effect was ratified. The fact that management, both in dismissing this worker and in preparing the new personnel schedule, was acting on oral instructions from its ministry was deemed irrelevant.[46] Sometimes even written authorization was not enough. In a 1986 case, the trial revealed that the elimination of the position of enterprise nurse was prompted not by reduced demand for medical services (as the ministerial order suggested) but by management's desire to get rid of this particular worker. The RSFSR Supreme Court reinstated the nurse, holding that ministry orders cannot be used to paper over a sham layoff.[47]

Along similar lines, the courts consistently held that only the sort of documentary evidence listed in the *Kommentarii* was acceptable. In a 1983 case, management proved that the ministry had ordered the reduction of personnel expenditures. It contended that this constituted authorization for the layoff. The *oblast'*-level court disagreed, basing its decision on management's failure to use the types of evidence sanctioned by the *Kommentarii.*[48] Appellate courts also criticized the predeliction on the part of trial courts to use the reports of commissions charged with evaluating workers' (particularly managers') qualifications as conclusive evidence of a bona fide layoff.[49] The higher courts held that the trial court had to look behind the report in order to assure itself that the conclusions were well grounded and, as a general rule, sent such cases back to the trial courts for new hearings.[50]

Once management convinced the court that the dismissal was a "layoff," the burden of proof shifted to the worker. In order to prevail, the worker had to rebut this evidence. The two most common rebuttal strategies relied on allegations that management was using the color of law to rid itself of an unwanted worker.

Workers often claimed that their dismissals were prompted by earlier criticisms of management policies. The USSR and RSFSR Supreme Courts consistently reiterated the illegal nature of retaliatory dismissals and directed the lower courts to investigate all such charges even when they were based solely on the oral allegations of the affected worker. Appellate cases brought before them in which the trial courts gave short shrift to such charges were uniformly sent back for new hearings with a notation to investigate more throroughly.[51] Even the fact that the criticism had been directed against a management team that was no longer in place and was not responsible for the petitioner's layoff did not stop the USSR Supreme Court from ordering a new hearing in a 1988 case.[52] The fact that virtually every communique from the high court that addressed labor law issues pressed this issue suggests, however, that the lower courts were slow to take workers' claims of revenge-inspired dismissals seriously. The data that I gathered in Moscow trial courts, reported in chapter 4, tend to buttress this conclusion.

The worker's claim to having been dismissed for criticizing management had the legal effect of shifting the burden of proof back to management. Management then had to convince the court, through a preponderance of physical evidence of the sort described above, that in laying off the worker, it had been motivated by business and not personal considerations. The testimony of the worker's supervisor and other managers, while relevant, was not considered sufficient to prove the legitimacy of the dismissal. Thus, the demands placed on the parties were very different. While oral allegations on the part of the worker served to shift the burden of proof, management was required to rebut these allegations with documentary evidence. Furthermore, as a 1990 RSFSR Supreme Court case illustrated, managers who were found to have dismissed a worker for criticism were subject to additional personal liability.[53]

The second fairly common rebuttal technique for workers was to allege that, after the petitioner's (worker A) departure, another person (worker B) was hired to perform the same duties worker A previously carried out, and that only the job titles differed. The *Kommentarii* forbad this sort of underhanded maneuver.[54]

The courts tended to be sympathetic to workers in such cases.[55] For example, in a 1975 case, an "inspector" (the worker A of this case) was allegedly laid off. Thereafter, another worker was hired as an "engineer" (the worker B of this case). Worker A claimed that, despite the different titles, worker B was actually doing his old job. Although management proved that worker B performed additional duties that worker A never had, the RSFSR Supreme Court held that management had to go further, that it had to prove that worker A was incapable of performing these additional duties. By the same token, as a 1986 case illustrates, downgrading the position after an alleged layoff was no more acceptable.[56] In that case, a "senior economist" was let go and a new position of "bookkeeper-economist" was created. Although the responsibilities and the salary of this new position were much less, the RSFSR Supreme Court ordered a new hearing on the question of whether there had really been a layoff or only a change in the job title.[57]

These cases illustrate the difference in the burden of proof placed on management and worker. When a worker petitioned for reinstatement, he or she did not have to prove that the layoff had been a sham. Yet management was required to prove conclusively that it was genuine through specific types of documentary evidence. However, in order to rebut management's prima facie case, a worker had only to allege, with no supporting evidence, that another worker was doing the same job under a new name. At that point, the burden shifted back to management and, once again, it was required to prove definitively that these unsubstantiated charges were unfounded.[58] Thus, the process appeared to favor workers over management.

Management's Duty to Transfer

The second question that a judge had to resolve when considering the merits of a laid-off worker's petition for reinstatement was whether management had complied with its statutory duty to transfer the worker to another job. This duty had two components: (1) the sort of job to be offered and (2) the scope of the job search undertaken on the worker's behalf.

The statutory language provided little guidance as to the sort of job the laid-off worker had to be offered. Consequently, the courts took the initiative in fleshing out the statute.[59] Over time, the rule that the worker had to be offered a job with duties comparable to those of his or her prior job became well accepted. If this was not possible, then other available jobs for which the worker was qualified had to be offered.[60] This rule was not changed in any material respect during the period under study.[61]

The courts tended to define "comparable" rather narrowly. For example, the RSFSR Supreme Court held that offering a plasterer a job as an insulator was not acceptable. In a more extreme case, the USSR Supreme Court found that, despite having offered a shoe salesman a job as a coat salesman, management had not fulfilled its duty. The court reasoned that the shoe salesman had expertise that was not transferable to the new position. In these two cases, the petitioners were reinstated because management was unable to convince the court that "comparable" jobs were unavailable.

The requirement that the offered job be "comparable" was designed to protect the worker. Consequently, if the worker volunteered to take on a noncomparable job, management was hard-pressed to refuse. This is well illustrated by a 1978 case in which management was scolded and ordered to reinstate three electricians and put them to work as bricklayers. Although the work was clearly not comparable, the petitioners had informed management of their willingness to take it on. The court held that if management had had the ability to offer this other work, it should have transferred rather than dismissed them.[62]

If there were no comparable jobs, the court could not demand that they be created. It could, however, inquire into whether there were any other jobs available for which the worker was qualified. In this regard, simply showing that none of the positions were within the petitioner's area of expertise was not sufficient. Instead, management had to provide the court with evidence regarding the required duties and demonstrate that the laid-off worker would be unable to perform them. Management was often placed in a difficult position when the personnel schedule indicated the existence of vacancies. In a 1990 case brought by a laid-off truck driver, the RSFSR Supreme Court was troubled by the presence of 28 vacancies for drivers and ordered a new hearing.[63] Similar proworker decisions resulted even when job titles and qualifications were very different. A good example is the 1987 case in which the RSFSR Supreme Court held that management had to prove affirmatively that the petitioner's lack of special engineering education should bar him from a vacant engineer position.[64]

As between the parties, the worker seemed, once again, to be in the more enviable position in terms of burden of proof. The worker had only to allege that a vacancy existed for which he or she was potentially suitable. Management then had to prove the worker was not capable of filling this position; the worker was not required to demonstrate his or her suitability.[65] The USSR Supreme Court confirmed the continuing validity of this basic rule, even after the February 1988 amendments to the Fundamentals and the RSFSR Labor Code.[66]

Turning to the second component of management's labor placement duty, it would be fair to say that initially management's duty to search for alternative positions for laid-off workers was broadly construed. In a 1973 "guiding explanation" *(rukovodiashchee raz"iasnenie)*, the RSFSR Supreme Court instructed the lower courts that layoffs were permitted "only if it is impossible to transfer the worker, with his consent, to other work." The Court went on to define impossibility as being the absence of the sort of work previously done by the petitioner "in the given enterprise or *in another enterprise*" (emphasis added).[67] Thus, management's duty extended beyond its own walls. Published case decisions demonstrate that the courts did hold management to this very high standard of conduct.[68] For example, the dismissal of a school teacher was held to be invalid and the teacher reinstated because the school administrators had made no effort to find her a job at another school. In its opinion, the court explicitly referred to the 1973 "guiding explanation" as the basis for its decision.[69]

The USSR Supreme Court addressed this issue in a 1980 "guiding explanation" and, in effect, overruled the earlier instruction of the RSFSR Supreme Court. The lower courts were directed that

> When considering cases involving the reinstatement of persons whose labor contracts were dissolved . . . [on grounds of redundancy], the court has an obligation to request and obtain from management evidence that demonstrates that the worker has refused a transfer to a different job or that management did not have the opportunity to transfer the worker, with his consent, to other work in the same enterprise."[70]

Thus, management's duty to find laid-off workers other jobs was curtailed to its own premises. Yet its job placement function was not eliminated entirely. Indeed, the USSR Supreme Court reconfirmed it in a 1988 decree[71] and, in 1990, the RSFSR Supreme Court returned two cases to the trial court for new hearings on the grounds that management had not expended sufficient effort to find jobs for the petitioners within the enterprise.[72]

Requiring management to make a good faith effort to find redundant workers acceptable jobs obviously hampered its capacity to rationalize the workforce and thereby increase its efficiency. During the Gorbachev years, Soviet labor law specialists criticized the law on those grounds. They argued that finding jobs for laid-off workers (or assisting them in so doing) should be the sole obligation of the state-sponsored labor placement bureaus *(biuro po trudoustroistve)*.[73] These bureaus had existed since the early 1970s but had never become much of a factor in labor policy, due largely to their woeful underfunding.[74] By the late 1980s, they were still not computerized.[75] The formal recognition of the inevitability of unemployment brought renewed attention to these bureaus.[76] Yet management was never officially relieved of its placement obligation vis-à-vis redundant workers.

Furthermore, the published case decisions and pronouncements of the USSR and RSFSR Supreme Courts indicate that workers' rights were rigorously protected in this regard. The higher courts routinely sent cases back to the trial courts if there was even a hint that they did not fully explore the worker's charges that vacancies existed for which the worker was qualified yet jobs were never offered to him or her. The pattern is the same as previously observed: unsupported oral allegations on the part of the worker were sufficient to shift the burden of proof onto management, which then had to disprove them affirmatively. Once again, the law (both substantively and procedurally) appeared to be on the worker's side.

Preferential Rights

The third and final issue that the trial court had to consider when deciding whether to reinstate a laid-off worker was whether management properly took into account his or her preferential rights (as compared to other workers) to remain on the job. The criteria to be used in making such determinations were spelled out in the RSFSR Labor Code and were never changed following the adoption of the Code in 1971.[77] Not surprisingly, the threshold criteria were productivity and level of qualifications. If a distinction could not be made on these grounds, the state provided an exhaustive list of other factors that must be considered. These included both work-related, for example, length of uninterrupted work service, as well as non-work-related factors, for example, family size and past military service.

The court did not consider the question of preferential rights unless the worker alleged that management had violated the law in this regard. If such a claim were made (usually in the form of an unsupported oral allegation), management was required to prove conclusively that the petitioner was the most appropriate person to have been laid off. If management could not sustain this burden of proof, the worker was reinstated.

The higher courts' attitude toward this issue was much the same as that exhibited toward allegations of retaliatory dismissals. To this end, the USSR and RSFSR Supreme Courts consistently instructed the lower courts that any claim by a worker that one of his or her co-workers should have been laid off in his or her place had to be taken seriously and investigated thoroughly. They gave force to their words by routinely overturning lower court decisions and ordering new hearings in cases in which the worker contended the trial court ignored such charges.[78] Even cases in which the relative abilities of the petitioner and his or her coworkers were examined in excruciating detail at trial were sometimes overturned. A good example is a 1989 RSFSR Supreme Court case in which on appeal the worker claimed that the data submitted by management failed to compare her with all possible candidates for layoff. She further claimed that the data regarding productivity was improperly interpreted by management and the court accepted management's interpretation without question. The RSFSR Supreme Court sent the case back for further study of this question of preferential rights.[79]

Summary

This survey of the statutory law governing layoffs and the published materials on its implementation reveals a striking consistency. At every turn, the law seemed to be on the side of the worker. The very fact that the law contained an exhaustive list of permissible reasons for dismissing a worker obviously served to benefit workers. Management was not permitted to dismiss a worker on a whim. It had to be able to justify its action as falling within one of the statutorily sanctioned categories. Moreover, management was consistently required to meet a higher burden of proof than were workers. The published case decisions indicate that the courts were rigorous in holding management to these legal standards.

The Law Governing Transfers

The Law Prior to February 1988

The second focus of the case study is the law governing internal transfers at the initiative of management. This law proceeds from the fundamental principle of contract law that neither party to a contract can unilaterally change its terms.[80] Following this logic, the Fundamentals and the RSFSR Labor Code provided that a worker could not be transferred without his or her consent.[81] On its face, this rule would seem to act as a profound constraint on management attempts to enhance efficiency. The apparent simplicity of this rule was, however, deceptive, for in order to grasp the full implications of this single sentence, it is necessary to persevere through a labyrinth of definitional issues.

Definitional Issues. The first of these is the definition of transfer. Under the pre-1988 law, a "transfer" *(perevod)* was deemed to have occurred when management demanded that the worker perform "other work" *(drugaia rabota)* or be relocated to a different "place of work" *(mesto raboty)* not stipulated in the labor contract or when management unilaterally changed the "essential conditions of labor" *(sushchestvennie usloviia truda)* for the worker. Such "transfers" were permitted only with the consent of the worker. Notwithstanding the fact that, according to prominent Soviet labor law scholars, the term "other work" was to be broadly construed,[82] management was far from hamstrung by the law. It could change the worker's "workplace" *(rabochee mesto)* or alter nonessential conditions of labor at its discretion.[83] Such changes were defined as "shifts" *(peremeshchenie)* and, in contrast to "transfers," did not require the worker's consent.[84]

Thus, the critical issue for management when contemplating a reorganization of the workplace in order to enhance efficiency was whether the changes made would be construed as "transfers" or "shifts." Management preferred the latter because no consent was required. Workers obviously preferred to have changes categorized as "transfers" because it gave them a voice in their future.

The statutory law provided a basic guideline for making this distinction. The RSFSR Labor Code provided that

> The shifting of a . . . worker to another workplace in the same enterprise . . . without a change in specialty, qualifications, position, or amount of pay, privileges, advantages, and other essential conditions of labor shall not be considered a transfer to other work.[85]

The RSFSR Supreme Court clarified that "a change even if in only one of these conditions is a transfer to other work demanding the consent of the worker."[86] The approach taken in this statute of having a nonexhaustive list of essential conditions in labor resulted in the courts playing an active role in this definitional question[87] and gave rise to two distinct lines of cases. On the one hand, there were cases in which a condition listed in the statute (a Core Condition) had been changed. On the other hand, there were cases in which management had changed a condition not listed in the statute but which the worker believed to be essential.

Distinguishing between the two types of cases is useful because different levels of proof were required for each. For example, a worker who claimed that management had unilaterally changed a Core Condition did not have to prove that the condition was, in fact, essential. That was assumed. In contrast, a worker who made a similar claim based on a non-Core Condition first had to prove to the court that the condition was essential. In such cases, the presumption was that it was not essential and, consequently, that the change was not a transfer but merely a shift that did not require the worker's consent.

Changing Core Conditions. Cases involving changes in Core Conditions were often fairly straightforward. In many instances, management had clearly changed the worker's specialty, qualifications, and position, thus giving rise to a transfer to which the worker's consent should have been sought. For example, demanding that a hotel administrator work as a floor supervisor *(dezhurnaia)* was held to be an illegal transfer by a trial court *(narodnyi sud)* in the Tadzhik SSR and the worker was ordered reinstated to her prior position.[88] Similarly, a Moscow suburban trial court held that sending a photographer to work as a third-class laboratory assistant was an illegal transfer and reinstated the worker.[89] In these cases, it was clear that the worker was being asked to do something to which he or she had not initially agreed, amounting to an attempt by management to change the labor contract unilaterally.

The changes did not need to be dramatic to warrant a finding that the labor function had been changed. A closer case is that of a woman hired in 1971 to tidy up a research laboratory who, after a coworker had been fired in 1975, was assigned the additional duties of cleaning up after the laboratory animals. She argued that these duties had not been stipulated in her labor contract and that management could not demand them of her without her prior consent. The RSFSR Supreme Court agreed, holding this to be a change in her labor function, that is, a transfer, and ordered her reinstated to her prior duties. In this case (as in many others), there was no detailed written contract that could be consulted.[90] Instead, the plaintiff had only an oral agreement with management. In this case, the plaintiff's allegations were buttressed by the four years of work experience during which she had never been asked to care for the animals. What happened in such cases is by now familiar from the survey of court practice involving dismissals: the worker made an allegation as to the scope of her duties that then had to be affirmatively disproved by management. Thus, the process as well as the substantive law favored workers by imposing a significantly heavier burden of proof on management.

In 1980s, however, management became more creative and the courts became more lenient. Take the example of a design engineer who was suddenly asked to prepare technical documentation for microfilm readers. Although outside the circle of tasks he normally performed, this task was part of his written job description *(dolzhnostnaia instruktsiia)*. Despite the fact that this document came into existence well after the plaintiff had been hired and so could not possibly have served as the basis for the plaintiff's labor contract, it was this piece of evidence that ultimately persuaded the RSFSR Supreme Court that the demands of management did not constitute a change in the labor function. The court was unsympathetic to the estoppel argument it had found so persuasive in the 1976 laboratory cleanup case described above. This would seem to represent an attempt by the court to loosen the reins on management while continuing to pay lip service to the sanctity of the labor contract.[91]

The Core Conditions consisted not only of a worker's labor function (specialty, qualifications, position) but also included wages and privileges, which likewise could not be changed unilaterally by management. A good example is the case of a worker who was moved from ordinary painting work to painting done on board a vessel. Despite the identical nature of the worker's duties, the RSFSR Supreme Court held it to be a transfer requiring the worker's consent because the pensionable age at the second job was 50 while it was 55 at the first. This change in the worker's pension rights was construed as a change in her privileges.[92] The case of a worker moved from his regular duties as a stoker in the boiler room of a fish factory to the boiler room of a dormitory attached to the factory provides yet another example of this tendency. Once again, the RSFSR Supreme Court was not swayed by the identical nature of the duties. Because the worker had received 12 days' vacation at the first assignment and only 6 days' at the second, the Court held that his privileges had been altered. As a result, this new assignment was deemed to be a transfer and so could be carried out only with the worker's consent.[93]

Similarly, in a reference book for labor inspectors, R. Z. Livshits, a prominent Soviet labor law scholar, wrote that a transfer requiring the worker's consent occurred when a worker's qualification level changed or even when his or her title changed. Even a seemingly innocuous change from "leading" engineer to "senior" engineer was considered a transfer.[94] Although some of these examples represent only incremental changes in what a worker did every day, they are, nonetheless, unambiguous examples of transfer under the pre-1988 law. When Core Conditions were involved, the law governing internal transfers was very rigid. A worker had only to demonstrate that management had changed one of these Conditions without his or her consent in order to prevail.[95] Management's hands were tied. The presumption that these were Core Conditions, that they were fundamental to every worker's labor contract, was not rebuttable but rather absolute.

Changing Non-Core Conditions. The dynamics were quite different when dealing with changes in non-Core Conditions. In such cases, the worker faced the presumption that the condition was not essential and so could be changed unilaterally at the discretion of management. In order to overcome this presumption, the worker had to prove that the condition was an integral part of his or her contract (whether oral or written) with management. Often this boiled down to the worker's word against management's. In such instances, the procedural conventions favored the worker.

This can be illustrated by examining the succession of cases involving workers who had been moved from one subdivision *(strukturnoe podrazdelenie)* of an enterprise to another. Although some Soviet labor law scholars have argued that, under the pre-1988 law, such a change was a prima facie transfer requiring the worker's consent,[96] the weight of authority suggests otherwise. Both the USSR and RSFSR Supreme Courts have stated unequivocably that such changes are not to be regarded as transfers unless the parties have specifically agreed that a worker would be placed in a particular subdivision or shop *(tsekh)* or unless the worker's labor function changes as a consequence of the move.[97]

Likewise, the pre-1988 editions of the official commentaries to the labor code set forth the general rule that moves between subdivisions are generally considered "shifts" not requiring the workers' consent.[98]

This rule would seem to have enabled management to reallocate its workforce among its subdivisions in a more rational manner. However, the published case decisions interpreting the rule demonstrate that it was virtually impossible to move a worker from one subdivision to another without impacting one or more of the Core Conditions.[99] In fact, management might have been in a better position had intraenterprise redistribution simply been listed as a Core Condition. At least the consequences would have been clear. Instead, the pre-1988 law required a laborious case-by-case analysis of the nature of the particular labor contract.[100]

The published case decisions provide several relevant examples. A 1981 case involved a woman who had been hired as a barmaid for the Kosmos cafe in Volzhskii. After some time, the cafe was closed and she was assigned to work as a barmaid in the Kulinarie cafe. Despite the identical nature of the work, she refused to report to the new assignment and so was ultimately dismissed on grounds of absenteeism.[101] Although the trial court sided with management, the RSFSR Supreme Court reversed, reasoning that the parties had specifically agreed that the plaintiff would work at the Kosmos and that she could not be reassigned without her consent. It should be noted that there was no physical evidence of the parties' agreement, only the plaintiff's word. Yet the RSFSR Supreme Court viewed this as sufficient in the absence of contravening evidence. As the plaintiff could not be reinstated to her old job, the practical import of the decision was to give the plaintiff a right to refuse any proposed reassignment.[102]

In a 1987 case that was also decided in favor of the worker, the court employed a different line of reasoning, one that had the USSR and RSFSR Supreme Courts' stamp of approval. The head of one technical design bureau was ordered to take over another such bureau within the same enterprise. Although the Minsk trial court ordered the plaintiff reinstated to his prior job, management appealed, and the decision was reversed by the Minsk city appeals court and then upheld by the Belorussian Supreme Court. The USSR Supreme Court disagreed, holding that management had illegally transferred the plaintiff. The Court reasoned that the duties of the two positions were sufficiently different to constitute a change in the labor function, clearly an essential condition of labor.[103]

The Court went on to offer management some unsolicited advice, noting that Soviet law permitted the plaintiff to be laid off and implying that this would have been the more prudent path. Although only dicta and therefore not binding on the parties, this language would seem to represent a shift in judicial thinking in favor of management. After all, a similar recommendation could have been made in the 1981 Kosmos cafe case discussed above, but was not.[104]

Excluding Workers from Brigades. This judicial empathy for the predicament of management (or perhaps nascent concern for efficiency) was also reflected in a series of substantive pronouncements and case decisions of the USSR and RSFSR Supreme Courts in the mid-1980s on brigade membership.[105] Brigades were organized groups of workers (usually 10 to 20) who shared responsibility for certain production tasks and enjoyed a fair amount of autonomy in terms of how those tasks were to be carried out and how the members were to be compensated for so doing.[106] Exclusion from a brigade was akin to a transfer. Typically, workers were kicked out of their brigades by the other members and challenged their exclusion on the grounds that it constituted a change in his essential conditions of labor.[107] From the individual worker's perspective, whether his or her work situation changed unilaterally by management or by a majority vote of his or her fellow brigade members made little difference.

The issue first arose in a 1984 case decided as a case of first instance by the RSFSR Supreme Court.[108] The plaintiff was a woman who worked at a samovar factory as a second-class polisher and was kicked out of a brigade by a vote of its members. She claimed that this constituted a change in essential conditions and was illegal because she had not given her consent. In particular, she argued that her exclusion would result in a 50 percent decrease in her premium. The RSFSR Supreme Court found this to be a shift not a transfer because she continued to work in the place, position, and qualification level stipulated in her labor contract.[109] The Court further held that, standing alone, a decrease in wages did not give rise to a transfer because her wages were based on a piece-rate system and so depended on the effort she herself expended.

The importance of this decision is reflected in the decision of the editors of the *Kommentarii* to include a detailed description of it in their analysis of the statute governing transfers.[110] Soviet labor law specialists criticized it on the grounds that the RSFSR Supreme Court failed to explain why changes in the wage level and the manner of working did not give rise to a transfer requiring the worker's consent.[111] After all, wages were a Core Condition.

Despite these apparent shortcomings, the USSR Supreme Court took the same line in its 1986 plenum. The Court decreed that

> the relocation to individual work of a worker who had been ejected from a brigade by . . . its members is not a transfer that requires his consent, provided it does not change the character of the duties that are stipulated in the terms of the labor contract.[112]

The Court went on to note that such a change should be considered a transfer only if working in a brigade had been stipulated in the labor contract.[113] The USSR Supreme Court reconfirmed this rule in 1987.[114]

Thus, the rule developed for brigade exclusions appeared to be virtually identical to that articulated for non-Core Conditions. Yet the courts' attitudes when confronted with this issue demonstrate that the similarities were merely skin deep. Prior to the mid-1980s, the courts tended to interpret the term "essential conditions of labor" rather broadly. They searched for a way to declare management's action to be an illegal unilateral transfer (rather than a shift). Often judges resorted to small and seemingly inconsequential changes in work conditions to justify their decisions. With brigade exclusions, just the opposite happened, that is, courts went out of their way not to find a transfer when, from a common sense point of view, it was present.

One might argue that the courts' attitudinal shift was due to their greater respect for decisions of the work collective versus those of management. Such an argument, however, is undermined by the courts' consistent failure to distinguish between brigade exclusions and transfers.

At the time, one could not be sure—although in retrospect it is clear—that the Supreme Courts' attitude toward being moved in and out of brigades marked a major shift away from a preoccupation with workers' rights and toward a concern with management's flexibility. This nascent shift in the balance of collective and individual interests was consummated with the legislative changes of February 1988.

The Law Governing Transfers after February 1988

The Substance of the Law. In February 1988, the provisions governing internal transfers were changed in parallel fashion in both the Fundamentals and the RSFSR Labor Code.[115] The impetus for these changes was the new Law on State Enterprises, adopted in July 1987, which was intended to be the cornerstone of perestroika.[116] This law dealt only peripherally with labor issues, but certain inconsistencies nonetheless arose between it and the long-standing Soviet labor law.

The first step in abating these inconsistencies was taken not legislatively but through the familiar tactic of a joint decree of the Central Committee of the Communist Party, the USSR Council of Ministers, and the official trade union organization. The decree, issued in January 1988, announced a campaign to rationalize the workforce. It represented a first effort to establish a safety net for laid-off workers, and focused on issues of labor placement, retraining, and unemployment compensation.

Intraenterprise transfers were mentioned only in the context of reallocating redundant workers.

When the Fundamentals and the RSFSR Labor Code were amended several weeks later to take account of this decree, the statute governing internal transfers was changed fundamentally. Several Soviet labor law specialists described the changes as "highly progressive" from the point of view of encouraging efficiency.[117] Management enjoyed more leeway in undertaking a reorganization of its workforce, and the relevant statutory language was clearer, presumably offering more predictability.

Most scholars, however, viewed these amendments as misguided.[118] Indeed, the head of the labor law sector of the Institute of State and Law wrote that "[t]his amendment has made Soviet workers practically defenseless against in-house maneuvering by management."[119] For these and other scholars, the most grating element of the new law was that it gave management permission to change "essential conditions of labor" without any input from workers. Workers who could not stomach the changes were to be cast aside. Many regarded this expansion of the rights of the state at the expense of individual rights as inappropriate and even repugnant in an era in which the Soviet Union was ostensibly reconstituting itself as a law-governed state *(pravovoe gosudarstvo)*.[120]

These scholars uniformly predicted that the new provisions would be a temporary aberration, that is, that the law would be changed back to its old form in short order. Indeed, the draft Fundamentals prepared by scholars at a key Moscow legal institute[121] in the spring of 1990 provided for intra-enterprise transfers to be treated as they were under the pre-1988 law. Under its terms, management would no longer be permitted to change "essential conditions of labor" unilaterally. Yet when the USSR Supreme Soviet took up the question of labor law in May 1991, the legislators limited themselves to revising the existing Fundamentals.[122] Although some elements of the 1988 amendments were changed back to their earlier wording,[123] the provisions governing transfers were left untouched.

Why was the law governing internal transfers changed in 1988? The legislative changes came before the elections that would transform the Supreme Soviets of the USSR and the RSFSR into at least quasi-democratic institutions. In early 1988, the Supreme Soviets were still rubber-stamp operations. These legislators automatically voted for any piece of legislation placed before them. Thus, talking with legislators about why these amendments were adopted proved to be useless.

More profitable were conversations with various members of the working group who had drafted the amendments to the Fundamentals submitted to and approved by the Supreme Soviets in early 1988. The group included scholars from the most prominent legal and labor policy research institutes and representatives of the official trade union and the government. The stories they told were far from consistent. Just about the only point of agreement was that the issue of intraenterprise transfers was highly contentious. What they could not agree upon was how the parties lined up when the question was being debated. Sometimes I heard that it was the state (in the form of the State Committee on Labor and Social Questions or *Goskomtrud*) versus the official trade union. In this scenario, the state favored giving management complete free rein in reallocating its workers while the trade union wanted to continue the practice of giving workers some say in their future. Others disputed this version, telling me that representatives of *Goskomtrud* and the trade union presented a united front in favor of enhancing management's flexibility and that it was left to the legal scholars to try to hold the line. These scholars were concerned not so much with the impact that the change might have on workers but rather that it represented a rejection of the contractual theory underpinning the law itself.

What really happened is known only to the members of the group. What is beyond dispute is that the February 1988 changes to the law were the product of compromise. As B. P. Kurashvili of the Institute of State and Law has noted

> it would be rash and dangerous not to see the contradictory, halfway, intermediate nature of the legislation that has been adopted. It is the form of a temporary compromise between radical and conservative approaches, between the initiators of fundamental reform and the inert bureaucratic *apparat* of management, which resorts to the phraseology of perestroika in order to maximize their conservative positions and proposals.[124]

What is also beyond dispute is that the statute governing intraenterprise transfers was considered important enough to fight over. After all, many amendments were made to the Fundamentals in February 1988, but it was always the transfer law that scholars brought up when I asked which of these were particularly difficult or controversial.

Definition of Transfer. The substantive changes to the law were threefold. First, the definitions of transfer and shift were tightened. While the distinction was retained, as were the legal consequences of the distinction, the statute went on to provide that a relocation to another subdivision or machine was also a shift, provided that the specialty, qualification level, and position remained unchanged.[125] Thus, the determination of whether consent was required came to be based solely on whether the labor function had changed. Changes in other conditions, regardless of whether previously regarded as "essential," were not taken into consideration.[126] Livshits praised this aspect of the new law:

> Implementation of this rule is not particularly difficult. It is clear that it is forbidden to transfer a lathe operator to the position of a metal craftsman, an engineer to the position of a technician, a doctor to the position of a laboratory assistant, etc. The difficulty arises when there is a dispute over whether the position to which the worker is being transferred is different from his previous position.[127]

Livshits relates the case of a fifth-level lathe operator *(tokar')* who was relocated from a repair shop to a mechanical shop within the same enterprise. Certain conditions of labor changed, including the level of premiums and privileges. The change was not deemed a transfer because the worker continued to be employed as a fifth-level lathe operator.[128] There is little doubt that this would have been considered a transfer requiring the worker's consent under the old law. Yet the courts did not completely abandon workers' interests. Obvious cases, such as demanding that a kitchen worker work as a supply clerk, were still recognized as transfers.[129]

When disputes arose over whether the labor function had changed, the critical piece of evidence was not the job title but rather the written job description *(dolzhnostnaia instruktsiia).* If this document included the newly demanded duties, then the change was not considered a transfer; it did not matter that management never requested that the worker perform these tasks.[130] Furthermore, their absence was not necessarily fatal. In contrast to past practice, management's demands that a worker master more advanced technology were likewise not be deemed to be transfers.[131]

The new rules obviously favored management more than the old rules. After all, management controlled the content of the official job descriptions. A worker could be hired and work for many years without ever seeing this document. While the *profkom* might be called upon to approve these job descriptions, its role was strictly consultative.[132] Changes in job descriptions were solely within the purview of management. On a deeper level, these rules helped management by providing a degree of stability and predictability that was previously absent.[133] No longer was there any doubt that a worker's relocation to another division within an enterprise was a shift that could be undertaken at management's discretion.[134] This is not to say that management had been given free rein but rather that the parameters of permissibility had been clarified, thereby giving management the freedom to plan and implement reallocations of the workforce without having to look over its shoulder constantly.

Changes in "Essential Conditions of Labor." The second major change in the law governing internal transfers concerned the legal consequences of management unilaterally changing the "essential conditions of labor" *(sushchestvennye usloviia truda).* The pre-1988 law treated such changes as transfers requiring the worker's consent. While not eliminated, the nature of the legal constraint on management was greatly lessened. The Fundamentals and the RSFSR Labor Code provided that

> A change in the essential conditions of labor is permitted in connection with changes in the organization of production and labor, provided that the specialty, qualification level, and position remain the same. The worker must be notified of changes in essential conditions of labor—system and amount of wages, privileges, work regime, establishment or elimination of part-time work, change in job title, etc.—at least two months in advance.[135]

Thus, change in essential conditions of labor became a distinct legal category, much like transfer and shift.[136] From the perspective of management, it fell in between those two. While managers were no longer required to obtain the worker's consent to the change in circumstances, they were not permitted to act unilaterally.

The law placed two limitations on management's ability to change a worker's essential conditions of labor: motive and notice. As to the former, changes were permitted only in connection with changes in the organization of production and labor. Unfortunately, the definition of this term varied depending on the circumstances.[137] The courts interpreted it rather broadly and even sanctioned the relocation of workers in order to eliminate a conflictual situation at the workplace.[138] Yet management did not receive carte blanche. Indeed, the RSFSR Supreme Court emphasized the importance of having the trial court look into the reason for the change and ordered that the prior conditions be reinstated whenever the change was motivated by personal animosity rather than the needs of production.[139] Clearly the goal was to facilitate efficiency-based work reorganizations while continuing to forbid management to act arbitrarily or punitively.

The two-month notice provision would also seem to limit management's freedom of action. However, in practice, the courts implemented this provision in a remarkably nonformalistic manner that tended to favor management.[140] Rather than rescinding the changes or imposing some other remedy of deterrence, the RSFSR Supreme Court instructed the lower courts simply to shift the effective date of the change so as to satisfy the notice provision.[141] For example, in a case in which a worker's wage level was changed without notice, the court ordered management to maintain the old level for two months.[142]

This provision governing unilateral changes in essential conditions of labor by management represented a significant reduction in the rights of workers. Previously, if a worker's wages were reduced or any other essential condition of labor were changed without his or her consent, the worker could sue to have the prior conditions restored. After the legislative amendments, this cause of action was open to a worker only if management acted maliciously. In all other instances, the worker had only to be notified of the impending change. From management's perspective, the new law was a positive development. It loosened the constraints on management, thereby permitting workers to be reallocated in order to enhance productivity. Yet the law was still far from ideal. The list of essential conditions continued to be nonexhaustive, which gave rise to a certain level of unpredictability for management.[143]

Consequences of Workers' Refusal to Accede to Changes. The third major change in the law was closely related to the second and also resulted in a cutback in worker's rights. The law was amended to provide for the dismissal of workers who refused to continue working on the grounds that their essential conditions of labor had been changed unilaterally.[144] The fact that they could be fired was nothing new. Previously, such dismissals were treated as layoffs, with all the attendant procedural rights outlined above. A number of workers challenged their dismissals under the transfer statute, arguing that in fact they were laid off. However, the courts were uniformly unsympathetic to such claims, consistently upholding the dismissal as related to the refusal to accept a transfer.[145]

There are several reasons why this seemingly meaningless distinction was important from a worker's perspective. First, when dismissed pursuant to the transfer statute, a worker did not have the right to appeal his or her dismissal directly to the local trial court but first had to challenge management's action in the commission for labor disputes *(kommissia po trudovym sporam* or *KTS)* and the *profkom.* Only after failing to obtain satisfaction from one of these in-house bodies did the worker have the right to press his or her claim in court.[146] The courts strictly enforced this obligation to exhaust all administrative remedies.[147] This tended to discourage worker complaints, both because of the time and effort necessary and because of the low level of respect commanded by the *KTS* and the *profkom* among workers.[148] In addition, *profkom* consent was required for layoffs, but not for transfer-related dismissals.[149] Although I have argued elsewhere that the *profkom* generally acted as a rubber stamp for management,[150] the fact that its consent was required did force management to justify the dismissal and may well have deterred management from acting in haste. Finally, when laying off a worker, management was legally obliged to make a good faith effort to find him or her a comparable job within the enterprise. If the worker alleged that this was not done, management had to reinstate the worker unless it could convince the court that doing so was impossible.[151] In contrast, no such obligation obtained when a worker was dismissed because he or she refused to continue working when the essential conditions of labor were changed. Thus, having a dismissal categorized as transfer-related (rather than as a layoff) was very much to the advantage of management.

Summary

The consistency observed in the survey of the law governing layoffs is absent with regard to the law governing internal transfers. The formalism that characterized the law prior to the 1988 legislative amendments appeared to operate as a constraint on management efforts to reorganize its labor force in order to enhance productivity and efficiency. This is not to say that such reorganization efforts were never undertaken or were doomed to failure but that management perceived the requirement of obtaining the consent of all affected workers as a significant obstacle. It may have contributed to the long-standing practice of hiring additional workers rather than attempting to use those already available in a more rational manner.[152] However, the demographic trends of the 1980s made these extensive methods of increasing output rather outdated.[153] Intensive methods of stimulating growth might have been found but were not, indicating the level of resistence or perhaps just the inertia of management when confronted with the need to rationalize its labor force.

Management was not entirely to blame. Recognizing the need to reallocate the workforce in a more efficient manner, Soviet policymakers could have amended the law so as to loosen the constraints on management. At the very least, the presumption that the Core Conditions were essential (and hence not changeable without consent) could have been made rebuttable. This would have allowed management to embark on wholesale reordering of the workforce under appropriate circumstances without having to worry that the process could be held up or even reversed by disgruntled workers. However, such changes in the law were introduced only in February 1988.

In light of these legislative changes, the courts seemed more willing to see management's point of view in transfer cases and, particularly during the Gorbachev era, to characterize a change in working conditions as a mere shift rather than as a transfer. Perhaps the difference lies in the February 1988 amendment to the law governing internal transfers, which unquestionably had a promanagement bent. Yet the statutory law remained murky, thereby leaving considerable room for maneuvering by the courts. In contrast to the proworker attitude exhibited in the published opinions in dismissal cases, the courts appeared to follow the proefficiency line taken by the statute when considering cases involving internal transfers.

Conclusion

Although the legal rules surrounding dismissals and transfers differ in the extent to which they favor the interests of workers or management, they were remarkably similar in that, according to the published materials, both appeared to be rigorously implemented. Notwithstanding some softening in the interpretation of some provisions relating to internal transfers in the late 1980s, the courts (particuarly the USSR and RSFSR Supreme Courts) took the rights granted to workers by the legislature seriously and required management to meet a very high burden of proof when it endeavored to dislodge a worker from a long-held job. The courts did their best to guarantee that workers' allegations of illegal activities on the part of management were checked out thoroughly and remedied whenever possible.

In the next chapter, I address whether this picture of courts that care deeply about protecting workers' rights has any basis in reality. In other words, does the tip of the iceberg revealed through statutory law and published case reports bear any similarity to the reality of everyday life in the Soviet Union?

CHAPTER 4

The Law in Practice: Implementing Labor Law in Soviet Enterprises and Courts

Introduction

The published appellate case decisions paint a picture of Soviet courts as rigorous, indeed even relentless, in their protection of workers, oftentimes holding management to a burden of proof that seemed to be virtually insurmountable. How well does this workers' rights-driven vision of Soviet labor law hold up when the law's implemention on a day-to-day basis is examined?

When moving from the rarefied world of the Soviet and Russian Supreme Courts into the more mundane world of factories and trial courts, the legal rights of workers that on paper seemed so well protected become largely meaningless in practice. Within the enterprise, management was expert at manipulating the law, both substantively and procedurally. The trade unions, in theory the champions of the worker, were thoroughly coopted by management. More surprising was the failure of trial courts to take up the cudgel. A willingness to accept management's evidence (whether documentary or testimonial in nature) concerning the legality of a dismissal was more common than the rigorous scrutiny found in the published case decisions. As a result, the proportionately higher burden of proof that the higher courts placed on management was easily satisfied and, in contrast to what the review of published materials would suggest, did not serve to strengthen workers' rights.

Methodology: Finding the Law in Action

The Soviet Union had no tradition of empirical legal sociology. Thus, notwithstanding the fact that I carried out my fieldwork in Moscow at the height of the Gorbachev era of *glasnost'* (during 1989 and 1990), the general attitude of scholars and practitioners to my research was hostile. Not understanding my goals, they reverted to their old suspicion of foreigners and assumed that my aim was to expose the dark side of state socialism. For the most part, official channels were closed to me. Indeed, simply getting into enterprises and trial courts quickly emerged as the major impediment to my research. The limitations on access forced me to stitch together data gathered from a variety of sources rather than from exhaustive case studies of particular factories and/or courts.

Soviet Scholars. I began the search for the law in action by interviewing scholars from various research institutes in Moscow who specialized in labor law and/or labor policy.[1] Scholars were insiders in the policy process. Given their lack of expertise in drafting laws, legislators routinely turned to legal scholars for assistance. For example, the 1988 amendments to the Russian Labor Code were prepared by a group of scholars, acting within the admittedly rigid policy guidelines set by the Central Committee of the Communist Party.

These interviews were of limited use in understanding the law in practice because, for the most part, the scholars' interest in the law extended only to its enactment and subsequent debates over interpretation. While I gained considerable insight into the reasons why various provisions of the labor laws had been changed, I learned little about whether these changes had had any real impact.

Access to Enterprises. I gained the necessary access to factories only through a variety of byzantine schemes and prolonged negotiations. The most successful technique was to have a Soviet friend or colleague prevail upon an acquaintance within an enterprise to talk with me. My freedom of action, however, was circumscribed by the terms of my access. I could not make demands but had to insinuate myself with the managers I met, hoping that over time I would be allowed to expand the scope of my research.

This strategy, albeit time consuming, worked remarkably well. I succeeded in carrying out research at seven industrial enterprises of varying sizes in Moscow and one large plant in Kaluga (a small industrial city 100 kilometers from Moscow). In all cases, I was able to talk with one or more managers who handled issues of labor relations, for example, the personnel chief, the head of the wage department, the chairman of the trade union committee, the in-house legal counsel. In a number of cases, I was able to go beyond interviewing managers to reviewing relevant records and attending meetings where personnel matters were handled. At two enterprises, I succeeded in organizing meetings with workers. Thus, despite my inability to study a single factory in depth, I have been able to weave a picture of what happens to workers threatened with an unwanted dismissal or internal transfer by piecing together information gleaned from my necessarily fragmentary access to these eight Russian enterprises.

The enterprises varied in terms of size and nature of production. All but one had more than a thousand employees and some had as many as five thousand. The nature of production ranged from foodstuffs to textiles to plastics to electronics. The one constant element was the high percentage of manual labor, but in this these factories did not differ from the vast majority of Soviet industrial enterprises.[2]

Access to Trial Courts. Trial courts constituted the final piece of the puzzle. After months of negotiations, the Ministry of Justice finally granted me access to the records of trial courts *(narodnyi sud)* in the *Proletarskii* and *Oktiabr'skii* districts of Moscow. The courts retained records for ten years. This allowed me to review files for labor-related cases for a significant time period, thereby gaining a deeper appreciation of the behavior of Soviet courts. I spent more of my time in the *Proletarskii* court and was able to examine all of the labor-related cases filed between 1983 and 1989.[3] This archive was more fruitful for two reasons. For one thing, the district was the site of many of the gargantuan state industrial enterprises that grew up during the Stalin era, including one of the largest Soviet auto plants, ZIL *(Zavod imeni Ligacheva)*. Also, my work went more quickly there because the clerk who maintained the records segregated the labor cases for me. Between 1983 and 1990, an average of 56 labor-related cases were filed annually at the *Proletarskii* court.[4] At the *Oktiabr'skii* court, I had to go through all of the civil cases myself in order to find those relevant to my research. Given that an excess of three thousand cases was filed each year, this proved to be an extremely time consuming activity. The *Oktiabr'skii* court was also less appealing because the district did not have a high concentration of industrial capital but was primarily residential, with a fair number of scholarly institutions.

I also observed court proceedings and interviewed court personnel, including judges, court secretaries, procurators, and people's assessors. No special permission was needed to attend trials. Civil trials were required by law to be open to the public and, while the parties often cast quizzical looks my way and sometimes even asked me what I was doing there, I was never formally asked to leave. Once I had spent enough time at courts to get a sense of how trials were conducted and the relationship between the parties and the judge, the usefulness of going to court diminished. Labor cases were rarely on the docket and, when they were, they were often dismissed or postponed.

Implementing Law in the Factory

The Problematic Nature of the Data

Upon gaining access to an enterprise, I faced the task of getting information on the implementation of the law governing dismissals and transfers.

I began by talking with managers and then worked at convincing them to grant me access to more detailed records. Two categories of records were most relevant to my concerns. The first was the minutes *(protokoly)* of the meetings of the enterprise trade union committee *(profkom),* at which all management-initiated dismissals (including layoffs) and transfers had to be voted upon. Theoretically, these records revealed the incidence of such actions by management, both successful and abortive. The *protokoly* of the sessions of the commission for labor disputes *(KTS)* constituted the second type of relevant document. Workers unhappy at having been transferred had to begin the complaint process with the *KTS.* In theory, these records provided an indication of worker satisfaction with management efforts to reallocate the workforce. I was able to review *profkom* and *KTS* records at four enterprises.

These data, while valuable, have to be used with caution. My interviews with personnel chiefs at a number of Moscow factories revealed that workers dismissed at the initiative of management were routinely given the option of resigning in lieu of being fired.[5] Management preferred resignations because it lessened their paperwork load. For workers, they were something of a mixed blessing. On the one hand, a resignation looked better to future employers than being fired or even laid off. When I asked why being laid off carried the same stigma as being dismissed for cause, I was told by workers and personnel directors alike that "a good worker would never be laid off." Workers could not conceal the terms under which they had parted because the statutory basis for dismissal was legally required to be noted in the "work book" *(trudovaia knizhka)* of the affected worker. This work book stayed with a worker for life and had to be presented to all potential employers. Consequently, the reason for dismissal had real practical significance, and workers could petition the courts to force former employers to change notations in their work books.[6]

On the other hand, workers who resigned had significantly fewer legal protections than did fired workers. Resignations did not have to be approved by the *profkom.* In addition, a worker who resigned and then reneged and wanted to be reinstated to his or her old job had first to petition the *KTS* and the *profkom* before a court would hear his or her claim. This was true even when the worker claimed to have been forced to resign by management. In contrast, a fired worker did not have to exhaust any administrative remedies but had the right to proceed directly to court with a petition for reinstatement. What this means in terms of the data is that the numbers given for dismissals and resignations, both on the enterprise and aggregate levels, often presented a picture that bore little resemblance to reality.

Thus, getting access to records that would permit an intimate view into the legal process within the factory became ever more critical. The purpose was to gain a deeper understanding of what actually happened when management wanted to fire or transfer a worker against his or her will. This, in turn, allowed me to assess the extent to which management complied with the letter and the spirit of the law.

The *profkom* and *KTS protokoly* constituted the only documentary evidence at my disposal. The discussions as to whether consent should be granted to a dismissal or transfer were transcribed verbatim and so provided a fairly reliable (or at least the best available) record of what happened. In the language employed, the nature and number of parties participating, and the time devoted to the dismissal or transfer the general attitude of the parties toward the underlying law surfaced.

Unfortunately, the maintenance of these records was slipshod, reflecting the fact that management attached little importance to them.[7] None of the four Moscow factories that permitted me access to this material had an intact set of records for any sustained period of time. One enterprise retained them for one calendar year. Another held them for five years, but when I began to go through them I found big chunks missing. Yet another located *KTS* records for the preceding three years but could find only six months of *profkom* records. When I reported that the records were missing, the response was a shrug of the shoulders. No one knew or cared what had become of these records. In fact, the typical reaction to a request to look at *profkom* and *KTS* records was incredulity—managers could not believe that these records that they had tossed aside in a dusty cubbyhole would be of interest to anyone, much less of value for scholarly research.

In many cases, management's lackadaisical attitude toward record keeping diminished the usefulness of the records themselves. All too often, the number of dismissals reported by the personnel manager for a given year did not match the number debated by the *profkom.* Greater diligence on the part of managers in this regard would have allowed for a more complete picture of life inside the enterprise. To some extent, *profkom* records that surfaced in my research in the archives of Moscow trial courts compensated for these shortcomings. The centrality of having obtained *profkom* consent to the legality of a dismissal meant that these records were always included in the case file. Certain patterns emerge that betray enterprise management's (acting through its surrogate, the *profkom*) underlying attitude toward law. Thus, even with all their flaws, these records represent an essential piece of the puzzle.

The Absence of Mass Reallocation of Workforce

Another incongruity that I discovered once I began spending time at Soviet factories was that the redistribution of the workforce, including mass layoffs and widespread internal transfers, that I had been led to expect was not taking place inside these factories. During the late 1980s, the Soviet press, both mass media and scholarly journals, was replete with articles discussing the policy of "release of labor resources" *(vysvobozhdenie trudovykh resursov)*.[8] Its purpose was to increase labor productivity through more efficient allocation of the existing workforce. Various governmental officials estimated that by the turn of the century as many as 40 million Soviet workers would feel the effects of this policy. This is not to say that all of these workers would be laid off. Ideally, most would be reallocated within the same enterprise and, where that proved impossible, provisions were made for short-term unemployment compensation.

Thus, I arrived in Moscow in September 1989 expecting to bear witness to a massive reallocation and rationalization of the Soviet workforce. As I noted in the preceding chapter, this had been one of the main reasons for selecting the law governing dismissals and transfers as the subject of my case study.

Attitude of Soviet Scholars. My conversations with scholars at Moscow research institutes concerned with labor law and labor policy more generally did little to undermine my expectations. They were well aware of the policy and, for the most part, viewed it as economically necessary and rational. More importantly, they believed it was being implemented vigorously at industrial enterprises. They contended that the Soviet Union could increase productivity and thus become competitive on the world market only by using the existing labor pool more efficiently. The demographic data indicated that the old style solution of simply throwing more workers at the problem was no longer feasible. A scholarly consensus emerged that the only solution was a massive rationalization of the workforce. Fears of unemployment did not cloud their scenario; they firmly believed that the enterprises would somehow reabsorb the most redundant workers.

Some were troubled by the move away from the worker-oriented labor policy of state socialism to a market-oriented labor policy that increased management discretion. The law on internal transfers, as amended in February 1988, became something of a lightning rod for their concerns. One scholar at the Institute of State and Law described it repeatedly as a "nightmare" *(koshmar)*.[9] The head of the labor law sector of this institute contended that "[t]his amendment has made Soviet workers practically defenseless against in-house maneuvering by management."[10] For these scholars, the most grating element of the law was that it gave management permission to change "essential conditions of labor" without any input from workers. Workers unwilling to stomach change were to be cast aside. Many regarded this expansion of the rights of the state (in the form of management of state enterprises) as inappropriate and even repugnant in an era in which the Soviet Union was ostensibly reconstituting itself as a law-governed state *(pravovoe gosudarstvo)*.[11]

All of these conversations with scholars were conducted at a fairly high level of generality. This was not my choice but theirs. While these scholars were willing to discuss the relevant statutory provisions and how they had been changed to accommodate this rationalization policy, they were pointedly indifferent to how (or even whether) the policy was actually being implemented, even when information about practice might have buttressed their arguments about the inherent unfairness of some of the changes. My incessant questions about practice puzzled them. Studying the law in action did not strike them as a worthwhile scholarly endeavor.

The Reality within Enterprises. When I began to talk with people involved in day-to-day labor policy in enterprises, I quickly discovered that this policy had had little impact in their world. My first interview was with a personnel director at an enterprise in north Moscow, employing less than two hundred people, that made and repaired television antennae. She had literally never heard the Russian catchphrase used to describe the policy for rationalizing the workforce. No effort had been made there to redistribute the workforce to increase efficiency.

One might argue that this is not terribly surprising given the size of the operation. But the fact that this was a small shop did not necessarily mean that featherbedding was absent. Overemployment was ubiquitous in the Soviet context. Furthermore, this was not a standalone enterprise. It was a constituent part of a large "production association" *(proizvodstvennoe ob"edinenie)* and had received no directives from above to institute a review of its workers' productivity as a precursor to a reallocation plan. This suggests that the higher organ was likewise unaware of this policy.

More convincing is the fact that, throughout the first half of 1990, I had similar experiences in every enterprise I visited regardless of its size. At one medium-sized (3,500 workers) Moscow electronics plant, I spoke at length with the in-house counsel, the personnel director, and the chairman of the trade union committee, the three officials intimately concerned with labor policy. None of them was familiar with the terminology used by journalists and scholars when discussing this reallocation policy. This experience repeated itself at two other Moscow factories (textile and plastics) of approximately the same size. Indeed, at each enterprise, I found myself in the somewhat awkward position of explaining the rationale of the policy to these managers.

More to the point, none of the enterprises I studied had undergone the sort of wholesale reallocation of the workforce contemplated by the government's policy. Although a thorough analysis of why enterprise management failed to heed the government's call to rationalize the workforce is beyond the scope of this chapter, several contributory factors can be suggested. Primary among these was the state's failure to change the underlying incentive system prior to its introduction of the labor rationalization plan. Throughout the 1980s, enterprise management continued to be rewarded for plan fulfillment. Other more efficiency-driven indicia of success, such as profitability, were conspicuous by their absence. Even increases in labor productivity were of little interest so long as an enterprise continued to meet its output targets. After all, the confiscatory tax structure meant that the enterprise itself reaped none of the benefits of enhanced output since more than 80 percent of profits had to be sent to the central authorities.

With Gorbachev's accession to political leadership in the mid-1980s, efforts began to dismantle the old administrative-command system, but these remained more in the realm of rhetoric than action. The problem did not lie exclusively in a lack of political will on the part of Moscow. The reforms were also stymied by enterprise managers who, over the course of decades of Soviet rule, had learned how to function and even thrive under the existing system. Inertia had set in. Until they could be shown that becoming more efficient would inure to their benefit in some concrete fashion, managers clung to the old ways.

This was reflected in labor policy within the enterprise. Managers were accustomed to a system under which the wage fund for the enterprise was determined largely by the number of workers. This, combined with the frequent need to "storm" at the end of the month in order to fulfill the plan, provided a powerful incentive to featherbed. Vague jingoistic slogans about the need to make the production process more efficient did not serve as sufficient incentives for serious restructuring. Changes in the rules governing wage funds in the mid-1980s had provoked some reductions but not the kind of mass reallocation of the workforce needed to spur productivity. The managers' reluctance was completely rational. So long as performance was judged on plan fulfillment, it was in their best interests to retain a cushion of excess workers to ensure that these targets were met in a timely fashion. Their behavior would change only when profitability and other more efficiency-sensitive criteria of success took hold.

Consequently, the number of dismissals for redundancy was smaller than I had anticipated. Sloppy record-keeping practices caused the details to elude me, which prompted me to expand the scope of inquiry to include all dismissals made at the initiative of management. Including other categories of dismissals was appropriate in that the legal issues and procedures were the same across the board. Unlike Western practice, layoffs were not treated differently. The rights and remedies available to workers dismissed on other grounds were likewise available to workers allegedly laid off.

While layoffs continued to be my primary focus, studying other types of dismissals proved helpful in understanding the balance of power between management and workers during the legal proceedings inside the enterprise.

Transfers within enterprises comprised the second element of the government's vaunted plan to rationalize the labor force. As with layoffs, the underlying policy goal was to increase the overall efficiency of enterprises. Indeed, the law was amended in 1988 in order to allow management greater freedom in distributing its workforce. Yet my research shows that the incidence of management-initiated internal transfers continued to be negligible following the legislative changes. Thus, in studying the law, the critical question becomes why management failed to take advantage of this seemingly golden opportunity to reallocate its workers in a more efficient manner.

Instituting a Layoff

Lack of Enterprise Autonomy. During the Soviet period, layoffs invariably originated outside the enterprise. In some cases, a layoff began with a decree from the USSR Council of Ministers which was then filtered through the relevant industrial ministries. In others, the process began at the ministerial level. While enterprise management could draw its ministry's attention to the need for a layoff, it lacked the power to act on its own. Instead, it merely implemented orders sent down from above.

Indeed, being acted upon in matters of labor policy was symptomatic of the general lack of autonomy of enterprises in the Soviet context. Under Stalin, a rigid hierarchy was established within the economy. Enterprises were agents not principals. Numerous efforts were made to enhance the rights of enterprises in the post-Stalin era, but the political muscle of the industrial ministries ensured the consistent failure of such reforms.

With Gorbachev's rise to power came a renewed call for enterprise autonomy. This time, however, the instigators were not merely obscure scholars and disgruntled enterprise managers but included Gorbachev and his cohort as well. They pushed for an end to the so-called "petty tutelage" of ministries, contending that control over day-to-day management matters, such as the production profile and manpower issues, would be more properly lodged at the enterprise level. The 1987 Law on State Enterprises represented an effort to increase the independence of enterprises legislatively. It failed. In practice, ministries continued to have tremendous leverage over enterprises. The fact remains that, in a shortage economy, ministries effectively controlled the flow of raw materials and other supplies. Ultimately, of course, the system disintegrated, and enterprises were left to fend for themselves. During the period under study, however, ministries remained in firm control, and, more to the point, enterprise management lacked the right to institute significant layoffs on its own authority.

The Layoff Process in Two Enterprises. The layoffs observed can be divided into three categories. The first were reductions that were marginal or preliminary in nature. Typically, they called for the displacement of very few real people. Instead, the existing vacancies on the personnel schedule were eliminated, thereby reducing the wage fund. The vacancies so eliminated tended to be white-collar positions. The net effect was to reduce overhead expenses. Two of the enterprises I studied had layoffs of this sort. The law was not brought into play because no one was actually dismissed. My review of trial court records reveals that this sort of layoff was often the first step; more substantial reductions typically followed.

The second were also reductions that, while sanctioned by the ministry, took place at the margins. Typically, only one or two departments would be affected and the number of workers would be comparatively small (less than 1 percent of the workforce). These were the sort of instances in which claims of sham layoffs most often arose. Such layoffs took place periodically in all of the enterprises I studied and were the most common type of layoff encountered in the trial court records.

The final category of layoffs were those involving deep across-the-board cuts in the existing workforce. Such layoffs took place at two of the enterprises I studied. When the process is examined, a pattern emerges with respect to the way it was carried out and the role played by law.

The Leather Plant. One of these factories was a 1,600-worker plant in the suburbs of Moscow that produced various items from artificial leather (the "Leather Plant"). Based on a decree of the USSR Council of Ministers that made certain changes in the rules governing wage funds, the Ministry of Light Industry ordered it to eliminate redundant workers. The ministry's order *(prikaz)* made specific reference to this decree. Ironically, given the ministry's usurpation of microlevel management powers, its decree also paid lip service to the importance of enterprise autonomy. The enterprise was part of a larger production association, and the management of this intermediate organ issued an order similar in tenor to that of the ministry.

One goal of the layoff was to reduce overhead, but production line workers were not exempt. Consequently, a two-pronged approach was instituted. In order to identify white-collar workers who were redundant or functioning at less than their full capacity, a commission was organized to evaluate these workers. (In Russian, this vetting process is known as *attestatsia.*) The members of the commission included, among others, the chief financial officer, the chief technologist and accountant, and the heads of the accounting, wages, planning, and legal departments. The ministry established the rules governing its activities. Members of the commission interviewed clerical, engineering, and low-level management personnel in order to determine the extent to which they met the needs of the enterprise as reflected in the written job descriptions and as communicated by upper management. Twelve positions were ultimately eliminated. Although the process was, by its very nature, highly subjective, those involved insisted that none of those affected complained or appealed the decisions.

The process of identifying redundant production-level workers was handled in a less rigorous fashion. In essence, the reponsibility was shifted onto the production shops *(tsekhi)*. The general director of the enterprise ordered each production shop chief to come up with a plan to reduce his personnel and gave them one month to identify suitable candidates for termination. At some shops, the foremen simply picked out the least productive workers.

More often, however, these decisions were made collectively, for example, the members of brigades (usually comprising less than ten workers) decided who was expendable. A meeting would then be held of the entire shop collective (approximately one hundred workers) at which the issue of whether to recommend dismissal to upper management would be debated. Although the records of these meetings are disappointingly sketchy, they do reveal that they were well attended, with more than 75 percent of the collective present. (This can be compared with a meeting of the enterprise party organization to discuss the pending layoff, which was attended by less than 5 percent of the workforce.) They further reveal the reluctance of workers to sanction the dismissal of one of their own, regardless of his or her work habits. For example, with regard to a worker who used only 30 percent of his or her time productively, the collective resolved not to recommend dismissal but rather to reexamine how labor was being utilized. Transcripts of interviews conducted with these workers by Soviet sociologists demonstrate their awareness of the widespread nature of featherbedding within the enterprise. Yet they did not want to be responsible for a fellow worker being identified as redundant and thus dismissed.

The final tally shows that 73 production-level workers (out of a total of 1,600 workers) were targeted to be laid off. As with their white-collar colleagues, management contended that none of those affected complained or appealed the decisions. I found no evidence of appeals by either category of worker.

The role of law in the process was marginal at best. Although a statement was made in one of the orders from the ministry to the effect that the law should be respected in carrying out the layoff, the relevant internal enterprise documents fail to specify the requirements set forth by the Russian Labor Code or even to mention that they exist. Thus, the instructions to production shops relating to the layoff failed to note that certain categories of workers, including war veterans and pregnant women, had a preferential right to remain on the job.

Of course, the discussion to this point refers only to the decision to implement a layoff and the identification of potential candidates for elimination. A number of additional hurdles remained for management before a worker could be terminated. Key among them was obtaining the consent of the *profkom.* Theoretically, there was every chance that illegalities would be discovered at that point and thwarted. The records, however, reveal that the *profkom* approved all of the proposed dismissals as a matter of course. The tendency to rubber-stamp management's personnel decisions was common in many Soviet enterprises.

The Electronics Plant. On a superficial level, law appeared to play a more vital role at the other enterprise that experienced a substantial layoff. This was a 5,000-worker electronics firm (the "Electronics Plant") located in a southern district of Moscow. As with the Leather Plant, the layoff was initiated from above. In light of the introduction of a tax on labor resources and the consequent reduction of the wage fund, the ministry ordered that every effort be made to eliminate redundant personnel. The general director responded by forming a commission whose task was to reformulate the personnel schedule *(shtatnoe raspisanie)* to take account of the newfound constraints on the wage fund. The chairman of this commission was the chief financial officer. Its task was first to eliminate all vacancies and, only if that proved insufficient, to embark on a search for candidates for termination. The layoff was aimed at white-collar workers; this enterprise had had a perennial shortage of production-level workers.

Shortly thereafter, a second commission was formed. Its sole purpose was to ensure that the layoff was carried out in strict accordance with the law. The chairman of this commission was the head of the legal department of the enterprise. The other members were the heads of the personnel and wage departments and the deputy chairman of the *profkom.* It is important to recognize, however, that the political clout of these individuals was marginal when compared with the top managers (mostly production-related) who made the key decisions. The commission was more symbolic than functional. The chief lawyer could recall no occasion on which it actually met, and I found no records of any such meetings.

In connection with her duties as chairwoman of this commission, the chief lawyer prepared a six-page, single-spaced, mimeographed pamphlet outlining the law governing layoffs. The style was Russian legalese and was little more than an almost verbatim copying of the relevant statutes from the Russian Labor Code. No effort was made to make this arcane language comprehensible to the average worker. While this document was freely available in the offices of the legal department, I found no evidence of it elsewhere. More to the point, during my conversations with workers and managers about the layoff and other dismissals, no one referred to it or even mentioned its existence.

The process of carrying out the layoff at the Electronics Plant had just begun in the summer of 1990 as my own research in Moscow was coming to an end. Consequently, the ultimate scope of the layoff is not clear. The head of the wage department, who was actively involved in the process, predicted that several hundred workers would be affected. Similarly, the role played by law in the overall process remains unclear. The apparent importance given to statutory compliance in the startup phase has to be weighed against the company's record in prior dismissals. The *profkom* was completely under the thumb of management. As a result, management had long had virtual carte blanche to fire workers at its discretion irrespective of the law. There is little reason to believe that this behavioral pattern was different during the 1990 layoff.

On a more general level, these two examples of broad-based layoffs reveal the relentlessly top-down nature of the process. The ministries dictated the timing and terms of these layoffs. Ironically, to a large degree, this inured to the benefit of enterprise management, which never had to take responsibility for this undoubtedly unpopular policy. The review of trial court records of laid-off workers petitioning for reinstatement between 1983 and 1989 indicates that this hierarchical quality of layoff decision making was widespread. It was common to virtually all of the layoff cases reviewed. The sort of entities involved ran the gamut from governmental agencies to construction firms to a large hotel catering primarily to foreigners.

In addition, the example of the two enterprises brings into relief the secondary role played by law in fashioning personnel policy. Although the Russian Labor Code is silent as to *when* a layoff is warranted, it does speak to the issue of *how* a layoff should be conducted. Indeed, it establishes an elaborate and seemingly rigid hierarchy of preferential rights. In practice, ministries and enterprise management paid little attention to these legal niceties. What emerges are the beginnings of a pattern that will become etched ever more deeply as we continue our review of the evidence. It is a pattern of paying lip service to the importance of complying with the law, all the while ignoring its basic tenor.

Management Tactics for Getting around the Law

Management was required by law to place redundant workers in comparable jobs within the enterprise whenever possible. Obtaining hard data on compliance was problematic because management rarely left a paper trail. For instance, if a place was found for a redundant worker, it was styled as a worker-initiated transfer, which could be carried out with less fuss than a management-initiated transfer, given that no *profkom* consent was required. Sometimes the door was opened by a disgruntled worker. The *profkom* records for 1987 at the Electronics Plant include the case of a worker being laid off who complained that management had not made sufficient efforts to find him other work. Management responded, in part, by noting that six other workers had simultaneously been declared redundant and that all of them had been placed successfully within the same enterprise. (This was the only record I ever found of these six workers.) Management saw its success in placing these other workers as conclusive evidence of its good faith in dealing with laid-off workers.

Alternatively, if an appropriate position was not available, it was standard practice to allow redundant workers to resign rather than be laid off, which, once again, could be done without involving the *profkom.* Despite management's admission that layoffs had taken place at the Leather Plant and a 1,000-worker bread and pastry enterprise (the "Bakery") between 1983 and 1989, the *profkom* records made no mention of them. This suggests that the laid-off workers resigned preemptively, in lieu of having the stain of being laid off recorded in their work books. But it was impossible to determine what actually happened to these workers.

Interviews with personnel chiefs revealed that they were well versed in management's job placement duties in cases of layoffs. These interviews further revealed that they had developed a whole series of coping mechanisms that allowed them to comply with the letter of the law while still getting rid of undesirable workers. When describing a layoff of approximately 100 clerical workers at Rezina (a 4,000-worker rubber products enterprise located in the center of Moscow), the head of the personnel department told me with great satisfaction how he had offered production-level jobs to these redundant workers, most of whom were women, knowing full well that his offers would be rejected out of hand. The working conditions at Rezina were not inviting; many positions were classified as hazardous on health grounds *(vrednye).*[12] Management had great difficulty attracting and retaining its workforce, and vacancies always existed. Not surprisingly, these former secretaries and bookkeepers did not flock to fill these vacancies but resigned quietly.

Court records revealed few instances of such blatantly questionable tactics. Presumably, when workers could prove that management had skirted the law in such an obvious fashion and were sufficiently motivated to pursue the matter in court, their cases were settled. The occasional case did, however, slip through. In a 1986 court case, a university-educated engineer deemed redundant was given the choice of working as a bookkeeper or a janitor. Along similar lines, in a 1988 court case, a teacher was offered positions as a coat checker or a cleaning woman.

Another tactic employed by management was to mask layoffs as other types of dismissals to which no job placement obligation was attached. This came to light as I was observing the in-house counsel *(iuriskonsul't)* at Rezina dispense legal advice to production shop managers. On a number of occasions, they came with questions as to how to lay off redundant workers. Coincidentally, all of the workers in question were of pensionable age. The *iuriskonsul't* chided them for going by the book and reminded them that the law allowed such workers to be fired on grounds of old age, with no questions asked. Later he confessed that he avoided the rubric of layoffs whenever possible. Few others were as candid, but a close reading of the *protokoly* suggests that many enterprises employed similar tactics to avoid what they viewed as unnecessary legal entanglements.

Obtaining *Profkom* Consent

The statutory requirement that management obtain the consent of the *profkom* before laying off a worker (or dismissing him or her on other legally permissible grounds) is supposed to act as a check on the discretion of management in personnel matters. To a certain extent, it served this function. But the effectiveness of the *profkom* within the enterprise was hampered by its unwillingness to buck management and by workers' perception of it as collaborationist.

Attitude of Legal Counsel. All of the *iuriskonsul'ty* with whom I spoke were well aware of this duty and were similarly aware of the penalty of automatic reinstatement for failure to obtain such consent in a timely fashion. Without exception, they claimed to live up to this obligation religiously, and the records bear them out. I found no evidence that the courts had reinstated a worker to any of the enterprises I studied on the grounds that the *profkom* had failed to give its consent to the dismissal.[13] In my review of seven years of trial court records, I found only two instances of reinstatements on the grounds of a failure to obtain *profkom* consent. In each case, the court characterized management's behavior as a "gross violation of the law." The fact that such cases are encountered so infrequently suggests that the statutory prerequisite of *profkom* consent has been well inculcated into the consciousness of enterprise management.

These *iuriskonsul'ty* further agreed that the change in the law in February 1988, which gave management the flexibility to seek and obtain *profkom* consent after the fact, had had little practical effect. The counsel for the Electronics Plant told me that she and her staff continued to operate under the old rules because even though it had become legally permissible to request *profkom* consent after the dismissed worker had appealed to the courts for reinstatement, doing so was procedurally messy (the trial was suspended until the *profkom* took action) and time consuming. Her legal department had long ago become accustomed to getting *profkom* consent before drafting the official dismissal order. She preferred not to rock the boat by introducing a new procedure that on the surface complied with the new law but that might or might not stand up to judicial scrutiny. Other *iuriskonsul'ty* echoed her sentiments. Given that in May 1991 the law was changed back to require preliminary *profkom* consent, their wariness proved to have been well placed.

A. I. Stavtseva, the head of the labor law sector of the Institute of Soviet Legislation, believed that the 1988 change worked to erode the protection of workers' rights. Speaking in early 1991, she claimed that enterprise trade union committees became more compliant as a direct result of this statutory change. She argued that the effect was to make denying consent an act of political defiance for the *profkom* in that it required them to affirmatively reinstate a worker after he or she had already been fired. Under the old system, *profkom* consent was just one of several prerequisites for firing a worker, and the *profkom* was not solely responsible for thwarting the desires of management. She further contended that the incidence of refusals to grant consent actually decreased. Her argument is provocative and even logical, but my data do not support it. Instead, they suggest that the tendency to rubber-stamp management requests for dismissal began long before 1988. Indeed, by that time the practice had become almost institutionalized in many enterprises.

Incidence of Profkom *Approval.* The Leather Plant described above illustrates the tendency to rubber-stamp management requests. A review of the *profkom* records for 1986–89 revealed no instance of a management request for consent to the dismissal of a worker being refused. The records were, however, incomplete, and so I asked management and trade union officials whether this was correct. They confirmed it, telling me that they could not recall the last time the *profkom* had failed to give its consent. I found a similar pattern of 100-percent approval over the same time period in the records of a 5,000-worker Moscow textile enterprise (the "Textile Factory"). The *iuriskonsul't* explained quite candidly that management did not regard the need for *profkom* consent as a real obstacle but rather as a bureaucratic annoyance. He said that he always prepared the official request to the *profkom* for consent and the order *(prikaz)* dismissing the worker so that both were signed by the enterprise director at the same time. A close examination of the records at his enterprise and at the Leather Plant revealed that the two documents usually carried the same date. Court records demonstrate that this practice was not confined to these two plants. In a 1983 case, the worker was given notice at 1 P.M., the *profkom* met and gave its consent at 3 P.M., and the official dismissal order was issued at 4 P.M.

Although the *profkom* was somewhat less compliant at other factories, at none of the enterprises I studied did the consent rate ever dip below 50 percent. For example, in 1986 and 1987, the two years for which I was able to find relatively complete *profkom* records at the Electronics Plant, the *profkom* approved, respectively, 100 and 70 percent of the management requests submitted.[14] At Rezina, a review of *profkom* records for 1989 (it retained its *profkom* records for only one year) revealed that the *profkom* had consented 92 percent of the time.[15] At the Bakery, the *profkom* records were more or less intact for 1986 and 1987.[16] During those years, the *profkom* gave its consent to 86 and 83 percent, respectively, of the requests submitted. The records were spottier for 1985 and 1988 but nonetheless reflect that the *profkom* consented at least 60 percent of the time.

One possible explanation for the behavior of trade union committees is that the cases submitted by management were meritorious. Certainly this was the consistent explanation advanced when I queried management and trade union officials about the suspiciously high incidence of *profkom* consent. In particular, *iuriskonsul'ty* consistently contended that they prepared the requests for consent with an eye to the law because they did not want workers reinstated on so-called technicalities. The chairman of the *profkom* at Rezina explained the record in similar terms. Interestingly, neither he nor his counterparts at the other enterprises I studied were defensive when discussing this issue. They regarded it as completely normal in most cases to grant consent for management to dismiss coworkers.

Nature of Profkom *Consideration.* This explanation begs the question of whether management's requests were, in fact, meritorious. Theoretically, it was the task of the *profkom* to make that determination. In many cases, however, the trade union committees took the good faith of management for granted and, assuming the worthiness of the request, granted consent without any independent review of the underlying facts.

This kind of pro forma consent was reflected in the *protokoly* of a *profkom* meeting, which consisted simply of a proposal and a resolution, with no presentation of the background or ensuing discussion. For example, a 1987 *protokoly* of the *profkom* at the Bakery contains the following exchange:

> The head of the personnel office: "The management requests that you give consent to the dismissal of [worker A] pursuant to article 33, point 4 [absenteeism]."
> Resolved: "To give consent to the dismissal of [worker A] pursuant to article 33, point 4."

This represented the full extent of the examination of the dismissal. It was not an unusual occurrence. In 1986 and 1987, 57 and 61 percent, respectively, of the dismissals received similar treatment, that is, no evidence was discussed, a practice that was not unique to the Bakery. At Rezina, for example, the *profkom* accorded such treatment to 62 percent of the dismissals that it considered in 1989. Likewise, at the Electronics Plant, 71 percent of the 1987 dismissal cases were considered in this sort of pro forma manner, and in 1986 all of the cases submitted to the *profkom* were approved with no discussion whatsoever.

Furthermore, the apparent lack of rigor on the part of the *profkomy* cannot be explained away as a matter of notetaking style. The same *protokoly* that contained these perfunctory approvals of dismissals requested by management often contained lengthy transcripts of debates among *profkom* members over other items on the agenda. This suggests that the lack of debate reported in the written minutes of the meetings was an accurate reflection of what actually happened.

My review of the records of a Moscow trial court between 1983 and 1989 supports the conclusion that *profkomy* tended to be perfunctory in dealing with dismissals.[17] The percentage of dismissal cases in which the *profkomy* took a pro forma approach ranged from a high of 71 percent in 1989 to a low of 44 percent in 1984. In other years, it hovered around 60 percent. These data, while problematic in that they are culled from many different enterprises, are in some ways more revealing than those collected at specific enterprises. After all, appealing to the courts for reinstatement is not the norm, and those who do so are usually openly alienated. In fact, these workers often threatened the *profkom* with judicial action. It would be logical to expect the *profkomy* to take special care in dealing with these workers, and the fact that they do not indicates that this a deep-seated behavior pattern.

At the same time, it is important to recognize that not all dismissals were handled in a pro forma manner. In organizing the data, I set up two additional categories: limited discussion and heated debate. The former included instances in which the facts supporting management's case for dismissal were given and one or more *profkom* members or outside witnesses offered their opinions. Although the *protokoly* invariably set forth the statutory basis for the dismissal, the discussion rarely centered on whether the management's request was legally justified. Instead, the testimony more often degenerated into character assassination. Typical is a 1985 case of alleged absenteeism at the Bakery in which a foreman testified

> She blames everyone else for her mistakes and takes no responsibility for how the brigade will function without her. All of the members of the brigade dislike her and want her thrown out of the brigade. She cannot be rehabilitated. She doesn't want to understand anything.

Another revealing example is provided by the case of the groundskeeper *(dvornik)* at the enterprise kindergarten whom management at Rezina was trying to lay off. The limited discussion focused not on whether a layoff had really taken place and whether reasonable efforts had been undertaken to relocate the worker elsewhere at Rezina but on the worker's inability to perform his assigned functions. A member of the *profkom* testified

> He cannot cope with the responsibilities of being a groundskeeper. The territory of the kindergarten is poorly tended, the children's area is not cleared, and the asphalt road surrounding the kindergarten is not cleaned up. The ice is not removed. I ask that you give your consent to his dismissal.

The *profkom* gave its unanimous consent to his dismissal without further discussion.

These sorts of statements by coworkers and supervisors—to the effect that the worker under discussion had poor work habits and/or a displeasing personality—were encountered frequently in the *profkom* records of all of the enterprises I studied. Often they served as the sole foundation for a worker's dismissal. While personality problems could have been legally relevant in cases of disciplinary dismissals, at most they should have been one of several contributory causes, not the only basis for a dismissal. In contrast, the law stipulated that layoffs had to be based on economic considerations. Consequently, recountings of character flaws—regardless of whether they affected the work environment—should not have been used to justify layoffs.

When the scope of inquiry is broadened to include the *protokoly* found in court records, a slightly different picture emerges. The practice of becoming sidetracked on extralegal issues of personality persisted. A good example is a 1984 court case of alleged absenteeism in which the testimony of the worker's supervisor and a *profkom* member focused solely on their view of her as a shirker and someone with whom her brigade did not want to work. On the other hand, this tendency was mitigated by the fact that corroborating evidence was more often made part of the record. For example, in cases of dismissal for drunkenness on the job, the fact that the worker was drunk would be supported not just by the testimony of his or her supervisor but by affidavits filed by two or three coworkers. On the other hand, it was rare to find a *profkom* demanding any nonopinion corroborating evidence, and the identical wording of the affidavits rendered them inherently suspect (though not in the eyes of the Soviet trial courts). A similar pattern of multiple supporting affidavits was also found in many cases of dismissal for absenteeism.

From a legal point of view, opinion statements about character were inherently prejudicial to the worker and had very little legal relevance. The *profkom's* task was not to pass judgment on the worker's character but rather to determine whether he or she had violated the Russian Labor Code and thus deserved to be dismissed. As the defender of workers' rights, the *profkom* should, theoretically, err on the side of the worker, not management.

As with the pro forma cases, the outcome in cases of limited discussion was predetermined but, in contrast, consent was occasionally denied. For example, at the Bakery in 1987, 30 percent of the cases engendered limited discussion and, of those cases, consent was given 86 percent of the time. The picture was somewhat different at Rezina in 1989. Although there was a limited discussion in only 23 percent of the cases, the *profkom* gave its consent in 66 percent of those cases. Workers were less fortunate at the Electronics Plant, where in 1987 there was limited discussion in 15 percent of the total cases, and *profkom* consent was granted in all of these cases.

Cases in which arguments broke out at the *profkom* session over the facts and/or the proper disposition were categorized as involving heated debate. Although this type of case arose least frequently, it was the category in which workers most often prevailed. At the Bakery in 1987, for instance, only 9 percent of management's requests for *profkom* consent to dismissal sparked heated debate, but the *profkom* denied consent in 75 percent of those cases. On the other hand, at Rezina in 1989 and at the Electronic Plant in 1987, heated debate broke out in 15 percent of the cases, but the *profkom* nonetheless gave its consent to all these dismissals.

The debate took several forms. As with the cases of limited discussion, the discourse rarely had much to do with the underlying legal issue. The success of workers at the Bakery, for example, was the result of a strategy of laying out the extenuating circumstances and then throwing themselves on the mercy of the decision-makers. One worker, whom management was attempting to dismiss for absenteeism, testified

> Please understand that I am completely at fault, but the situation unfolded as follows. My father had an operation, and I had to go to him, and I spent all of this time [that I was absent from work] with him. If you don't believe me, I will get a document that says it was just so. If you want, you can transfer me to any job, just don't fire me.

Her supervisor then reported that she was a good worker, but that her brigade wanted nothing more to do with her. After some additional discussion, the *profkom* decided that, while this worker should be disciplined, she did not deserve to be fired. She was transferred to the night shift. In similar cases, the *profkom* gave second chances to a recovering alcoholic and a worker who argued that his family situation had contributed to his troubles at work but that he now had that under control. In none of these cases did the *profkom* regard the law as central or even relevant to its decision as to whether to grant or deny its consent.

Management's legal obligations played a more visible, though ultimately marginal, role in several layoff cases. Although the cases arose in different enterprises, the fact pattern is consistent. The worker appears at the *profkom* meeting at which his or her layoff is to be debated and alleges that management made no effort to find comparable work or that a suitable job exists but has not been offered. Management sidestepped responsibility in a variety of ways.

In a 1987 case at the Electronics Plant, it succeeded in shifting blame onto the worker, contending that the worker had refused to accept numerous suitable job offers and had failed to appear for job counseling sessions. The *profkom* did not demand that management support its allegations with documentary evidence such as personnel schedules or even affidavits from those who had made the job offers. Instead, management's claims were accepted at face value. The discourse quickly degenerated into personal attacks on the worker, with one *profkom* member stating, "I consider it inadvisable to keep such a worker, who does not fulfill his responsibilities, at the factory." The worker was, in fact, laid off by unanimous vote of the *profkom*.

In a 1989 case at Rezina, the worker contended that the layoff was a sham, organized specifically to get rid of her. She further claimed that an outsider had been hired to fill a vacancy for which she was qualified. The *profkom* did not press management on these issues, allowing it to slide by with a postlayoff personnel schedule reflecting no vacancies. The bulk of the discussion focused on whether the worker had a conflictual relationship with her supervisor. The testimony of her coworkers was contradictory. One person testified that "for the past two years, there has been no bickering. It all started right before the layoff." But another person claimed that "I have worked with her since she came into the department. She arrived with a chip on her shoulder. I have no desire to work with her any longer." Despite the lack of clarity and the failure to address the critical legal issue of job placement, the *profkom* did not hesitate to approve her layoff unanimously.

Thus, the statutory requirement of obtaining *profkom* consent failed to serve as a bulwark against management's manipulation in personnel matters. The political balance of power within the enterprise favored management. The *profkomy* were reluctant to exercise the few legal rights they had in a way that might undermine their standing with management. The result was a system in which the *profkom,* which should have vigorously protected workers' rights, did little more than rubber-stamp management decisions.

Internal Transfers

Given the willingness of enterprise management to manipulate the law governing dismissals, its behavior regarding internal transfers of workers came as something of a surprise. The degree of controversy over the February 1988 statutory changes, reflected in interviews with leading Soviet scholars (see chap. 3), led to the hypothesis that the number of internal transfers made at the initiative of management would have increased dramatically following the statutory amendment and that these transfers would be the subject of controversy within enterprises. What I found was just the opposite: the number of internal transfers had not changed, and no increase was expected in the near future. Furthermore, the reallocation of the workforce in a more rational manner was neither a top priority for managers and nor of particular concern to workers.

Indeed, the responses of management officials to my questions about internal transfers were remarkably consistent. I was told that the number of such transfers had traditionally been low and that when workers were transferred it was almost always at their request. I was also told that the incidence of intraenterprise transfers at the initiative of management had not increased in recent years. The actual numbers quoted were usually less than ten per year, constituting less than 1 percent of the workforce. Although the numbers were higher at the Bakery (between 20 and 30), this level had remained constant for the last five years and, as a percentage of the total work force, was still only about 2 percent.

My conversations with workers revealed that internal transfers barely registered on their list of priorities. They were preoccupied with wages, housing, labor conditions, pension rights, and other issues of daily survival. Internal transfers were not something they worried about or even contemplated. I was impressed by the strong sense of loyalty they felt to the shop in which they worked. For them, being transferred from one shop to another was akin to being transferred to another enterprise. They simply did not regard it as being within the realm of the possible. This indicated that neither the workers with whom I spoke nor any of their immediate circle of acquaintances had ever been transferred at the initiative of management.

Despite the fact that this information did not correspond to my hypothesis, it nonetheless rang true. The very fact that I kept hearing the same story in different settings was, in and of itself, convincing. In addition, in virtually every interview, when I would bring up the question of internal transfers, a look of utter surprise would come across the face of the official or worker with whom I was talking, as if he or she could not figure out why an American had come all this way to ask them about something so unimportant. Typically, they quickly grew impatient with my detailed questions on this topic. This attitude was not present when we were discussing layoffs or unemployment.

Commissions for Labor Disputes. A disgruntled transferee had to complain first to the *KTS* and then, if not satisfied, to the *profkom* before he or she could petition the local trial court. Thus, the incidence of appeals of transfers to these in-house adjudicatory bodies provides some insight into the overall incidence of transfers. A direct correlation would, however, be inappropriate given the tendency of workers not to take legal action to enforce their rights, even when they had been clearly violated.[18]

Yet the data are so lopsided that they tend to buttress the claims made by management in interviews. The docket of the *KTS* was dominated not by claims of illegal transfers but by wage disputes. My review of the *protokoly* of *KTS* meetings for the last ten years at the Textile Factory revealed not a single instance of a transfer-related claim. Of the annual average of only four cases, more than 70 percent involved wage disputes.[19] The *KTS* records for 1989 and 1990 at Rezina revealed only one transfer-related claim out of the few cases (12 in two years) considered. This claim was not pursued to the *profkom* level. At the Electronics Plant, the *KTS* averaged 13 cases annually for 1986–90, of which on average nine were wage-related and two involved transfers. No material increase was seen in 1988–90. Indeed, the only year when there were more than two transfer-related cases (in 1986 there were no transfer claims) was 1987 and that was due to three virtually identical petitions that the *KTS* ultimately dismissed on jurisdictional grounds.[20] When those cases are taken out of the calculation, the annual average of transfer-related cases drops down to 1.6.

Despite the fact that the *KTS* sided with management in more than half of all these transfer-related claims, not a single one of them was appealed to the *profkom*.

Implementing the Law in the Lower Courts

Dismissals

Workers who had been dismissed with the blessing of the *profkom* and who believed that their rights had been violated had only one option under the law if they wanted their old jobs back: they had to appeal to the court for reinstatement. This was true regardless of the statutory basis for the dismissal, and it was true even when the dismissal was a layoff and so was prompted by economic considerations ostensibly beyond the control of the workers or management.

The preceding chapter laid out in some detail the legal rules dictating the process by which courts were to consider reinstatement petitions of laid-off workers. As a threshold matter, the courts required management to demonstrate that the layoff actually took place. Assuming it did, the worker had an opportunity to rebut by arguing that it had been a sham designed not to ameliorate economic difficulties but targeted specifically at removing him or her. The court was then supposed to turn its attention to whether management had satisfied its statutory duty to make all reasonable efforts to reallocate the redundant worker within the enterprise. Finally, the court addressed the question of preferential rights.

The review of the published decisions of appellate courts gave rise to an image of activist courts rigorously protecting workers' rights by holding management to a high (but sustainable) burden of proof. The courts seemed to recognize and take account of the inevitable inequality of the parties by requiring only oral allegations by the worker of wrongdoing on the part of management to shift the burden back to management. At the same time, the courts required management to rebut these charges and sustain its own affirmative burden of proof through clear and convincing documentary evidence.

However, a very different image emerges from my review of the records of labor-related cases filed in two Moscow trial courts between 1983 and 1989. It is a picture of courts going through the motions in a tired and dispirited fashion. Although they enforced the letter of the law, close examination revealed the rote nature of their behavior. Judges seemed to have a checklist of the evidence needed to lay off a worker. Regardless of the worker's allegations, if management submitted the requisite evidence, the courts tended not to push the matter any further, that is, they did not look behind the documentary evidence in order to try to discern whether personal animosity actually prompted the layoff. This tendency to value form over substance worked to the benefit of management.

Proving a Layoff Occurred. The courts' fetish for documentary evidence was most clearly played out with regard to the threshold issue of whether the dismissal was due to an economic-based layoff. The case files typically included the order or decree of a superior organization regarding the layoff. These orders could be very detailed. Indeed, in some instances, the ministerial decree went so far as to list the positions and salary obligations to be eliminated, although it stopped short of providing specific names. The courts found this evidence, standing alone, convincing. In their opinions, judges consistently referred to these ministerial orders as satisfying management's burden to prove that an economic layoff had occurred.

Furthermore, the proworker fastidiousness exhibited in the published appellate court opinions was absent in the trial court records. Although the trial courts demanded written evidence, they were not picky about the sort of evidence. Typical of this behavior pattern is a 1988 case in which the court accepted a letter from the superior organization suggesting cutbacks in the wage fund as evidence that a layoff had taken place. Along the same lines, in a 1986 case, the court found an affidavit signed by six enterprise management officials to be sufficient to sustain management's burden of proof. More troubling was the tendency of the courts to accept the reports of commissions charged with evaluating workers' qualifications as evidence of the fact that a layoff occurred. Doing so directly contradicted the guidelines set down by the supreme courts. Indeed, the compliant attitude of the trial courts stood in sharp contrast to the published case decisions in which management was required to submit conclusive evidence that the layoff had been ordered from above.

Thus, it is no coincidence that I found no lower court case in which management failed to sustain its initial burden of proving that a layoff had taken place. This was true even when the documents submitted by management clearly raised the specter of personal vendetta. In numerous cases involving large organizations, the plaintiff-worker turned out to be the only one to have been affected by the layoff. The suspicions thus raised would seem to have been confirmed in a 1988 court case in which a secretary's supervisor had written a letter to upper management several months before her layoff was conceived in which he complained that she had a "nonresponsible attitude toward her duties." (Ironically, the defendant in this case was the main office of the official Soviet trade union organization.) I frequently encountered a past history of conflictual relations between the fired worker and the enterprise management. Sometimes, as in the 1988 case of a dispatcher who had previously been reinstated by the court on technical grounds, the case at hand did not represent the first attempt on the part of management to get rid of the worker.

In all of these cases and, in fact, in virtually every layoff case I reviewed, the worker claimed that the layoff had been a sham. The courts consistently sloughed off such contentions with a notation in their opinions that no supporting evidence had been presented at trial. Of course, this begged the question of just how workers were supposed to gather evidence given their position of virtual powerlessness vis-à-vis management. The published appellate cases hold that the worker only has to create a presumption, based on oral allegations and factual coincidence, but the trial courts were less sympathetic to the proof problems of workers. In private conversation, one trial court judge who specialized in labor cases characterized laid-off workers as "troublemakers" who deserved their fate.

The failure of workers to prevail on claims of sham layoffs cannot fully be laid at the door of an unsympathetic judiciary. It was also due, perhaps in equal measure, to the workers' repeated failure or inability to state a coherent argument. Typically, the claim would be raised in the complaint and then not again until the trial, where it would come down to the plaintiff's word against that of management officials, whose defense was buttressed by a mountain of documentary evidence. Although Soviet law gave these plaintiffs pretrial discovery rights, I found no layoff case in which the plaintiff petitioned the court to bring in additional evidence. As a result, the evidentiary record inevitably tipped in favor of management. The worker-plaintiffs' lack of legal representation also worked to their detriment throughout the judicial process, particularly at trial. In only 15 percent of the layoff cases I reviewed over a seven-year period did the worker have counsel.

Thus, generic claims by workers that they were singled out for unfair treatment lost every time. More specific allegations that the dismissal had been prompted by the worker's prior criticism of management were likewise undermined by a lack of corroborating evidence. Arguments that someone else had been hired to do the plaintiff's job after he or she had been laid off were made much less frequently and were much less successful than the published appellate court opinions led me to expect. Indeed, I found only one such case in which the worker prevailed. Management had claimed that the newly filled position of dispatcher differed materially from the similarly titled job that the plaintiff had held and that the plaintiff lacked the educational credentials and experience to carry out these new tasks. Ironically, management's case was undermined by its own records. Prior (and unrelated) to the layoff, a review of staff competency had been undertaken, and the report stated that the plaintiff was fully competent to carry out all of the functions assigned to the new dispatcher. Consequently, the court ordered the plaintiff to be reinstated to her prior position. This was, however, an exception. Other efforts along these lines failed because the workers lacked definitive proof of double-dealing by management.

Management's Duty to Transfer. Once management decided to eliminate redundant workers, the Russian Labor Code stipulated that, whenever possible, it had to transfer such workers to other positions within the enterprise. In order to comply with this duty, the positions offered had to be comparable to those being vacated. By the same token, the law did not oblige management to create make-work positions in order to avoid having to lay off workers.

The implementation of this legal duty gives rise to two issues: whether vacancies existed that management failed to offer to the displaced worker and whether the positions offered were comparable. In resolving these issues, the published appellate court opinions suggest that workers are in a favorable position vis-à-vis the burden of proof. The appellate courts (including the Supreme Courts) consistently held that workers need only allege that management had abrogated its placement responsibilities in order to shift the burden of proof onto management. In contrast, management had to prove definitively that it had complied with the law.

The review of trial court opinions, however, indicates that the situation was a bit dicier than that in practice. This point can be illustrated by looking at the issue of how to define comparability. The previous chapter detailed an appellate case in which the court held the positions of coat salesman and shoe salesman to be noncomparable and ordered the worker reinstated to his prior position. An analogous lower court case arose in 1983 in which a woman deemed redundant as a worker in the room service department at the Rossiia hotel argued that management's offers of waitressing jobs in the coffee shop *(bufet)* and the restaurant of the hotel involved different skills and training and were not comparable to her prior position. Her argument fell on deaf ears. The court found the positions comparable and held that management had fulfilled its statutory obligation.

What this case and most layoff cases demonstrate is a disturbing tendency on the part of courts to accept the word of management with no questions asked. Indeed, when the record of this 1983 Rossiia hotel case is probed more deeply, it becomes clear that six of the nine workers to be laid off refused all of the jobs offered to them and that each of these workers was offered at least four other jobs. Perhaps this was a coincidence, but the facts allow the inference that management was making propositions that it knew would be declined, a clear violation of the spirit of the law. Yet the court never asked management to explain what had happened. It looked only at the bottom line—the displaced workers had been offered "comparable" jobs and had declined them—and was satisfied.

Unfortunately, this case was not unique. A trend emerges in which the court equates management having made alternative job offers with its having acted in good faith. The trial courts were particularly inclined to believe management when it could show that the displaced worker had been offered more than one position (regardless of the position) and/or that a special commission had been formed to facilitate the reallocation of displaced workers within the enterprise. Most of the time, however, all it took was one offer of an alternative position. In a 1984 case, the court found nothing suspicious in the fact that a redundant "senior engineer" was offered a position as "engineer" in the same department with a 24 percent wage cut. It accepted at face value management's argument that the new job did not represent a retitled and lower-paid version of the plaintiff's prior job and that the plaintiff was not overqualified for the new job. The worker's argument to the contrary was given no credence.

Along similar lines, trial courts tended to accept management's word that no vacant positions existed. Although before and after personnel schedules were submitted in many cases, in contrast to what was seen in the published appellate court opinions, the trial courts did not insist upon this sort of corroborating documentary evidence. The same was true of cases in which management admitted that some positions stood vacant but claimed that the plaintiff lacked the education or other qualifications necessary to fill them. The published opinions hold that management has the burden of proving the inappropriateness of the displaced worker for the available position. In practice, however, the tables were turned, and workers were required to demonstrate that they were capable of doing the job.

Workers were able to win such cases only when the evidence (even that provided by management) was incontrovertible. In a 1988 case, a senior engineer won reinstatement by proving that a vacancy for a senior engineer had existed from the moment of his layoff, albeit in a different department. Management submitted a letter to the court in which it argued that the plaintiff lacked the necessary educational background and claimed that the plaintiff had been offered many other jobs that were within his capabilities, all of which had been rejected out of hand. The plaintiff quarreled with the charge of unsuitability for the senior engineer position. The court responded by asking management to compare the plaintiff to his co-workers based on seven objective criteria. This document demonstrated that the plaintiff was qualified and provided the grounds for his reinstatement.

This case also demonstrates that trial court judges were sympathetic to workers who could show that management had blatantly violated the law by offering them positions for which they were vastly overqualified. For example, in the 1988 case of the secretary at the main office of the official Soviet trade union organization, the court ordered her reinstated on the grounds that the proposed jobs of filing clerk or maid at the Sputnik hotel (owned by the official trade union organization) were well beneath her level of qualifications and so not comparable. Consistent with the holdings in the published decisions, the court did not require the plaintiff to prove that there was a vacant position that she could fill. It seems to have been a case in which the behavior of management shocked the conscience of the judge.

Cases in which the plaintiff prevailed were the exceptions. In the vast majority of cases, the worker was unable to sustain the burden of proving that management had not fulfilled its statutory duty. The point here is that the trial courts imposed a burden on workers that, given their lack of access to enterprise records, proved extremely difficult and often impossible to sustain. In contrast to the appellate courts, the trial courts were not satisfied with oral allegations from workers but required affirmative proof from the worker that, despite the presence of available comparable positions, management had failed to transfer a redundant worker within the enterprise. This directly contradicts the guidelines of the Supreme Courts and the holdings in analogous case opinions published in the *Kommentariia.*

Preferential Rights. The final issue that trial courts regularly addressed in layoff cases was whether management properly took into account the laid-off worker's preferential rights (as compared to other workers) to remain on the job. The decrees of the supreme courts clearly instructed trial courts to consider carefully claims by workers that their rights in this regard had been violated. The published appellate court opinions indicated that cases in which trial courts failed to do so were regularly sent back for new hearings.

Notwithstanding this black letter law, the record of the trial courts that emerges from unpublished sources is mixed. Workers routinely argued that their preferential rights had been disregarded. Sometimes the trial courts took these claims seriously, but more often they did not. Furthermore, there appears to have been no underlying principle that served as a predictor of the courts' behavior.

One might hypothesize that workers who were able to document their right to preferential treatment were more likely to have their claims taken seriously by the courts. The records indicate that this was only sometimes the case. Certainly, there were many instances of poorly documented claims that were ignored by the courts. By the same token, in a 1983 case, the fact that a worker presented a medical certificate attesting to her invalid status (which under the Russian Labor Code should have given her preferential rights vis-à-vis her co-workers in case of a layoff) did nothing to convince the court that it was a meritorious claim. Yet in a 1984 case the court reinstated a worker based only on her unsubstantiated testimony about her sterling war record and number of years on the job. Along similar lines, in a 1988 case, a worker won reinstatement based on her statements about her family situation. More often, however, such claims were ignored by the court or dismissed by a single line in the opinion stating that no supporting evidence was presented at trial.

As with claims of sham layoffs, one might hypothesize that these workers lacked the knowledge and sophistication to put forward a coherent legal argument concerning their preferential rights. Although they were undoubtedly hampered by a lack of legal counsel, that alone could not have been the decisive factor because none of the workers in the cases in which preferential rights were at issue were represented by counsel.

Thus, it is not clear what distinguishes winners from losers. What is clear is that the trial courts paid very little attention to the instructions of the higher courts on how to assess petitions alleging violations of management's duty to respect workers' preferential right to remain on the job. The record indicates that, rather than routinely looking into such claims, the courts took judicial notice only haphazardly.

Trends Extending beyond Layoffs

Two themes recur during the review of layoff cases. Trial court judges had a tendency to value form over substance. Judges appeared to have reached consensus on what documentary evidence was needed to justify a layoff, and so long as the right sort of evidence was filed they rarely quibbled over inconsistencies raised by plaintiff-workers. Causally intertwined with the formalism exhibited by trial courts was the unwillingness or, more likely, the inability of workers to rebut the case presented by management by presenting a coherent and affirmative argument of their own.

When the sphere of inquiry is expanded beyond layoff cases to other dismissals made on the initiative of management, we find that these trends are ubiquitous. The Russian Labor Code permitted management to dismiss workers when (among other reasons) they were absent from their assigned workplace for more than two hours and when they were drunk on the job. A careful examination of these cases brings the trial courts' formalism into sharper relief. In most cases, a worker's drunkenness was established through affidavits from coworkers and/or supervisors stating that the plaintiff looked drunk or smelled of alcohol on the day in question. In one 1983 case, a co-worker noted that the plaintiff had "conducted himself like a hooligan." These affidavits were usually no more than two or three sentences long and were almost always worded identically—as if they had been dictated by a third party. Preprinted forms requiring only a signature were used in a 1986 case. The courts consistently failed to demand more objective proof of intoxication and, in a 1986 case, went so far as to hold that medical certification was neither required nor relevant.

The trial courts were unconcerned by the fact that the sole support for management's allegations of intoxication on the job came from the impressionistic affidavits (often confirmed by in-court testimony) of individuals who were beholden to management for their livelihood. Indeed, the relationship of dependence seemed not to penetrate the courts' consciousness insofar as their opinions often stated that "[t]he court has no basis not to trust the evidence of the witnesses." The courts seemed more concerned with having some kind of authoritative-looking evidence that would hold up on appeal than with achieving a full airing of the underlying facts. Of course, behaving in this manner allowed the trial courts to process cases very quickly. Management understood what the court wanted and formulated its evidence accordingly. That, in and of itself, was not a problem; over time, procedural conventions would be expected to develop. Its insidious nature, however, stems from the fact that the courts consistently failed to study the evidence filed: they were satisfied when the formal prequisites had been met.

No doubt the courts' formalism contributed to the passivity of workers in the judicial process. As in layoff cases, workers dismissed on grounds of absenteeism or drunkenness on the job only rarely attempted to mount an affirmative case. Typically, they made no effort to undermine the credibility of management's witnesses by pointing out their strong incentive to paint their employer in the best possible light. They also failed to discredit management's evidence by drawing the court's attention to the fact that the affidavits of intoxication (and unauthorized absences from the workplace) were suspiciously similar.

More puzzling was the workers' failure to argue that they had been singled out for censure while others who engaged in similar behavior escaped unscathed. A good illustration of this is a 1984 case in which a senior engineer was fired after participating in an after-hours birthday celebration on the premises of the enterprise at which alcohol was consumed. While her dismissal was within the law, it does raise the question of why she alone was punished. Neither the plaintiff nor her counsel raised this issue in the pleadings or at trial.

Even stronger potential candidates for affirmative claims that the petitioner was being treated differently from other workers that were similarly situated can be found among cases of alleged absenteeism. In a 1983 case, a driver failed to report for work because his car, which he used in his work, was being repaired. He assumed that he would be of little use without his car. His complaint implied, but did not assert as a defense, that it was standard practice at his enterprise for drivers without cars to stay home. Rather than look into whether this was the accepted practice, the court rubber-stamped the dismissal.

A music teacher fired in 1986 for failing to report to school every day was a bit bolder in asserting this sort of "pattern-and-practice" claim. She argued that her teaching schedule did not require her constant presence. Not only did the court not investigate her allegation, it allowed management to reshift the focus to her competence. At one point, the judge permitted testimony from the school principal in which he criticized how she corrected homework assignments. This whole line of inquiry was, of course, legally irrelevant to the absenteeism case.[21] Such testimony undoubtedly reinforced management's portrayal of the teacher as a shirker and contributed to the court's rejection of her petition for reinstatement.

A 1988 case provides a final example. A worker was dismissed for being absent from his appointed workplace between 1:30 and 5 P.M. on a single day. While admitting that he left without permission, the worker attempted to justify it by claiming that he had been doing work-related shopping. Management easily demonstrated that such was not the case. Yet neither the plaintiff nor the court pressed management as to whether it dismissed all workers who played hooky for an afternoon. The court was concerned only with whether the technical statutory requirements had been met. Determining that they had, it held the dismissal to be legal.

Transfers

My review of the court records indicates that claims of illegal transfer were rarely filed. In 1983, only one of the 42 labor-related cases involved a transfer. In 1986, none of the 48 labor-related cases raised this issue. In 1988, two of the 52 labor-related cases involved transfers, while in 1989, no claims of illegal transfer were made.[22]

As with the information from the *KTS* records, relying on the number of cases filed to prove the presence or absence of a given phenomenon is problematic in the Soviet context. However, when taken together with evidence from interviews and enterprise records, this approach tends to buttress the conclusion that intraenterprise transfers were far from common, and certainly legal disputes over such transfers were rare indeed. This evidence also suggests that the incidence of such transfers had not increased significantly following the easing in early 1988 of legal and other constraints on management's ability to reallocate its workforce.

Conclusion

On a superficial level, law appeared to be important to Soviet labor policy on the enterprise level during the 1980s. The ministerial decrees regarding layoffs consistently cited relevant legislation and instructed subordinate enterprises to obey the dictates of the law in carrying out the layoffs. Within the enterprise, requests from management to the *profkom* always referred to the statutory basis for the dismissal, and dismissals were regularly submitted for *profkom* approval. Appearances can, however, be deceiving. In this case, the glow begins to fade when the purpose of the law is recalled: to protect workers from arbitrariness on the part of management in personnel matters. While the law requires management to jump through a number of bureaucratic hoops that are theoretically designed to deter capriciousness on the part of management, its deterrence effect has been marginal. The records show that the trade union committees have been coopted by management, thereby effectively eliminating what should have been the most important structural limitation on management discretion. In practice, the law did not matter, that is, it did little to constrain managerial discretion or to protect workers' interests.

The courts seemed to take up where the *profkom* left off. Rather than bending over backward to protect workers' interests, as the published materials would suggest is the case, the trial courts I studied were doing just the opposite. They were invariably in management's corner. Their preference was manifested not by open declaration but by a face value acceptance of management evidence and by sloughing off workers' charges that management acted illegally. Just as the courts, through their tendency to formalism, have lowered the burden of proof placed on management, so too have they raised the burden on workers. Given that workers are rarely legally literate and even more rarely represented by counsel, it comes as no surprise that they often came up short.

The information gathered in enterprises and trial courts clearly demonstrates that the February 1988 change in the law governing internal transfers had no impact. Contrary to the expectations of policymakers and scholars, easing the restrictions on management's discretion did not encourage management to redistribute its workers so as to increase efficiency. Instead, managers paid no attention to the change and simply continued on as they always had. Thus, the law on transfers made no difference in reality because economic markets remained static.

Similarly, the absence of real market forces tended to marginalize the effect of the law on layoffs. Just as important, however, was the failure of trade unions and lower courts to take this law seriously, which, in turn, had the effect of undermining the law's legitimacy among workers. The reasons for this will be explored in the following chapters, in which I examine the structural and cultural obstacles to making law matter in Soviet and post-Soviet society.

Part 3
Obstacles to the Emergence of a Legal State in the Soviet Union

CHAPTER 5

The Courts

Introduction

Although the published case decisions paint a picture of activist Soviet courts, ferreting out the truth whenever management sought to obscure it, the records of day-to-day practice revealed a passive institution, content to go through the motions in order to build a record that would stand up on appeal. Typically, this behavior was not the product of ex parte pressure on the judge from management (or local Communist Party officials) but reflected the usual operation of a ritualistic, almost apathetic, judicial process. In many ways, it mirrored industrial production within the Leninist administrative-command economy, in which the primary concern was not the quality of the output but meeting the quantitative targets established by the plan.

Trial court judges routinely accepted management's evidence at face value, while rejecting workers' allegations out of hand. A judicial process that values form over substance inevitably favors management. Workers could be buried in a blizzard of documentary evidence, and management was secure in the knowledge that the courts did not look behind the documents. The result of the courts' hands-off behavior was that the parties were not equal before the law. While management had access to the necessary "evidence" and could use it to good advantage, thanks to the availability of in-house legal counsel, workers had access neither to enterprise records nor to meaningful legal assistance. Judges could have acted as equalizers—and both the published materials and the ideology proclaiming the paternal role of judges suggest they were supposed to—but the data indicate they did not. For Soviet judges, the bottom line was not doing justice but maintaining the status quo.

Why were the Soviet courts so lethargic and what changes in the judicial system would be necessary to make law matter? Underlying these questions is the assumption that law cannot matter reciprocally in a society in which courts have been effectively coopted by those with political power and are generally held in low esteem by the citizenry.

The shortcomings of the Soviet judicial system are well known and little would be gained by recounting yet another litany of horrors. What is needed instead is some perspective on the Soviet case—a systematic analysis of what makes courts important political actors in the Western context and what role courts play in the evolution of a legal system in which law matters reciprocally. The most fruitful approach is not to idealize any single country by putting forward its judicial system as a model for the former Soviet Union but to sketch out in fairly broad strokes an ideal type that takes advantage of broad comparative experience. The ideal type provides a framework for analyzing and evaluating the reality of the Soviet judicial system and allows us to pinpoint those features that act to frustrate efforts to reshape the role of law in post-Soviet society.

Courts: An Ideal-Typical View

Courts, in terms of the functions they fulfill and the role assumed by the judge, vary widely among countries. The Anglo-American tradition differs from the European civil law tradition, and American courts differ from British, just as German courts differ from French.[1] Debates rage among legal scholars over the extent to which courts do and should engage in so-called judicial lawmaking and whether judges should be passive receivers of the evidence presented by the parties or should actively seek out the truth. These debates, while of intrinsic interest, have little bearing on my inquiry. They take for granted that law and, by implication, courts matter in a reciprocal fashion. My question is more basic: what causes courts to become a vital part of political and social life?

By taking a minimalist approach and reducing contemporary Western courts to their very essence, we see that courts in these societies are governmental institutions that impose penalties for antisocial behavior and resolve disputes pursuant to law, but do so in a generally impartial fashion. They are reasonably accessible (even if not equally so in an economic sense) to all strata of society. Furthermore, Western courts do not exist in isolation but are embedded in a governmental structure that respects the need for judicial impartiality.[2] Perhaps more importantly, Western courts are part of stable societies that respect and trust in the integrity of the institution and the decision makers and are willing to resort to the law to settle disagreements.

Impartiality

The practice of judicial impartiality means that in deciding cases the courts, both institutionally and in the person of the decision maker, are guided principally by the law and that in settling factual disputes and in interpreting the law generally applicable legal or community standards will govern. In finding facts and applying general principles of law or community standards, impartial judges are not predisposed in favor of either disputing party (including governmental parties) on political or personal grounds.

Of course, impartiality can rarely be achieved completely. As Shapiro and others have argued, no decision maker can ever be completely impartial. Judges have values.[3] They have ambitions. They may have some lingering dependence on, and loyalty to, those to whom they owe their job.[4] But as Justice Cardozo cautioned, a judge "would err if he were to impose on the community as a rule of life his own idiosyncrasies of conduct or belief."[5]

Furthermore, the law itself is rarely neutral. In favoring some values or policies, it favors certain groups within society. This favoritism cannot help but spill over into the process of adjudication. A judiciary that strives for impartiality in particular cases may favor some interests in general, but it is quite different from one that is not impartial in particular cases.[6] Procedural requirements, such as rules of evidence, may frustrate the achievement of impartial results. Such outcomes do not reflect on the decision makers as individuals but on the law itself. Indeed, this is the essence of what Nonet and Selznick refer to as the "historic bargain" by which courts receive limited autonomy in procedural matters on the condition that they do not meddle in substantive policy making.[7]

Institutional Impartiality. Impartiality has both institutional and individual dimensions. The former is more commonly referred to as judicial independence. Like the rule of law, the term *judicial independence* has often been used imprecisely and, over the years, has taken on considerable political baggage. Many commentators use the term without clarifying what they mean by it, while others use it too inclusively.[8] The distinction between the institutional independence of the judiciary and the impartiality (or integrity) of individual judges is critical. As Becker notes, "much independence may exist without much impartiality and much impartiality may exist without much independence."[9] A decision maker may be motivated to be dispassionate but may be undermined by a lack of institutional independence, and vice versa.

I am using the term *judicial independence* to refer to the institutional independence of the judiciary. In practice, this means that the judiciary stands to some extent apart from the rest of the state apparatus. At the very minimum, it assumes that no outside state (or parastatal) entity has the right to interfere or does, in fact, interfere regularly in the resolution of individual cases. This does not necessarily require the sort of strict separation of powers that characterizes the American system. The incorporation of the judiciary into the executive branch in civil law systems does not compromise its independence. On the other hand, the functional clarity that results from a formal segregation of judicial from other governmental functions tends to reinforce independence.

How is judicial independence secured? The goal is to foreclose or at least limit the ability of those with political power to influence the judicial process. No blueprint for policy options exists that will guarantee this outcome. A number of factors enter into the calculation, including selection procedures, tenure, salaries, promotions, and norms concerning ex parte communication with judges. Each is important because each has a direct impact on the long-term relationship between judges and the political power structure. A comparison of Anglo-American and European experience reveals very different patterns, all of which have their pluses and minuses, but all of which provide for a minimal level of institutional independence for the judiciary.

Judicial selection and tenure provide a contrast. There are three methods by which most judges are chosen: (1) appointment by a political executive, (2) popular or legislative election, or (3) a competitive examination process. None is inherently preferable; the choice depends on a country's legal and political system and culture and frequently reflects a mixture of the options (depending on the level of the court).

Within civil law systems, trial court judges are generally selected through competitive examinations,[10] although higher court judges are often appointed.[11] Young people enter the judicial corps upon graduation from a university legal faculty and stay for their entire career.[12] The job security is comparable to that of other civil service jobs and promotion to higher courts is based on technical merit and seniority rather than on political intrigue.[13] Although this selection system has been widely criticized for turning the judge into "a civil servant, a functionary,"[14] it has also been praised for insulating judges from outside political pressure.[15]

In contrast, the judiciary in common law countries is not composed of career civil servants. Instead, service on the bench typically follows a distinguished career as a lawyer or politician.[16] In England, higher court judges are appointed and, by statute, must be barristers with at least ten years' experience (most have been practicing law for 20 to 25 years).[17] In the United States, by contrast, selection processes varies. Federal judges are chosen by the president (confirmed by the Senate) and enjoy life tenure. State court judges, on the other hand, are typically elected,[18] though often they are initially appointed by the governor and later confirmed by popular election.[19] The procedure, as well as the term of office, depends on state law. While the recruitment of judges is more overtly political in the United States than in Europe and political leaders (as well as interest groups) work for the appointment or election of judges from the political parties they favor,[20] the rigid separation of powers, combined with the long terms of office of state court judges and life tenure of federal judges, tends to ensure the institutional impartiality of the American judiciary.

The institutional integrity of the judiciary may be compromised by outside control (whether legislative or executive) of matters relating to the internal operations of the courts. There is, after all, an inevitable tension between the desire for judicial independence and the desire to have courts facilitate the political agenda of those in power. This tension is most evident in authoritarian regimes[21] but is ubiquitous.[22] To this end, laws may be passed to limit the tenure of judges[23] or to permit removal at the discretion of the executive[24] with the express intent of getting rid of gadfly judges. In addition, in most countries, the legislature sets judicial salaries and operating budgets. This creates a danger that the power of the purse will be used to undermine the institutional independence of the judiciary.[25] Ultimately, therefore, independence rests on the existence of norms and social forces (e.g., opposition parties, free press) that condemn such use of legislative power.

Individual Impartiality. Perhaps more important than institutional factors in ensuring that courts become and remain respected political actors is the personal impartiality of individual judges. The plain meaning of "personal impartiality" would suggest a requirement of impeccable integrity and moral character. While necessary, such qualities are not sufficient. Also important is a desire, in essence, to do justice and uphold legitimately established legal values.

The first element in the impartiality equation is, however, objectivity. Impartial decision makers listen to both sides of a dispute and examine all relevant evidence before reaching their decision. As this implies, there is no specific preconceived role that a judge must play in order to ensure objectivity. The civil law tradition calls for judges to become part of the process rather than to remain above it. Continental judges routinely question witnesses and review all of the evidence, which for the most part is unfiltered by the restrictive rules of admissibility that exist in the United States.[26] In contrast, the American tradition of adversarialism requires judges to allow the parties to run the show in the courtroom.[27] This laissez-faire style was the norm until the rise of complex litigation in recent years forced judges into a more activist role.[28] As Resnik argues, "[b]oth before and after the trial, [American] judges are playing a critical role in shaping litigation and influencing results."[29] The point is that none of these models is inherently better than the others; all have advantages. Yet each is capable, assuming otherwise hospitable conditions, of giving rise to objective decision making.

An equally important element of individual judicial impartiality is the incorruptibility of judges. To a large extent, this depends on the moral character of individual judges and the sanctions placed on bribery and intimidation by society. On the other hand, if judges receive adequate salaries, financial temptation presumably diminishes. If salaries are permitted to erode, practice shows that judges resign or drift into varieties of soft or hard bribery. Over time, the quality of the judiciary and the standing of its members within society is undermined.[30]

Finally, the personal qualities of objectivity and incorruptibility are complemented by a desire to do justice.[31] What does it mean to "do justice"? As a threshold matter, it assumes that judges will look to the law when resolving disputes and be intellectually capable of legal analysis, breaking down disputes into legally cognizable issues. Yet the vision is not of judge as machine, mechanically applying law to controversies as they arise.[32] It is a more Solomonic vision, in which judges enforce the law rigorously but are able to look beyond it, when necessary, to embrace the prevailing community standards.[33] After all, despite the best efforts of legislators, statutory law cannot possibly anticipate every situation. In both civil law and common law systems, judicial decisions act to fill the gaps. In a society in which law matters reciprocally, judges are guided by, and respond to, the concerns of society in their decision making.[34] Impartiality, therefore, implies a certain dedication to the task, a willingness to invest energy, physical and moral, in the search for just decisions.

There is, of course, a danger in encouraging the judiciary to take an expansive view of law. This is well illustrated by the Nazi period, during which judges were told by the Grand Criminal Panel of the Supreme Court:

> the judiciary . . . can fulfill the task imposed upon it by the Third Reich only if it does not remain glued to the letter of the law, but rather penetrates to its innermost spirit; the judiciary must do its part to see that the goals of the lawmakers are achieved.[35]

Yet the slope is not as slippery as it might appear at first glance. The courts exist within a governmental and societal context, and when that context is totalitarian it is unrealistic to expect the courts to stand alone as a bulwark of responsiveness to democratic ideals. History shows that when a political system is in crisis or is threatened, courts become largely powerless.[36]

What is the source of individual judicial impartiality—this objectivity and incorruptibility combined with a desire to "do justice"? The short answer is that it is largely cultural. Thus, it is important that judges think of themselves as impartial and that their views be shared by society.[37] But where do these images come from? One source is undoubtedly the socialization process that is part and parcel of legal and judicial education.[38] The need for judges to be impartial (both personally and institutionally) is a deeply held principle (or perhaps legitimizing myth) of both the civil law and common law legal traditions. Another closely related source is the professionalization of the judiciary: the professional training of judges leads to a more detached and impersonal attitude and so reduces the impact of personal sentiment and bias.[39]

How is the impartiality of individual judges secured? The fallibility of mankind suggests that some mechanism more concrete than good intentions is required. The ability to appeal decisions to higher courts constitutes the primary method for keeping judges on the straight and narrow. The right to appeal, even when unexercised, acts as a latent threat and greatly lessens the willingness of judges to depart from established legal standards.[40] Moreover, appeal systems require lower courts to keep records of the evidence and often require judges to write opinions justifying their decisions, which tends independently to reinforce norms of legality and impartiality.

A number of additional political and legal mechanisms are used in the West to buttress the accountability of judges. Judges who are elected, as in many American state courts, have to be reelected and are subject to recall campaigns.[41] Removing appointed judges is more difficult, although most systems provide for removal in cases of clear misbehavior.[42] The challenge is to devise removal mechanisms that ensure that judges are not forced out because the political authorities disagree with the content of their decisions (assuming such decisions are in basic accord with the law) but only when they have done something to bring shame to their judicial office.

The question of judicial immunity must also be faced. It seems only fair that a citizen wronged by a judge who has breached his or her official duties be given some opportunity for recourse. Whether the state assumes vicarious liability or the judge is held personally liable, or some combination of the two, is not really the issue.[43] More important is that judges not be allowed to escape responsibility for their actions but be held legally accountable in some fashion.

Also critical to ensuring the impartiality of judges is the specter of public criticism. Merryman describes this as potentially "the most effective of all informal disciplinary mechanisms."[44] Of course, its effectiveness assumes a press that is free to gain access to, discuss, and criticize judicial decisions. Furthermore, as Rheinstein notes,

> [the] proper functioning [of public opinion] depends on the existence in the community . . . of an awareness of the profound significance of the judicial office and its proper functioning, and of a ready willingness to insist upon and, when necessary, to enforce judicial faithfulness to law.[45]

The informal approval or disapproval expressed by their colleagues on the bench, the practicing bar, and the scholarly community can also have a powerful effect on the behavior of judges.[46] As this implies, the presence of a politically independent, activist bar, and a general atmosphere of political pluralism is helpful in ensuring the accountability of judges.

Accessibility

Achieving a high degree of judicial independence and impartiality in decision making is a hollow achievement if citizens do not make use of the courts. One reason why people decline to mobilize their rights through the legal system has already been suggested; namely, a widely held belief that the judges or the judicial system are inherently biased or corrupt. An equally powerful rationale for opting out is an inability to gain access to the system.

What does it mean to say that a legal system is accessible? Complete and equal accessibility is not feasible. Rather, the question is whether most citizens consider the legal system to be a realistic avenue for resolving disputes and, if so, whether they can get their disputes resolved by a legal institution (court or other forum) without undue delay or expense.[47] Also relevant is the complexity of the system; that is, whether a relatively well-educated person can file a complaint or mount an effective defense on his or her own. If some type of assistance is required, it does not necessarily follow that the system is inaccessible. Instead, the inquiry shifts to whether such assistance is available at a reasonable cost.

Indeed, the legal systems of most Western liberal democracies are characterized by a high level of complexity. Complexity entails a need to rely on lawyers and hence high costs, which often diminish accessibility for claims involving low economic stakes, that is, where litigation costs exceed potential revenues.[48] To some extent, contingency fees and public subsidies (legal aid) compensate. But not fully, for lawyers and other legal professionals act not only as facilitators but also as gatekeepers, discouraging the assertion of some claims and defenses.[49] Subsidies, moreover, always fall short of achieving completely equal access: the wealthy and the state always have some advantages.[50]

Notwithstanding the complexity of Western legal systems, access can be enhanced through the introduction of inexpensive and procedurally simple forums in which small claims can be pursued. Similarly, publicly funded agencies that are charged with enforcing the law, for example, police, occupational safety inspectors, civil rights agencies, and housing code inspectors, may help to empower the "have-nots" in their disputes with the "haves." Most national systems place the burden on citizens to mobilize their rights rather than on government to take affirmative steps to enforce citizens' rights, but the critical issue is whether the mechanism of mobilization is clear and feasible for citizens.[51]

Governmental and Societal Context

Implicit in the analysis thus far is a recognition that courts do not exist in a vacuum. They are a constituent element in a broader governmental and societal context, which determines the extent to which courts are valued, used, and contribute to law mattering in a reciprocal sense. The key to the role of courts is not the form of government but the presence of political pluralism. The pluralist ideal requires that all groups within society be able to participate in the political process without fear of the consequences.[52] The citizenry feels free to bring disputes to the courtroom, to debate differences openly, and to continue that debate in the media if it disagrees with the decision rendered. Likewise, members of the press have the right and power to speak their minds about the work of the court without fear of being thrown into jail for contempt. And organized political opposition groups are free to use criticism of the courts (and the regime's use of them) as a way of winning political support.

Ideally, this political and social pluralism is complemented by a self-conscious recognition and acceptance within society and among political elites of the critical need to maintain the impartiality of the judiciary. This constitutes an admission that, while judges are unquestionably political actors, they are somehow different from those who staff the legislative and executive branches. Although their decisions often have political implications, and political calculations may play a role in the decision making process, judges should, at the most fundamental level, be guided by the law and not by the entreaties or threats of participants or interested outsiders.

Does this amount to an argument that courts can be impartial and command the respect of the citizenry only in a democracy? Not necessarily. History presents us with numerous examples of judicial systems, such as the ecclesiastical courts of the eleventh and twelfth centuries[53] and the English courts of the eighteenth and nineteenth centuries,[54] that functioned impartially and independently despite being situated in a decidedly nondemocratic context. When judicial impartiality and independence flourish, it reflects a compromise among societal forces to achieve stability at the expense of triumphing in particular cases through direct intervention. The desire for predictability in economic and social relations acts to unite societal forces in putting an end to outside interference in legal proceedings.[55]

Courts: The Soviet Reality

On a superficial level, courts appeared to fulfill much the same function in the Soviet Union as in the Western democracies. Soviet courts purported to resolve disputes in an impartial fashion and to be generally accessible. Although the claims of accessibility may well have been warranted, the claims of impartiality were much overstated.

Nowhere is the contrast sharper between the law on the books and actual practice than in the realm of judicial behavior. The 1936 and 1977 Soviet Constitutions stated unequivocally that judges were independent and subject only to the law in rendering decisions. Soviet legal scholars consistently asserted the independence of the courts and, as proof, cited this constitutional language. In contrast, Western and emigre legal scholars agreed that the defining feature of the Soviet judicial system was its dependence on the state and the Party. This is hardly surprising given the close identification between the law and the state and the cooptation by the Party of state functions.

My purpose is to push past the tired clichés about Soviet judges' lack of independence to look at the broader question of why the courts were relegated to the sidelines of Soviet society and why this continued despite the perestroika-era reforms. The ideal type developed in the preceding section serves as an analytical tool. By breaking down judicial behavior into its institutional and individual dimensions and examining the political and social context, the reasons for the dependence of the judiciary on outside forces come into sharper focus.

Impartiality

Before I embark on the analysis of the level of impartiality within the Soviet judiciary, a brief reminder of my working definition of impartiality is in order. Recognizing it as a relative concept, its presence is judged by the extent to which decisions are rendered dispassionately and in accord with the dictates of the law and, when the law is vague or silent, in accord with prevailing community standards. It therefore has both an institutional and an individual dimension.

In the Soviet context, this distinction between the institutional and individual components of impartiality is particularly important but rarely made, either by Soviet or Western commentators. The lack of impartiality and its primary cause were self-evident: the influence of the Party was pervasive and had a devastating impact on the ability of the judiciary to assert its independence, both institutionally and individually. Because it all seemed so obvious, scholars have made little effort to examine the absence of impartiality in a more systematic fashion. Doing so now, as we look beyond the Soviet period into an unknown future, is essential. Instilling impartiality is not a simple matter of lifting the stranglehold placed on the Soviet judiciary by the Party. Instead, it is necessary to untangle the knot and separate the strands into those that undermined institutional and individual impartiality. Only in this way can we come to terms with the long-term legacy of Leninism on the courts and make a coherent argument about the preconditions for enhancing the judiciary's impartiality in the post-Soviet period.

Institutional Impartiality. Institutional impartiality is a function of the extent to which the state imposes itself into the judicial process. Notwithstanding the bold constitutional proclamations, courts enjoyed very little autonomy from the state during the Soviet period. They were treated as an organ of state power—as an instrument to be used at the discretion of the state or Party.

Ministerial Subordination. The Soviet courts were subordinate to the Ministry of Justice. Similar hierarchical patterns are found throughout much of Western Europe and do not necessarily undermine the institutional integrity of the judiciary. The impact of the structure was different in the Soviet Union because the Ministry's functions were not merely administrative but extended to the "organizational guidance" *(organizatsionnoe rukovodstvo)* of the courts. As the Chief Justice of the Soviet Supreme Court noted in a July 1989 interview, "under the guise of organizational guidance, the Ministry of Justice has interfered in literally all aspects of the activities of the courts."[56]

The Ministry also served as the "transmission belt" to the courts for policy initiatives of the Party and the state. These were usually issued in the form of joint decrees of the Central Committee of the Party and the Council of Ministers but also appeared in the form of guiding explanations from the republic or All-Union supreme courts.[57] Campaigns against various forms of socially unacceptable behavior, such as drunkenness, hooliganism, parasitism, and poor labor discipline, were a constant of Soviet political life.[58] These crusades were always introduced with great fanfare and became the preoccupation of the media for a time. Feifer comments that

> [s]o pointed and so overwhelming was the legal campaign [under Khrushchev] that the women who cleaned the streets near the university were aware of its direction. Surely no judge could fail to understand—no imagination was required of him.[59]

The courts were expected to participate enthusiastically. Most often this meant altering sentencing policy in criminal cases[60] and, in civil cases, adjudicating with policy goals in mind.[61]

In other cases, the Party made its wishes known in a more surreptitious manner. The Soviet Union and its progeny often failed to publish laws, particularly those with troubling political implications.[62] Judges were made aware of these laws as the need arose and thereby became collaborators in the conspiracy of silence.

Selection, Tenure, and Promotion. The policies of selection, retention, and promotion also tended to compromise the institutional impartiality of the judiciary.[63] Although trial court judges were elected directly by the public, and higher court judges were selected by the corresponding level of the legislature,[64] the Party controlled the process quite thoroughly. One candidate was proposed for each position and thus, as an American scholar of Soviet law notes, "nomination was tantamount to election."[65] The key was not competence—until the late 1980s there were only minimal educational and no experiential prerequisites—but political reliability. Consequently, most (if not all) Soviet judges were Party members.[66]

Judges who failed to follow the Party line were drummed out of the corps at the next election.[67] Kaminskaya (a former defense lawyer in the Soviet Union) explains that

> In practice, . . . every judge knows that the approval of his candidacy for reelection, and consequently his continuance in the profession, depends on the Party's assessment of his record.[68]

As with the initial selection process, political reliability, that is, adherence to the views of the Party, was the key to tenure. The relatively short five-year terms gave the Party an opportunity to reevaluate the performance of the judiciary regularly and make adjustments as necessary.[69] The assessment process was ongoing; regular meetings were held at which Party officials reviewed the performance of judges.[70] Their interest extended beyond the courtroom to include the overall professional conduct of judges. Indeed, one justice of the Soviet Union's Supreme Court was denied renomination because he had written an article deemed too critical of the existing legal order.[71]

The long arm of the Party also reached into promotion policy. Like other countries with a civil service style of judiciary, promotions to higher courts were ostensibly based on objective criteria such as competence and seniority. Certainly these factors played a role. But the "cardinal criterion" was an absence of reversals.[72] Also relevant was the speed with which judges disposed of cases.[73] Just as important as job performance, however, was Party membership and other indicia of political dependability.[74] Markovits argues that, as a result of the political responsibilities that came with promotion, many East German judges "were happy to remain in inconspicuous posts."[75] The same was undoubtedly true in the Soviet case.

Budgetary Constraints. The state's (and by implication the Party's) control over the operating budget of the courts and the salaries paid to judges gave it additional leverage over the institution of the judiciary. The material conditions under which Soviet judges worked were far from ideal. As one citizen asked in 1989, "Why is justice in our country rendered in shacks?"[76] Perhaps his characterization was overstated, but not by much. In contrast to the gleaming marble edifices that housed Party officials, Soviet trial courts were housed in old wooden buildings that were dingy, dark, poorly heated and maintained, and difficult to find.[77] Typically they lacked the basic amenities of a cafeteria (or *bufet*) and a cloakroom presided over by a domineering babushka, which were present in virtually every other public building in the Soviet Union.[78] In a 1989 interview, the Soviet Minister of Justice estimated that one third of Soviet court buildings were "absolutely unsuitable for the administration of justice."[79]

In addition to the crumbling state of the physical plant, the state's failure to provide basic administrative support made the work of Soviet judges more difficult. Judges were expected to manage a large caseload on their own.[80] Not only were they not part of the computer age, often their chambers lacked even a functional typewriter. Of the labor-related cases I reviewed in the *Proletarskii* people's court in Moscow between 1983 and 1990, an average of 41 percent of the opinions each year were handwritten. Similarly, the record of the court proceedings was handwritten and somewhat haphazard.[81] The judge's secretary, who was typically just out of high school or in his first years of university night school, took notes on the proceedings. I found no instance in which these scribblings had been transcribed into a more legible and, therefore, usable form. Judges had no law clerks to help them research legal issues that arose, and the trial court buildings contained no law library. One judge showed me a battered copy of the official commentary to the labor code, in which the many changes made during the Gorbachev years had been pasted and paper-clipped. This constituted her law library.

The salaries paid to judges were also indicative of their low status. During the Soviet period, judges' salaries consistently lagged behind the national average.[82] Although comparable to the salaries received by lawyers *(advokaty),* lawyers routinely supplemented their income with under-the-table fees, an option not readily available to judges.[83]

Judges were also forced to rely on local governmental and Party organs to provide them with housing. Obtaining suitable housing was a perennial problem for all strata of Soviet society, and judges were no exception. In 1989, the Soviet Deputy Minister of Justice revealed that "[a]t the present time, more than 3,000 [Russian] judges either do not have a residence of their own or lead an existence on the brink of homelessness."[84]

The fact that the state was so miserly in its funding of the judiciary constitutes strong evidence of the lack of importance placed on courts within Soviet society. As one people's court judge commented, "[w]here there is no independence in the material and economic sense, there is no independence in the political sense."[85]

The Effort to Reform the Courts under Gorbachev

Gorbachev's tenure in office was marked by a willingness to discuss openly the shortcomings of the Soviet political and social order not seen since the Khrushchev "thaw" of the late 1950s. This *glasnost'* extended to the legal system and, more specifically, to the courts. Scholars and policymakers alike acknowledged the low status of the courts and their personnel as an obstacle to creating a law-based state *(pravovoe gosudarstvo).* In the late 1980s, a systematic effort was made to shore up the independence of the courts. Through constitutional amendments and legislative initiatives, structural barriers were erected in the hopes of putting an end to the cooptation of the judiciary by political forces, which had become routine under Soviet power.

The 1989 Law on Court Structure endeavored to change the relationship between the courts and the Ministry of Justice. No longer was the Ministry charged with the "organizational guidance" of the courts; its functions were limited to the "organizational maintenance" *(organizatsionnoe obespechenie)* of the courts.[86] Presumably the goal was to create a more traditional European administrative-supervisory relationship.

But the Ministry had not been the primary obstacle to institutional independence. Enhancing the status of the courts required the removal of the Party from the judicial process. This was no simple matter. The Party's tentacles reached into virtually every aspect of the process. In December 1988, the constitution was amended to change the selection procedure and, in 1989, the Law on the Status of Judges[87] confirmed and refined these new procedures.[88] Trial judges were no longer to be elected by the public but were to be selected by the legislature at the next higher level.[89] The electoral reforms of 1989 had given rise to a more independent legislature that no longer merely rubber-stamped Party-approved initiatives and nominees.[90]

The Ministry of Justice was responsible for selecting the nominees. Its choices were then vetted by a special "qualifications panel" of judges *(kvalifikatsionnye kollegii)* chosen by their fellow judges at their annual conference.[91] Objective criteria for selection were introduced, for example, qualifying exams, formal legal education, and at least two years of legal experience. The tenure of all judges was extended to ten years. The legislative body that elected a judge had the power to remove him but was required to consult with the qualifications panel before doing so.[92] All told, this represents a valiant effort to exclude the Party from the process. As one English scholar of Soviet law has commented,

> there has been set up the foundation of a career structure for Soviet judges, monitored and controlled generally by elected representatives of the body of judges. This seems on paper to be a reasonable compromise between the divergent requirements of ensuring judicial competence whilst not compromising their integrity.[93]

The legislation and the accompanying debate also recognized the need to improve the material conditions under which judges worked. Apropos of this is a 1989 statement of the Soviet Minister of Justice: "If [being a judge] is an honored profession, if this is a respected profession, if this is a profession that is valued highly by the state, then it follows that appropriate financial and other conditions should be provided."[94] Indeed, the salaries of judges were almost doubled, and promises were made regarding future expenditures to renovate court buildings.[95] A 1989 law required local officials to find suitable housing for judges within six months of appointment. The feasibility of the law was questionable,[96] but at least the problem was openly acknowledged and discussed.

Too little time elapsed between the introduction of these structural innovations and the collapse of the Soviet Union to make any definitive claims as to their effectiveness. Certainly they seem to represent steps in the right direction. Yet my conversations with Moscow trial court judges in the early 1990s indicate that little immediate effect was felt. A question that remains to be addressed is whether the lack of impartiality within the Soviet judiciary was due primarily to the routinized institutional interference (and lack of support) or whether the ultimate cause was the absence of individual impartiality, which is rooted in culture and is more difficult to eradicate.

Individual Impartiality. We have previously identified three facets of individual impartiality of judges: objectivity, incorruptibility and a commitment to basic principles of justice and legality. Each was problematic in the Soviet context.

Objectivity. An objective judge determines the outcome of a dispute based on the evidence placed before him and does everything within his power to ensure that both sides of the story are fully aired. His decision is not influenced by the identity of the parties and/or the extent of their political or economic power.

Soviet law attempted to mandate judicial objectivity. The 1977 constitution required judges to render decisions based solely on evidence presented in court. Furthermore, primary responsibility was placed on the judge for ensuring that all relevant evidence was sought and heard. As Feifer notes

> The Soviet judge . . . is an active player—the *most* active, questioning and examining, carrying out the Civil law tradition that the court itself must direct the search for truth rather than limit itself principally to the evidence offered by the "sides." (emphasis in original)[97]

Soviet commentators accepted and promoted this paradigm of the activist judge.

My research contradicts the common wisdom. It indicates that judges more often reacted to the evidence presented by the parties and only rarely took an activist role in the proceedings. In the labor cases I reviewed, the trial judge consistently failed to probe either the workers' allegations of improper management behavior or the reliability of the documentary evidence submitted by management. In many cases, judges declined to subpoena witnesses requested by workers and often overlooked the incestuous relationship between management and its witnesses when determining credibility. As a result, the evidence was inevitably skewed in favor of management.

Not surprisingly, the trial court judges I interviewed denied that this bias was the result of their behavior. While admitting that workers were often less knowledgeable about the legal system than management and, furthermore, that they were typically not represented by counsel, the judges did not regard these disadvantages as fatal flaws.[98] They believed the system compensated by requiring the judge—in his role as truth seeker—to take the lead in questioning witnesses and determining the reliability of other evidence. In theory, this might be adequate, but in practice it fell short due to the tendency of judges to accept management's evidence at face value.

This behavior on the part of judges in labor cases stemmed in large part from a lack of sympathy for workers. On numerous occasions, trial court judges confessed that, in their view, most workers who petitioned for reinstatement after having been laid off (or dismissed on other grounds by management) were "troublemakers" with little substance to support their claims. They did not see such remarks as betrayals of their judicial obligation to be objective but rather as statements of fact that, in turn, caused them to regard reinstatement claims with a suspicious rather than an open mind.

Incorruptibility. Just as the institutional integrity of the Soviet judiciary was compromised by its subjugation to the Party so too were individual Soviet judges. Party officials were able to dictate the outcome of specific cases[99] and, on occasion, were even able to use to the courts as vehicles for pursuing private vendettas.[100] This "telephone law" was most common in cases with clear political overtones but was also present in more mundane cases. Although not the norm, the specter of outside interference had an insidiously corrosive effect as judges learned to censor themselves in order to avoid incurring the wrath of the Party.[101]

With the death of Stalin in 1953 and the consequent end of mass, state-sponsored repression, fear ceased to be a significant motivating factor in judges' behavior. The Party's power over individual judges stemmed from its control over selection, retention, and promotion. The periodic performance reviews discussed earlier went beyond judges' responses to policy directives to encompass their overall political reliability. One key indicator of loyalty was a willingness to toe the line in particular cases when so ordered by Party operatives—that is, to obey "telephone law."[102] Given the Party's control over the judicial selection process, the latent threat to get rid of judges who refused to follow instructions was quite potent. Kaminskaya describes an encounter with a judge who was weeping because she had been told to give a lighter sentence to a convicted criminal than she thought he deserved. Kaminskaya notes that the judge never contemplated not doing as she was ordered.[103] Nominations for trial court posts were made on the local level, thereby giving local Party officials considerable leverage over judges. Indeed, some argue that over time the ability to intervene in court proceedings became almost a perquisite of Party influence.[104]

Although Western and emigre commentators have long agreed that "telephone law" was a reality of Soviet life under Brezhnev and Khrushchev (disagreeing only as to the frequency with which it occurred), it was not until the policy of *glasnost'* took hold under Gorbachev that their Soviet counterparts openly acknowledged it. The ensuing discussion generally confirmed the conclusions of Western scholars and buttressed the claims made in emigre memoirs. One trial court judge complained that courts had been "a tool in the hands of the Party . . . ," and noted that "[i]n most cases, the opinion of the leaders of the Party and government was above the law."[105] Furthermore, exposing the interference did not end it. A 1988 survey of 120 trial court judges revealed that half were pressured by officials in specific cases.[106]

Interestingly, the trial court judges I interviewed in early 1990 refused to speak openly about Party interference (either past or present) in the decision making process. While admitting that it might have taken place elsewhere, they staunchly denied that it had undermined their own impartiality. Markovits reports similar conversations with East German judges in the period immediately preceding reunification. She comments that "[w]hatever independence these judges enjoyed must have been more fragile than they can now admit to themselves."[107] The same might well be said for Soviet judges. On the other hand, the reticence of Soviet judges in 1990 might also have been prompted by continued Party loyalty. At that time, a majority of judges (and all of the judges I interviewed) were still Party members and, as had been true for the entire Soviet period, were reluctant to criticize the Party or expose its flaws to foreigners.

With the dissipation of the power of the Party in the early 1990s, many feared that the newly empowered legislative branch was stepping into its shoes in terms of pressuring the courts in specific cases. As Yuri Feofanov, *Izvestiia*'s legal commentator, noted, "[i]n the final analysis what difference does it make whether it is a party functionary or a democratic deputy who has the right to order the court around?"[108] In a February 1991 interview, a member of the USSR Supreme Court confirmed that members of the USSR Supreme Soviet had repeatedly attempted to influence the outcome of pending cases. He claimed to have resisted such overtures but, like Markovits,[109] I found myself wondering about other untold stories in which his resolve had not proved so steadfast.

Doing Justice. The final component of individual impartiality is a commitment on the part of judges to basic principles of legality. Such a commitment assumes a respect for the written law, but goes further and demands that judges understand, embrace, and enforce the deeper values that unite society. In order for the end result to be just, the values espoused must be shared by the community, not imposed on its members in a repressive fashion by a politically powerful elite. At the same time, the judiciary cannot lose sight of the need for a certain degree of consistency in the law.

While Soviet judges were encouraged to depart from the written law, their touchstone was not the community but the Party. In the years immediately following the October Revolution, this took the form of "revolutionary justice." The existing statutory law was rejected as hopelessly bourgeois, and judges were instructed to pay attention to class origins and other indicia of political reliability. Certainly Party activists believed that this constituted "doing justice," but the effect was to undermine the legitimacy of law as it was bent beyond recognition in order to serve the needs of the Party (or its members). The idea of justice as a steady beacon guiding judges was lost as principle routinely gave way to politics and a particular kind of defensive, partisan politics, designed to maintain the Party's power.

By the 1920s, much of the statutory law had been reformulated to the satisfaction of the Party, which allowed judges to rely increasingly on statutes in their decision making. But the Party never allowed the law to operate in a truly autonomous fashion. Instead, it continued to use the courts as a wholly manipulable instrument of policy implementation, both on an institutional and individual level.[110]

A number of Western commentators have argued that the principal function of Soviet courts was educational and that judges took on a quasi-parental role within the system. It was not just that their decisions were intended to serve as lessons to the surrounding community, for that is a fairly universal feature of courts. More telling was the behavior of Soviet judges within the courtroom. According to Feifer, "a family council atmosphere prevail[ed]," with the judge as patriarch.[111] Judges did not resolve disputes in an arms-length fashion according to the laissez-faire model of judicial behavior. Nor were they "managerial judges," as described by Resnik, balancing the procedural demands of complex litigation. Instead, they put themselves right in the middle of the dispute and did not hesitate to castigate the parties (or even witnesses) for what they perceived as anti-social or anti-Soviet behavior, regardless of whether such behavior was at issue in the case. Feifer praises the informality of the proceedings and implies that the lack of attention to procedural details allowed judges to focus on the more important question of doing justice.[112] Markovits agrees, noting that, "[s]ocialist law has never been very finicky about procedural precision; what counted was substantive justice."[113]

But this argument loses sight of the instrumental function of law during the Soviet period. Law was not seen as the glue holding society together. Law held no awe; the Party viewed it as one of many means by which policy goals could be forced onto society. Judges were a cog in this policy-implementing machine. Their willingness to look beyond the written law does not necessarily mean that substantive justice was the end result. After all, the values espoused by these judges were those of the Party and were often not shared by the community.

On a more practical level, this Solomonic image of Soviet judges does not correspond to the reality I observed. The judges I spoke with were struggling to cope on a day-to-day basis with their heavy caseloads. Feeling powerless to challenge the status quo, they concerned themselves with avoiding reversal on appeal and retaining their jobs rather than with substantive justice. This gave rise to a conservatism and legalism in their decision making that is common to civil service style judiciaries but was exacerbated in the Soviet case by the long shadow of the Party. After all, for Soviet judges to survive and prosper, it was not sufficient merely to avoid legal controversies and otherwise to satisfy their superiors in the Ministry of Justice. They also had to be concerned with political correctness and so had to avoid antagonizing Party officials.

The impressions gleaned from interviews and observations of courtroom proceedings were supported by the case files I reviewed in which judicial behavior was notable for its passivity and attention to the letter of the law. Rare indeed was the labor-related case in which a judge looked beyond the prima facie case submitted by management to the underlying equities. Getting by, rather than doing justice, seemed to be the motivating force.

Explaining the Lack of Individual Impartiality. The "leading role" of the Party in Soviet society was the most obvious reason for the relative lack of individual impartiality of Soviet judges. Certainly it goes a long way toward explaining their behavior under Stalinism. The ability of Party apparatchiks to use strong-arm tactics to enforce their orders made efforts at resistance futile. Furthermore, the massive turnover of judicial personnel following the October Revolution and the introduction of litmus tests for political reliability in the recruitment process meant that judges generally supported the goals of the Party and believed in the need for unity within the Party ranks.

With the dismantling of the state terror machine following the death of Stalin (1953), judges no longer had to fear for their own personal safety (or that of their family) if they refused to go along with Party recommendations in particular cases. As previously noted, however, the Party continued to control a number of quality-of-life issues—job security, housing, salaries—which gave its officials considerable leverage over judges.

But the source of the problem went far deeper than what Ginsburgs has described as the "bear-hug of systematic Party supervision of the judicial record."[114] Over time, Soviet judges became accustomed to this relationship of dependency, as did society at large. Judges were viewed not as sages but as political hacks on sale to the highest bidder, which was usually but not always the Party.[115] A significant percentage of Soviet judges were women, indicating the low prestige of the profession.[116] There was an absence of cohesion within the ranks—an esprit de corps—that might have allowed them to stand up to outside interference. As a result, the best and the brightest did not seek judicial careers. Most judges in Moscow were graduates of night law school rather than the prestigious law faculty of Moscow State University. Legal education, like much of the Soviet educational system, was geared more to rote memorization than to stimulating independent thinking.

Thus, merely eliminating the Party is unlikely to lead to energetic impartial judges. In contrast to their Western counterparts, Soviet judges have been socialized to be dependent. Neither their self-image nor their low standing in society is likely to improve quickly. Indeed, the fact that in the early 1990s legislators felt free to interfere in pending cases, thereby taking up where Party officials left off, serves as a strong indication that the cultural pattern of judicial dependency is deeply rooted and that changing it is destined to be a slow and gradual process.

Securing Individual Impartiality. This dependency also infected the appellate process. In theory, the ability to appeal trial court decisions serves as a powerful incentive for impartial decision making. In the Soviet case, it served only as an incentive for conservatism insofar as avoiding reversals was the key to advancement. When reviewing cases, appellate courts took a highly legalistic approach, focusing primarily on the written record. Furthermore, the time pressure, combined with the lack of sufficient resources to prepare a comprehensive file (including a transcription of courtroom proceedings) for the appellate court, causes appeals to act as less of a check on trial court practice than is ideally desirable.[117] This mechanical approach to judging (both on the trial and appellate levels) is common to continental judicial systems, but the pluralism that characterizes most West European democracies tends to compensate by encouraging public discussion and criticism (if warranted) of judicial decisions.

The closed nature of Soviet society meant that such potential watchdogs were muzzled. Alternate political parties or social groups not authorized by the state were forbidden. The press remained under tight state controls until the late 1980s. What criticism that did emerge through samizdat reports of judicial improprieties in the Brezhnev-era dissident trials had extremely limited circulation within the Soviet Union.[118] The authors were subject to public villification by the regime and ran the risk of criminal prosecution for anti-Soviet activities.

As elected officials, Soviet trial court judges were ostensibly accountable to the voters and could be recalled. In practice, however, the elections were charades in which the single Party-endorsed candidate received the rubber-stamp approval of the electorate. The Party controlled the nomination process and, consequently, judges answered to the Party. On occasion, the "grass-roots unpopularity" of a judge affected renomination,[119] but typically the Party's stamp of approval was a function of political loyalty, not competency.

The law did not allow Soviet judges to be held liable for mistakes (whether inadvertent or intentional) made in the course of deciding a case. Formally, judicial immunity was absolute. But the malleability of the system allowed judges to be persecuted if they contravened Party policy. Indeed, judges could be made the object of vendettas if they offended Party officials.[120] The law lacked the power to rein in this sort of vigilante behavior, and other potentially forestalling mechanisms had been outlawed.

In the West, the presence of an independent bar works to enhance the impartiality of judges on a day-to-day basis. Although the Soviet bar *(advokatura)* enjoyed de facto independence, Soviet commentators agree that "self-governance [was] a fiction with no practical meaning."[121] The Ministry of Justice controlled salaries and membership and dictated the structure of the units *(kollegia)* into which lawyers *(advokaty)* were organized. The *kollegia* were inadequately funded, and their offices *(iuridicheskie konsul'tantsii)* lacked modern legal support services.[122] They were threadbare in the extreme—lawyers met with clients in small cubicles furnished with only chairs and a table—and bore little resemblance to plush Western law firms (or even storefront community law offices).[123]

Advokaty were not generally highly respected. When questioning average citizens about the societal value of lawyers, an American scholar was told that they were "useless, unimportant players in stage-managed performances."[124] Soviet judges seemed to share this view. *Advokaty* complained that judges paid no attention to their points of law and claimed that judges frequently wrote their opinions before hearing final arguments. They described themselves as "an unwanted stepchild"[125] "play[ing] second-fiddle in the courtroom."[126] Their belief that they were more legally literate than judges only increased their frustration over their impotence. The indifferent and often scornful attitude of judges vis-à-vis *advokaty,* combined with their lack of respect in society more generally, meant that Soviet lawyers' ability to affect judicial behavior was limited.

With Gorbachev's rise to power came an increased recognition of the importance of law that impacted favorably on the *advokatura.*[127] Lawyers began to demand and receive greater independence from the state and, in doing so, began to coalesce as a group and thereby elevate the influence and prestige of the bar. The Ministry of Justice relinquished its control over admissions to the bar and introduced a more flexible fee structure.[128] It created a new bar association, the Union of Advocates, untainted by prior collaboration with the Party.[129] Furthermore, the relaxation of press censorship gave disgruntled lawyers an outlet to voice their criticisms of the bench.

The legislative and constitutional changes to the structure of the judiciary made in 1988 and 1989 also increased the accountability of individual judges. As previously noted, the Party was taken out of the selection process, and the legislature was given the power to elect and recall judges. The drafters feared that legislators might abuse their power by threatening judges with removal if they did not go along with the legislators' wishes in particular cases. The danger of legislative imperialism was, to some extent, ameliorated by having judges elected by legislative bodies on a higher level and by providing that the qualifications panel had to be consulted prior to initiating any effort to recall a judge.[130]

Perhaps most importantly, the 1988 amendments to the Constitution (article 155) declared impermissible any outside interference in the work of the courts. The 1989 Law on the Status of Judges concretized this provision by stipulating that those who attempted to influence judges improperly would be subject to criminal liability.[131] While these changes are important and necessary if the former Soviet Union is to become a law-based state, it remains to be seen whether they will be vigorously enforced and thereby effect a fundamental change in behavior.

Accessibility

In contrast to the record on impartiality, Soviet courts can be compared favorably to Western courts in terms of accessibility. Initiating a claim in a Soviet civil court was a simple matter, requiring only a brief statement of the facts. Indeed, many of the reinstatement petitions I reviewed were one-sentence documents stating simply that the petitioner had been fired and believed his or her dismissal was unfair. Sixty percent were handwritten and, while one third of the petitions did make a specific statutory reference, it was usually to the article of the labor code that served as the basis for the dismissal. It was required that this information be noted in the worker's permanent work record and made available to the worker and prospective employers. Thus, its inclusion in complaints indicated neither broad knowledge of the law on the part of the petitioner nor participation by a lawyer. In no case did I find the sort of elaborate legal and factual argumentation typical of American pleadings.

Once in court, the absence of legal counsel—in the cases I reviewed less than 20 percent of workers had lawyers—was more problematic. Enterprise management appeared in court regularly. It had the benefit of in-house counsel and, consequently, presented its position more adeptly.

For most workers, however, the reinstatement petition represented their first brush with the legal system and, as the preceding chapter demonstrated, they consistently missed or bungled opportunities to undermine management's case. Feifer's observations on a broader spectrum of civil cases in the early 1960s suggest that this is nothing new. He concludes that "[e]ven to the untrained ear many facts go undisclosed, and seemingly essential questions go unasked."[132] While the seeming lack of complexity of the Soviet legal system makes legal counsel appear superfluous, lawyers may be necessary in order to prevail over more experienced opponents.

Accessibility is a more expansive concept, requiring not merely the ability to file a claim with the court but, more importantly, to pursue it in a meaningful fashion. This distinction is critical in the Soviet case. While petitioners had few barriers to initiating claims in Soviet courts, a lack of knowledge and experience (assuming they had no lawyer) frequently rendered their prosecution efforts futile. Among other things, they were ill equipped to gather and effectively marshal the relevant evidence, to make persuasive legal arguments, and to call and question witnesses. Upon closer examination, the apparent accessibility of Soviet courts fell short of constituting an ability to participate fully in legal proceedings.

Workers often complained about the delays attendent to court proceedings. In fact, seeking postponements was a common stalling technique of management, and there was no legal limit on the number of delays that could be granted. But even at their worst, the delays experienced in the Soviet context were minimal compared to those that are commonplace in the United States.[133] Most of the labor-related cases I reviewed were heard within ten days of filing. There was no elaborate pretrial discovery by the parties. Instead, the judge would issue subpoenas for materials deemed relevant to the resolution of the dispute. In labor cases, a standard list of documents to be reviewed existed, but the parties could request that additional materials be produced or that particular individuals be compelled to testify in court.[134] Ideally, the case was resolved at the first hearing, assuming the presence of the parties and necessary witnesses. Delays to accommodate missing parties were not uncommon but usually amounted to no more than a week or two. Cases were typically resolved within a month of filing.

Furthermore, pursuing one's rights through the legal system was not terribly expensive. Filing fees were nominal. Lawyer's fees, while substantial, did not constitute a barrier to entry because cases could be filed without outside assistance. The fee schedule, established by the Ministry of Justice and in effect until 1988, stipulated that labor-related cases were to be handled free of charge and set strict limits on the fees that could be charged in other areas. In practice, this fee schedule was a formality. Litigants routinely made supplemental payments to lawyers privately in order to guarantee satisfactory representation.[135] The amounts demanded could be quite large and may well explain the reluctance of workers to engage legal counsel in their reinstatement petitions.

Notwithstanding the ease of access into the Soviet legal system, the fact remains that average citizens tended not to pursue legal remedies when their rights (whether labor-related or other) had been violated.[136] The cost of obtaining legal counsel seems appealing at least as a partial explanation until we recall that lawyers were generally viewed as unnecessary to the process of dispute resolution. This suggests that difficulties in obtaining legal representation (or even a lack thereof) did not undermine the accessibility of the Soviet legal system.

Accessibility, while necessary, is not sufficient to ensure regular use of the courts by average citizens. Markovits argues that the failure to use law to resolve disputes under state socialism was instrumental and stemmed from the inadequacy of the remedies provided by law.[137] While this is a compelling argument in the East German context, my research, which centers on the implementation of certain Soviet labor laws for which the remedies were quite appealing, indicates that it is less persuasive in the Soviet case.[138] In the Soviet Union, the problems went deeper; there was a general distrust of the courts that, in turn, found its source in the relative absence of institutional and individual impartiality within the judiciary.

Governmental and Societal Context

Impartial courts flourish in an atmosphere of political pluralism in which judges are publicly held to account by citizens, members of the press, and legal scholars. Within society, a basic respect for, and appreciation of, the critical importance of an impartial judiciary is also a necessary foundation. The rulers and the ruled alike must have a sufficiently strong desire for predictability and stability such that they are willing to agree not to intervene in particular cases. While these societal preconditions can be isolated from one another for purposes of discussion, they tend to be mutually reinforcing and so to develop in tandem.

Soviet courts were embedded in a governmental and societal context that did little to encourage impartiality and, on the contrary, encouraged dependency. The ideals of "legality" and the "rule of law" were not highly valued.[139] As we have seen, law was not viewed as an interactive process involving state and society but as a one-way projection of state authority that reflected the interests of those in power.[140] Similarly, the courts were expected to toe the line. Indeed, the courts' consistent failure to stand up to the Party when its policies contradicted the basic ideals of legality undoubtedly contributed to undermining the courts' legitimacy in the eyes of the citizenry.[141]

The political pluralism that characterizes the Western liberal democracies and buttresses judicial independence was neither present nor contemplated within the Soviet Union until the late 1980s. The Party declared itself to be ruling in the name of society and allowed no challenges to its authority. Public debate was stage-managed, and participation in the political process was strictly circumscribed. Any criticism of official policy was discouraged and, at times, was punished quite severely. In essence, the Party coopted the state and effectively silenced dissenting voices in society through fear.

Comparative experience tells us that courts do not long retain their impartiality within repressive regimes. Efforts to assert their independence typically result in the removal of offending judges or the closing down of the courts. The Soviet courts were not an exception to this general rule. Recognizing the potential power of independent courts, the Bolsheviks quickly remade the judicial system in their image. As I have noted, they instituted a structure that was permeable to outside influence and recruited judges on the basis of political loyalty, not intellectual acumen.

Under such conditions, it is not surprising that the courts developed into a static and conservative institution. Soviet courts did not have the policy role that their Western counterparts have increasingly assumed. Soviet judges took on the role of the stereotypical nineteenth-century laissez-faire judge by limiting themselves to resolving the dispute at hand on the basis of the evidence presented. To assert themselves further into the dispute—to attempt to look beyond the superficial facts to basic questions of fairness—was too risky politically. The judges that survived and thrived in the Soviet context simply went along; they did not rock the boat.

Conclusion

Much of my discussion thus far has focused on the past, but the legacy of the past weighs heavily on the present and future of the former Soviet Union. The dependence of the judiciary on the Party was initially created and reinforced through structural means, that is, the Party's control over the selection, retention, and promotion of judges. Over time, however, the behavioral patterns became ingrained as judges grew accustomed to looking over their shoulders and thinking about the political fallout of decisions rather than concerning themselves solely with their justness. Under such circumstances, merely eliminating the Party is not sufficient. Yet the analysis of the Soviet judicial system in terms of my ideal type suggests that the problems go deeper, that even when the strings are cut, the old pathologies persist. The evidence indicates that the new political elite—the legislators—are stepping into the shoes of the Party, thus inaugurating a new variety of the old "telephone law."

Thus far, the reforms instituted focus on structure. Under Gorbachev, efforts were made to enhance the power and prestige of courts in Soviet society. The goal was to insulate judges from outside interference.[142] To that end, structural barriers were erected, beginning with the process of choosing judges and continuing right through to the disposition of individual cases. Changing structure is much easier than changing behavioral patterns. On the positive side, Russian policymakers recognize the need to change the way judges think about themselves and are perceived in society. Steps are being taken in this direction, such as increasing judicial salaries, introducing objective criteria into the selection process, and criminalizing efforts to interfere in judicial proceedings. But reinvigorating the courts has been given relatively low priority in post-Soviet Russia, which is struggling to transform its entire economic and political structure.

CHAPTER 6

Economic Incentives, Labor Unions, and Legal Culture

Introduction

In the preceding chapter, I argued that law never came to matter in the reciprocal sense during the Soviet period because the state failed to supply an energetic, independent judiciary that endeavored to do justice in specific cases. But that is not the whole explanation. Failure on the institutional supply side was complemented by a failure of social demand for law that mattered. Law failed to matter because enterprise management did not take its legal obligations seriously and because workers did not demand their rights. The Soviet Union had no civil "legal culture" that valued and demanded legal integrity.

What explains enterprise management's attitude toward law? Soviet law imposed certain obligations on management as it sought to rationalize its workforce.[1] In cases of layoffs, management was required to offer the redundant worker comparable positions within the enterprise, if such positions were available. More importantly, management had to request and obtain the consent of the enterprise trade union committee *(profkom)* before issuing a dismissal order. The law placed similar restraints on management discretion when transferring workers within the enterprise. In theory, the law acted as a constraint on management discretion by requiring that its personnel decisions be legally justified and confirmed by the *profkom.*

In practice, however, the legal prerequisites to layoffs or internal transfers were not meaningful hurdles for management. They were mere inconveniences. By the 1980s, Soviet managers had become adept at building a record—even when their actions blatantly contradicted the law—that would win both *profkom* consent and, if necessary, judicial approval.

This raises deeper questions: Why did law become so marginalized within the Soviet enterprise? Why was management so willing to skirt the law? In other words, why did the law fail to restrain management behavior vis-à-vis workers?

There is, of course, no single answer to these questions. But several important contributory factors come into focus when the question is restated in comparative terms, that is, why do Western managers tend to pay more attention to the law than did their Soviet counterparts?

First, Western managers operate in the context of the market. At the very least, this suggests the presence of a reasonably fluid labor market. Aggrieved workers generally enjoy the option of exit.[2] To compete effectively, employers must recruit and retain competent employees. Information regarding enterprise management's attitude toward organized labor and its compliance record in terms of legal regulations governing equal opportunity, worker safety, and environmental issues is available to workers and can be an important factor in employment decisions. Also, enterprises run the risk that systematic violations of the law will be publicized and will trigger negative reactions by customers, sources of capital, and stock traders. In a highly competitive market, this can be important.

Second, Western trade unions tend to curb the excesses of management by acting as vigorous advocates of workers' rights. The unions' clout stems from their legislatively granted power at the bargaining table and their power to halt production by striking when management fails to live up to its obligations.[3]

Third, workers in the West are often willing to mobilize the law, when necessary, to keep management in check.[4] This activism once again raises the basic issue of the role of law in society. After all, if citizens generally respect the law, their attitude is likely to be reflected in the workplace.

Examining the question comparatively highlights the importance of the underlying institutional framework. The three factors identified above tend to complement one another in the Western context, working to even the balance of power between labor and capital. That is, while market pressure, independent labor unions, or legal culture *alone* may not be sufficient to guarantee management compliance with labor law, acting together they achieve a certain synergy. The operation of these factors was deeply intertwined in the Soviet context. But because of the differences in the underlying institutional framework, they tended not to level the playing field and only further strengthened the position of enterprise management.

The sort of differentiation of power generally found in Western enterprises was lacking in Soviet firms. The main organ of power within Soviet society was, of course, the Communist Party. Within the enterprise, both management and trade unions served at the pleasure of the Party.[5] Although workers unquestionably had certain latent power,[6] the trade unions suppressed (rather than facilitated) its expression. As a general matter, workers failed to mobilize the law, even when they believed their legal rights were clearly violated. In part, their behavior stemmed from a lack of knowledge. But a more powerful causal factor was their lack of trust in law as a means of achieving justice.

The Role of the Economic Incentive System

The nature of the economic incentive system that prevails within a society has a significant impact on enterprise behavior, particularly the extent to which management complies with the law. Paradoxically, critics of capitalism in the West have often seen the market-induced profit motive primarily as creating incentives for corporate lawlessness. It cannot be denied that sometimes management's interest in the bottom line causes it to skirt or even disobey the law. But the Soviet experience suggests that markets invite lawlessness far less than does state socialism and provide as well stronger incentives for compliance.

Market Capitalism: Profit, Competition and the Labor Market

Market economies are generally characterized by sustained patterns of private trading with the goal of maximizing profit. Most resources are allocated not by governmental fiat but through private agreements in which all parties seek to maximize profits. Similarly, most prices are not determined administratively but are negotiated based on supply and demand in the market as a whole.

In the contemporary market capitalism of Western Europe and North America, the "invisible hand" championed by Adam Smith[7] has given way to overt government intervention on many fronts.[8] Moreover, as Hurst cautions, "though law does not create the market, law may be needed to keep the market itself in being."[9] Thus, in most nations, laws now exist that endeavor to bring some degree of predictability to economic transactions and to discourage the development of monopolies in some (but not all) market segments. Moreover, large corporate conglomerates shift many markets away from the Smithian model of atomistic small firms in most (if not all) market segments. But the essence and the individualistic ethic of the market remain unchallenged.

For the most part, profitability determines the success of an enterprise and the fate of its management team operating within the market context. Managers seek to keep the cost of labor low while simultaneously maintaining high levels of productivity (both quantitative and qualitative). Thus, in order to succeed, enterprise management has to attract and maintain a highly qualified and motivated workforce, particularly in the increasingly technologically sophisticated industrial world. Furthermore, it must do so in the context of a highly competitive labor market in which workers are generally free to move from one job to another.

At the same time, workers—especially the most skilled and most productive workers—are also seeking to maximize their interests. At the most elemental level, they look for jobs with high wages, attractive benefit packages, and promising career opportunities at companies with solid financial bases. (In the market context, collateral benefits tend to be confined to work-related matters such as health insurance and pensions.) Because competitors face similar constraints in the market, the financial packages offered by different companies often turn out to be remarkably similar, and so the most desirable workers turn to less tangible factors when making their decision. In such cases, the reputation of enterprise management within the marketplace for fair dealing in labor relations and for maintaining a clean and safe work environment may become a significant factor in the job search process (and in deciding whether to exit). One of the key indicators of a desirable workplace is a relatively unsullied record of compliance with labor laws and regulations on occupational safety, equal opportunity, and related matters.

Management and labor are locked into a relationship of mutual dependence.[10] While management creates job opportunities, workers are free to leave if better opportunities present themselves. The presence of a highly competitive labor market means that management has to offer more than high wages to the most mobile and attractive prospective workers. Corporate reputation matters.[11] The expense of recruiting and training new workers only strengthens management's interest in not losing skilled and conscientious workers. Thus, obeying the law—at least insofar as it affects labor relations—generally serves management's interests.

This is not meant to imply that capitalism gives rise to some sort of legal utopia where managers never run afoul of the law. To the contrary, management violations of legal norms—whether due to rational calculations based on the likelihood of escaping detection or due to incompetence or shortcomings in internal corporate monitoring schemes—are not uncommon in capitalist systems.[12] In particular, the large wage and flexibility disparity between union and nonunion firms in the United States creates an incentive to violate regulations concerning union organizing.[13] But violations tend to be the exception rather than the rule for most well-established enterprises.

State Socialism: The Plan

The dynamics were completely different under Soviet-style state socialism. The "invisible hand" of the market was replaced by the many hands of the state. The institutionalization of a comprehensive national economic plan represented an effort to eliminate the chaos and inequality inherent in the market, while maximizing efficiency. Although pronounced gaps in wealth and status persisted during the Soviet period, the experiment nonetheless had more success in achieving relative equality within society than in encouraging efficiency.[14]

Plan fulfillment took the place of profitability and competitiveness as the basic motivating force within the Soviet economy. Not surprisingly, economic actors accommodated their behavior to the realities of the administrative-command system that grew up during the Soviet period. In this section, I outline the incentives underlying this system and explore how they operated to undercut the authority of law. Guided by the preceding discussion of Western practices, the focus is narrowed to two specific questions. First, why were Soviet managers less concerned than their Western counterparts with retaining a skilled workforce? Second, what motivated Soviet workers to stay or to leave a given enterprise?

Management Incentives. Making sense of management behavior under state socialism requires a basic understanding of how the underlying economic system actually worked. The starting point for this inquiry is the role of the plan. Dissatisfied with the chaos and inequality that is an inevitable aspect of market transactions, a decision was made in the late 1920s to rein in market forces and to direct the economy affirmatively through a national economic plan.[15] By the 1930s, the plan had come to encompass virtually all aspects of the economy, including the balancing of inputs and outputs and the determination of prices and wages. A huge bureaucratic structure, headed by the state planning agency *(Gosplan)* and including the industrial ministries, sprang up in order to generate and administer the plan.

At the level of the firm, the plan dictated the production profile and set targets for output. The plan also specified the sort of workforce necessary to meet these goals[16] and set upper limits on the total amount that could be paid out in wages. Although the plan was imposed from above, enterprise managers—both directly and through the industrial ministries—played an important role in setting the general parameters. As part of the planning process, managers would estimate their production capacity and would detail the inputs (both raw materials and labor) required in order to meet these targets. Negotiations ensued under which *Gosplan* tried to maximize planned output and minimize input levels, while managers tried to maximize inputs and to resist unrealistically high production targets. Managers were left in a catch-up position—always struggling to increase their guaranteed allocation of supplies. Indeed, the process often left managers in a no-win situation. If they failed to meet the annual plan targets, they faced almost certain dismissal and disgrace. On the other hand, if they fulfilled the plan, the targets would inevitably be increased in the next year, and the cycle would begin anew.

The absence of the market meant that Soviet managers could not simply purchase deficit items. Indeed, enterprises had only limited authority to enter into contracts on their own authority without prior ministerial approval. Yet, as the pioneering work of Berliner and Granick so graphically demonstrates, these managers were far from passive.[17] They understood that their job security and the priority of the enterprise in subsequent planning cycles depended on meeting the current plan targets.

As a result, managers devised a series of coping strategies that aimed at ensuring plan fulfillment. Enhancing efficiency and competitiveness was an occasional consequence but was rarely the stated goal. Supplies (including labor) were hoarded, and production was integrated vertically so as to avoid reliance on outsiders.[18] On the labor front, management endeavored to pad the personnel schedule. The goal was to push the wage fund as high as possible in order to afford managers maximum flexibility. It became commonplace to have a cohort of workers literally standing around until the days immediately preceding the end of the plan period. At that time, in a desperate effort to fulfill the plan, all available resources—including labor—would be thrown into the mix. Thanks to the high incidence of unskilled, manual labor within Soviet industry, production could be increased by simply adding more workers.[19] Clearly, such "storming" tactics had a deleterious effect on the quality of the output.[20] But quality was largely irrelevant—only quantity counted when it came to measuring plan fulfillment. As Berliner notes, "Soviet management thinks and works, as it were, on a piece-rate basis."[21]

Why was plan fulfillment so critical? During the 1930s, when the push for rapid industrialization was in full swing, enterprises strove to meet plan targets as a reflection of their patriotism. Managers were also motivated by fear because those who failed to meet the often unrealistic goals of the First Five-Year Plan (1928–32) could easily find themselves on trial on charges of "wrecking" production, a process from which few escaped unscathed.[22]

As economic relations settled into predictability, certain patterns emerged. Meeting plan targets brought the promise of bonuses *(premiia)* for workers and management alike. These *premiia* were not inconsequential: the difference between 99 and 100 percent plan fulfillment could mean a difference of up to 30 percent in annual income.[23] Performance in preceding years was an important factor in subsequent negotiations with *Gosplan,* particularly when pressing for enhanced state support.

Failure to fulfill the plan brought personal disgrace and often dismissal for top managers. For the enterprise as an institution, it meant decreased prestige, which translated into greater difficulty when bargaining with ministerial and planning officials for supplies as well as a lower level of priority vis-à-vis investment. Moreover, the failure of the state system to provide essential inputs, whether as a result of miscalculations in the plan itself or nonperformance of contractual obligations by another enterprise, did not constitute an acceptable excuse for not fulfilling the plan. Under such circumstances, hoarding was a completely rational response. At the same time, it is important to recognize that the ultimate sanction of the market for an unsuccessful firm, namely, bankruptcy, was rejected on ideological grounds in the context of state socialism. Regardless of how poorly an enterprise performed, it continued to limp along thanks to state subsidies—the so-called soft budget constraint implicit in state socialism.[24]

Having outlined the planning system, I can now step back and assess how it shaped management's attitude toward workers and affected its attitude toward law. While retaining a workforce sufficient to meet the production goals established by the plan was essential, Soviet managers tended to pay less attention to the specific attributes of individual workers than did their Western counterparts. Put bluntly, workers were regarded as a fungible commodity. I have already alluded to the two main reasons for this nonchalance. Perhaps most important was the high concentration of manual labor within Soviet industry. Buttressing this, however, was the demographic profile of the Soviet workforce. Until the 1980s, the work-age population consistently exceeded the available jobs. As a result, management had the luxury of answering demands for higher levels of output through extensive methods (increasing the number of workers) rather than intensive ones (increasing the productivity of individual workers). Labor turnover was a matter of indifference: training costs for manual laborers were minimal, and replacement workers could easily be found. Thus, management's view of workers as plentiful and easily interchangeable was not far off the mark.

By the 1980s, the demographic data indicated that the work-age population was actually decreasing in major urban centers in the Soviet Union.[25] These data, combined with the stagnant performance of the Soviet economy in the late Brezhnev period, caused Moscow's economic policymakers to recognize the importance of stimulating labor productivity through intensive means. Reform programs designed to spur on workers were introduced periodically with great fanfare only to fizzle out in short order due to lack of interest on the local level. These programs, which were often targeted at on-the-job discipline, attempted quick fixes for deeply rooted problems.[26] They failed to address the chronic inefficiency of the Soviet economy.

Because the underlying incentive system remained the same, enterprise management's behavior actually changed very little in response to these new economic realities. Logic dictates that, in a tightening labor market, manual labor should be phased out in favor of higher-yielding mechanized forms of labor. But enterprise management lacked the authority to initiate capital investment projects, and the state policy on investment continued to favor new construction projects over renovation of existing capital stock. No hue and cry went up among enterprise managers about the shortage of workers. They were, after all, accustomed to muddling along with fewer resources than they would like.

The difficulty of changing ingrained behavior patterns was demonstrated in the late 1980s, when Gorbachev initiated the policy of "freeing up labor resources" *(vysvobozhdenie trudovykh resursov),* under which enterprise managers were tasked with boosting productivity through more rational deployment of their workers.[27] In late 1990, the central government decreed that increases in the wage funds of state enterprises were permitted only when productivity increased.[28] No longer was the wage fund to be bumped up automatically upon the hiring of additional workers. Although the policy contemplated layoffs, the goal was to increase efficiency primarily by transferring workers within the enterprise. In chapters 3 and 4, I explained how the labor code was amended to facilitate such transfers. But managers uniformly failed to take advantage of this newly granted right. Had they done so, they would have been able to shape their workforce to better meet production needs and perhaps even improve the working conditions. A full discussion of the reasons for this missed opportunity falls outside the scope of this chapter, but the absence of a competitive spirit—a drive to excel—no doubt played a critical role.[29]

Furthermore, management's paramount concern was fulfilling the plan. The state concurred. Neither the planning officials nor their colleagues at the industrial ministries cared much about how the desired production levels were maintained. These authorities conveniently looked the other way as enterprise managers cut legal corners (and did far worse) in order to assure themselves of a sufficient supply of labor and raw materials. They cared even less about the extent to which enterprise management complied with legal norms regarding the work environment. As I documented in chapter 4, enterprise managers routinely took a pro forma attitude toward the statutorily guaranteed right of workers not to be fired arbitrarily. Reprisals from above were rarely forthcoming. Similarly, safety regulations, both environmental and occupational, were enforced haphazardly at best. Enterprise-level management shared with its superiors a bottom-line mentality that failed to see beyond the immediate goal of fulfilling the plan.

Under such circumstances, enterprise management was not terribly concerned with its reputation in the community. Its primary interest was in pleasing its superiors in the hierarchical chain. Placating workers came in a distant second.

Management attitudes toward law might have been different if the balance of economic power had been skewed more in its direction,[30] and if the incentive system had been geared toward efficiency and other qualitative indicators of success rather than being limited to gross output.

As to the former, periodic efforts were made to curb the control of industrial ministries over the day-to-day affairs of enterprises. Perhaps the most serious of these efforts in the pre-perestroika era was launched in 1965 as part of a far-reaching reform package spearheaded by then Premier Kosygin.[31] A new law on state enterprises was enacted that placed certain limits on the right of the ministries to countermand the plan for an enterprise and allowed enterprise management to demand reimbursement for out-of-pocket expenses that resulted from fulfilling "illegal" *(nepravil'nyi)* ministerial orders.[32] This new law was, however, doomed from the start.[33] It lacked meaningful enforcement mechanisms and was unrealistic in its assumption that enterprise managers would sue the very ministerial officials on whom they relied for help in obtaining raw materials.[34] Notwithstanding the law, the ministries' "petty tutelage" quickly reasserted itself.[35] Enterprise management remained firmly under the thumb of the industrial ministries.

The next serious effort to reconfigure the balance of power within the economy came in the late 1980s.[36] Devolving power to the enterprise level emerged as one of the principal goals of perestroika. State planners were instructed to scale down the number of mandatory production targets to those absolutely essential for continuation of basic state functions. These targets, known as "state orders" *(gosudarstvennye zakazy* or *goszakazy),* still had to be met. But enterprise management was given complete authority over the disposition of all production in excess of that required to fulfill these *goszakazy.* The goal was to loosen the administrative controls over the economy and to introduce, albeit tentatively, market forces into the Soviet economy. Not surprisingly, the representatives of the old guard—ministerial and planning officials—managed to thwart this goal by issuing state orders that took up almost 100 percent of available production capacity.[37] In principle, enterprise management had become more autonomous, but in reality very little had changed.

As this implies, the failure (at least in the short run) of Gorbachev's effort to increase enterprise autonomy was due largely to the raw political power of the ministries and the planning apparatus. Over the seven decades of Soviet power, the administrative-command system gave rise to a bureaucratic elite who stubbornly clung to power. The members of this "new class" refused to acknowledge that the system that had been so effective in rapid industrialization in the 1930s had long outlived its usefulness, as the stagnation *(zastoi)* of the Brezhnev years so clearly demonstrated.

The shortcomings of the law made it easy for the bureaucrats to trump enterprise management. The new state enterprise law, which became effective on January 1, 1988, set forth the rights of enterprise management in general terms but did not specify how these new rights could be enforced.[38] More importantly, the law lacked a clear definition of what constituted a "state order." The ministries took advantage of this loophole. By categorizing most orders as *goszakazy,* they stopped the effort to introduce market forces dead in its tracks.

The triumph of the bureaucrats was, however, short lived. By the time of the August 1991 putsch, the administrative-command system lay in ruins. A full explanation of the reasons for its collapse is well beyond the scope of this chapter, but two factors stand out: the layoffs and other cost-cutting measures imposed on the ministries[39] and the rising tide of entrepreneurial activities that grew up in the wake of the legalization of new forms of economic activities. For my purposes, more important than the proximate causes of the collapse is that the managers of state enterprises stood on the sidelines as it happened. As always, their energies were devoted to meeting the plan targets or, in the perestroika lexicon, fulfilling state orders. Indeed, their lives became even more frantic as long-term suppliers deserted them for the quick money offered by the new entrepreneurs. Survival, not statutory compliance, was their top priority.

Workers' Incentives. Like their Western counterparts, Soviet workers strove to make a good life for themselves and their families. But they operated within a very different economic system, which shaped their interests and expectations of the workplace. Finding a job was typically not a problem; unemployment had been largely eliminated thanks to the rapid industrialization drive of the 1930s.[40] Moreover, since the end of World War II, each successive generation of Soviet workers enjoyed improved standards of living.[41] No one got rich from his or her take-home pay, and many yearned to live better, but basic needs were satisfied.[42] On the surface, economic equality among ordinary workers appeared to have been largely achieved within Soviet society.

But workers expected more than just a pay envelope from their place of employment. Many social welfare burdens that in the market context are shouldered by the individual were routinely assumed by the enterprise under state socialism. In particular, enterprise management found itself responsible for housing its workers, providing day care and kindergartens for workers' children, procuring big ticket consumer goods for distribution among workers (e.g., cars, refrigerators, televisions, video recorders) and even providing staples such as food and clothing.[43] Typically, these perquisites were doled out on the basis of seniority. A worker might wait years, even decades, to receive suitable housing.[44] This system provided a powerful incentive for workers to remain at the same job, since they would automatically be sent to the back of the line if they went elsewhere. The reputation of an enterprise for respecting (or not respecting) workers' rights and compliance (or noncompliance) with environmental and occupational safety regulations receded into the background when compared with these more pressing needs of everyday life.

The internal passport system also limited workers' mobility.[45] All Soviet citizens had these identification documents specifying their legal residence. Permanent residence permits *(propiski)* were particularly important in the large industrial cities. Obtaining permission to move to one of these cities could be difficult—the quickest route was to marry[46] a resident of the desired city or to be offered a job there.[47] Enterprises were reluctant to hire nonresidents because doing so imposed an immediate obligation to provide housing for them. (Local residents, in contrast, could be expected to live with their parents indefinitely.) Taking such jobs was risky for nonresidents. During the five years it took to receive a *propiska,* these workers, known as "*limitchiki,*" had none of the legal protections afforded to long-term residents.[48] *Limitchiki* could be fired and sent back to the provinces at a moment's notice.

A labor market of sorts existed in the Soviet Union. Enterprise management made hiring decisions, and most workers had the right to quit on two-weeks' notice.[49] At the same time, the peculiar features of the administrative-command system made the Soviet labor market unusual. Wage fund restrictions, established by the ministries in collaboration with planning officials, constrained management's discretion in making manpower decisions. The overpowering need to fulfill the plan caused management to hoard workers, which undercut the capacity of the labor market to stimulate efficient enterprise behavior. While Soviet workers were technically free to leave and seek employment elsewhere, practical concerns frequently dictated that they remain at the same job for sustained periods of time. The desire to prevail within the labor market did not motivate management to improve the overall work environment (including statutory compliance) in an effort to attract workers.

Indeed, the irrelevance of law emerges as one of the consistent themes of this review of management and workers' incentives in the Soviet context. Managers had to maintain a workforce sufficient to ensure plan fulfillment but, as in other aspects of production, were concerned more with quantity than quality. Thus, the sheer number of workers assumed more importance than did their technological sophistication. Workers were interested primarily in the enterprise record on security housing and other collateral benefits. The workers' lack of concern with whether management complied with the law contributed to the failure of the law to act as a constraint on enterprise management's behavior.[50]

The Role of Trade Unions

Given the inability of the Soviet economic incentive system to catalyze enterprise management to obey the law, it is appropriate to look elsewhere for sources of constraint. Trade unions were one potential institutional source. In theory, the function of trade unions is to represent and defend workers' interests. In theory, holding management to a rigorous standard in legal matters by monitoring its behavior and publicizing divergences fits within this rubric.

Trade Unions under Market Capitalism

The sorts of trade unions that exist in the Western industrialized democracies and the legal structures that underlie them vary widely. The role that unions play within a country depends on the history of industrial and class relations as well as on the contemporary institutional and cultural realities.[51] This makes detailed cross-national comparisons rather perilous and, in fact, that is not my purpose here.[52] Instead, my analysis is pitched at a high level of generality and seeks to identify the key unifying features of Western trade unions and to analyze why these features give rise to unions that are capable of constraining arbitrary and illegal behavior by management under certain circumstances.

Unions reflect the differentiated nature of Western society. At the most basic level, they express a recognition of the fundamental difference between the interests of workers and management. Similarly, the potential for conflicting interests among workers is acknowledged and reflected in the existence of a wide variety of skill- and industry-based unions.

In the United States, the divergence of interests between labor and capital is reflected in a highly antagonistic relationship on the enterprise level that expresses itself most clearly during campaigns for recognition[53] and negotiations over collective bargaining agreements.[54] Management, as the representative of capital, has the advantage. Nevertheless, unions, operating under the federal labor law regime, have some weapons that endeavor to even the playing field.[55] Labor unions' clout is derived in significant part from their legislatively granted right to strike. By halting production, either within a single enterprise or an entire industry, unions can force management to pay attention to the needs of workers.[56]

American unions have specific powers that act to force management to comply with the law. Under federal labor law, they can sue to force management to comply with the terms of the collective bargaining agreement, which are usually enforced through contractually established arbitration procedures. They also serve as a watchdog, monitoring and publicizing management's record on equal employment, workplace safety, the environment, and other related issues. They can complain about violations to governmental regulatory agencies. In addition to their obligations to the collective, unions represent individual workers in disputes with management (often in formal grievance procedures) and, if necessary and warranted, provide them with legal counsel. Furthermore, the system has certain built-in checks and balances. Workers have the right to sue their union when they believe it has behaved in an arbitrary, discriminatory, perfunctory, or bad faith manner in carrying out the duty of fair representation owed to the workers.[57] Perhaps more importantly, workers have the right to replace local and national union leaders through regularly scheduled elections and to vote to remove the union from the workplace.

But unions now represent only about 16 percent of American wage and salaried workers, down from about 26 percent in 1953.[58] What function do they serve in the nonunionized sector? Starting from the premise that American management is generally hostile to unions, largely because of the competitive advantages nonunionized firms have over unionized firms, it follows that the specter of unionization has an ameliorating influence on management behavior.[59] Unions, after all, build constituencies by documenting unfair or illegal management practices and by contending that they could remedy matters. If management minimizes such practices, unions may find it more difficult to gain a toehold among workers.

Antagonism is not the inevitable result of acknowledging the divergence of interests between labor and management. In many countries of Western Europe, where union power is less fragmented than in the United States and collective agreements tend to encompass all firms in an economic sector, unions often work collaboratively with management on the enterprise level in order to maximize, as far possible, both productivity and the protection of workers rights.[60] Union leaders frequently head national bureaucracies and are relatively independent from individual firms. Also, unions are financed by voluntary membership and must take actions that elicit rank-and-file support. Hence, they usually remain mindful of their role as advocates for workers and do not allow themselves to be completely coopted by management. Moreover, the structure of democratic corporatism that exists in much of Western Europe contemplates a formal role for labor in setting national policy and influencing the content of labor relations, income security, and workplace safety laws.[61] This is also true in noncorporatist countries such as Germany.[62] Having played a key role in creating and extending legal protection for workers, labor unions (and labor political parties) gain a stake in ensuring a reasonable degree of implementation.

Trade Unions under State Socialism

Both in form and substance, Soviet trade unions bore only a passing resemblance to their Western counterparts. One official trade union existed in the Soviet Union: the All-Union Central Council of Trade Unions *(Vsesoiuznyi Tsentral'nyi Sovet Profsoiuzov-Union* or *VTsSPS).* Formally, its principal functions on the enterprise level were twofold: to stimulate production and to protect workers' interests. The underlying assumption was that these two functions complemented one another, reflecting a deeper assumption that the interests of workers and management were one and the same under state socialism.

The *VTsSPS* purported to represent all strata of working people, from general directors of huge state enterprises to charwomen. Everyone belonged. Although it was theoretically possible to opt out, few did.[63] Two reasons were commonly cited. First, refusing to join or renouncing membership was a hassle. Paperwork had to be completed and filed with Moscow and that made staying in the union the path of least resistance. The membership dues, at 1 percent of wages, were nominal and painless because they were deducted automatically from employees' pay.[64] Second and perhaps more importantly, workers did not want to risk losing the social benefits controlled by the *profkom,*[65] such as housing and access to the vacation home(s), kindergartens, and youth camps owned by the enterprise.[66] Absent the danger of loss of support via exit, Soviet unions (unlike their Western counterparts) did not constantly have to prove themselves worthy of worker support. Worker support was assumed and, therefore, irrelevant.

The role of trade unions in the Soviet Union was established at the Tenth Party Congress in March 1921.[67] Faced with calls from competing factions within the Communist Party for strongly independent unions and, in the alternative, for their complete subjugation to the Party and the state, Lenin engineered a compromise that allowed for limited independence of unions within the context of a strong state. He envisioned trade unions as serving as a school of management for workers during the transition to communism.[68] As Ruble has argued, however, the dualistic vision that emerged embodied an "essential ambiguity. . . . Industrial unions generally cannot promote higher labor productivity and improve the lot of the laborer at the same time without compromising either or both of these goals."[69]

Typically, protecting workers' rights came in a distant second when resolving this ambiguity. Under Stalin, no other choice existed. But even after his death, the pattern persisted. In the *profkom* records for the 1980s that I reviewed, the agenda was dominated by organizing and reporting the results of quarterly "socialist competitions" *(sotsialisticheskoe sorevnovanie)* for achieving the highest productivity within the enterprise, not by efforts to improve working conditions. This remained true even after the *VTsSPS* officially renounced its production-related functions in 1989 and pledged to devote itself solely to protecting workers' interests.[70]

The trade union was also charged with monitoring management's compliance with workplace safety regulations. Indeed, within the *VTsSPS* was a "labor inspectorate," and the inspectors were supposed to visit enterprises periodically in order to verify compliance.[71] They were empowered to levy fines if management failed to live up to its obligations. In each of the eight enterprises I studied, I asked managers about their relationship with this agency. Although they all knew of its existence, not one of these managers had ever encountered an inspector, much less been assessed a fine. At some of the enterprises, conditions seemed relatively safe—which might explain this lack of attention. This was most definitely not the case, however, at the rubber goods plant (Rezina) I studied in Moscow, where working conditions were so difficult and potentially hazardous *(vrednye)* to the workers' health that many were permitted to retire five years before the legally mandated retirement age.[72]

During the Soviet period, the *profkom*'s preference for management over workers seemed to have become ingrained. As I documented in chapter 4, despite their statutory (and arguably their fiduciary) duty to scrutinize all management-initiated dismissals, trade union committees routinely rubber-stamped management's requests to dismiss workers. Rather than acting as the steadfast protector of workers' rights under the law, the *profkomy* acted as a facilitator, enabling management merely to go through the motions. Their attitude was no less perfunctory than management's. Had the trade union been willing to stand up for the workers it supposedly represented, law might never have become so marginalized in the workplace.

Why were Soviet trade unions so passive in their dealings with enterprise management? The most obvious reason was their patent lack of independence from both enterprise management and the Communist Party. Management exercised direct financial control over the chairman and vice chairman of the *profkom*—the only members to be freed from their normal work duties and occupied solely with union business. Although the *VTsSPS* paid their basic salaries, enterprise management was responsible for their bonuses. This arrangement clearly compromised the independence of the *profkom* since the payment of bonuses was discretionary and thus could be used by management to influence the outcome of *profkom* decisions. Moreover, because bonuses depended on plan fulfillment, union leaders also had a material stake in whether the plan was met, which goes a long way toward explaining why *profkomy* were consistently more attentive to their production-related duties than to protecting workers' rights.

A good argument can be made that the primary constituency of the *profkom* was not the workforce but management. Indeed, the members of the *profkom* (particularly the chairman and vice chairman) owed their positions to management. Although candidates were technically elected by the workers, the list of candidates was typically put together by management working together with the Party committee. More often than not, these candidates were themselves managers and not production-level workers. In 1987, only 4 percent of all *profkom* chairmen and vice chairmen were drawn from the ranks of workers.[73] The *profkom*'s lack of sympathy for workers' concerns is therefore hardly surprising.

The *profkom*'s open allegiance to management contributed to its lack of legitimacy among workers. The recognition of its inability to win the respect of the workers caused the *profkom* to edge ever closer to management, thereby increasing its dependence and its predilection toward passivity. The dynamic was circular and self-perpetuating, resulting in a labor force that was deeply alienated from the official unions. A 1989 survey revealed that only 10 percent of workers rated the authority of the union as "high" and only 7 percent viewed the unions as having the potential to assist with workers' concrete problems.[74] This contempt for the official union was likewise reflected in my conversations with workers. When visiting an auto plant in Kaluga in July 1990, I met with several groups of workers. My question whether they would go to their trade union representative if they had a dispute with management was consistently greeted with gales of laughter. This disdainful reaction was repeated time and again in factories in Moscow and in private conversations with workers, who uniformly dismissed the *profkomy* as being "in the pocket of management" *(v karmane administratsii)*.

The structural constraints within which Soviet trade unions operated also contributed to the polarization of relations with workers as well as to their overall passivity. The system did not encourage workers to rely on the *profkom* to act as their champion in case of disputes with management. When a dispute arose, it was the *profkom* that first considered its merits.[75] The *profkom*'s role was that of impartial decision maker, not worker advocate. In practice, impartiality was rarely exhibited and, as chapter 4 suggested, the *profkomy* tended to side with management. Of course, the worker had the right to press his or her claim in court. But because the *profkom* had already publicly disavowed the worker's claim, the worker was unlikely to appeal to it for legal assistance and, by the same token, the *profkom* was unlikely to be receptive to such an appeal. Theoretically, the worker could then go over the head of the *profkom* and appeal directly to the *VTsSPS* for assistance, but in my review of trial court records and my conversations at various enterprises, I encountered no such cases.

In the West, unions cement their authority by negotiating collective bargaining agreements that in the main serve their members' interests and force management to live up to the agreement's terms.[76] Collective bargaining agreements also existed in the Soviet Union, and their terms were the result of negotiations between management and the *profkom.*[77] But these agreements were largely meaningless.[78] They were framed in vague and declaratory language that merely obliged management to try to improve working conditions or accomplish other goals. Workers had no recourse if management failed to live up to its promises.[79] The very fact that the *profkom* participated in this charade only lessened its stature in the eyes of the workers.

The enterprise-level trade union organization was thoroughly coopted by management. It served management's interests rather than defending (or even paying attention to) workers' rights. Indeed, the interests of the union and of management were so deeply intertwined as to be inseparable. The sort of restraining influence exercised by unions in Western industrial democracies was absent by design in the Soviet Union. As late as February 1991, a *VTsSPS* representative, during an interview with me, continued to insist that there was no divergence between the interests of the workers and management. Given the day-to-day reality of the *profkom* as the handmaiden of management, it could hardly be expected to emerge as a vigilant protector of the rule of law within the enterprise.

The Gorbachev years saw the first serious reassessment of the role of Soviet trade unions since Lenin's day. Soviet scholars, freed by *glasnost'* to express their true opinions, began the process. In a 1987 article in the influential Party-sponsored journal, *Kommunist,* the *VTsSPS* and enterprise trade unions were criticized for having become bogged down in bureaucracy and for having sidestepped their obligation to defend workers' interests.[80] The *VTsSPS* did not react immediately. Indeed, as one prominent Soviet labor law scholar commented, "[p]erestroika did not reach the trade unions quickly."[81] The widespread wildcat miners' strikes of 1989 and the subsequent bubbling up of new independent trade unions served as the catalyst.[82] At its congress in September 1989, the *VTsSPS* passed a resolution committing itself to defending workers' rights and abdicating responsibility for stimulating production.[83]

The abrupt change in direction was regarded positively by policymakers. Both Gorbachev and his prime minister, N. I. Ryzhkov, gave numerous speeches stressing the importance of invigorating the trade unions.[84] At first glance, it seemed to be a step in the right direction, marking the beginning it seemed of a new era in which the *profkomy* forced management to obey the law. Unfortunately, that was not to be the case. Closer examination reveals the *VTsSPS*'s words were hollow rhetoric designed to win the respect and loyalty of the workers it had so long taken for granted.

The effort to reform the unions failed on the enterprise level for two reasons. First, the workers did not fall into line. They remained deeply skeptical about the ability of the official trade union to change. Second, the behavior of the *profkomy* remained more or less the same, suggesting that the workers' skepticism had been well founded. The members of the trade union committees had been trained to carry out certain tasks, and they simply could not change either their behavior or their way of thinking overnight.

Legal Culture and the Role of Law

In an ideal world, the moral force of the law alone would be sufficient to ensure compliance. But in a world in which all seek to maximize their interests, nowhere does this hold true in its pure form.[85] Law is not inherently self-realizing; it must either be mobilized from below by the citizenry or enforced from above by the state.[86] As a result, the compliance level varies widely among societies and even within a single society, depending on the subject matter of the law.

Labor Law and Legal Culture in the West

What about labor law? In most Western industrialized democracies, several factors coalesce to transform labor law into a relatively potent force in economic and social relations. First is the nature of the political process. Labor policy, as reflected in legislation, regulations, and the institutional structure of dispute resolution, is not simply unilaterally promulgated by the state. Rather, trade unions and other representatives of workers' interests are able to take part in the policymaking process. While they may not always succeed in pushing through the provisions most favorable to workers, they win sometimes.[87] Even when they lose, the process and the resulting law gain legitimacy by their very participation—that is, by the reciprocal nature of the political process.

This, in turn, gives rise to a legal culture in which workers, like other citizens, take their legal rights seriously and are willing to take affirmative steps to force management to live up to its obligations under the law. Their ability to do so is buttressed by the existence of a cadre of activist lawyers who act to even the stakes between the repeat-player managers and workers, who are typically first-timers.[88] In a more general sense, an independent bar acts as a gadfly, keeping management on the straight and narrow.

Labor Law and Legal Culture in the Soviet Union

The Soviet Union, however, presents quite a different case. As I argued in chapter 2, the powerful used law crudely as an instrument for achieving policy goals and thereby undermined the legitimacy of law. Although the official trade union often gave its stamp of approval to new laws, this was an empty gesture given that the union was subordinate to the Communist Party. As such, its sanction was a formality and did not reflect an effort by the authorities in Moscow to take the interests of workers into account when setting labor policy. As a result, workers did not see law as shielding them from the arbitrariness of the state or its agents but as a source of that arbitrariness.

Why was law marginalized in the Soviet workplace? This question requires us to probe more deeply into the attitudes of workers and management toward law in order to better appreciate the obstacles to changing these attitudes.

Management Attitudes toward Law. The evidence indicates that the law did not act as much of a constraint on Soviet management. Over the years, managers became expert at meeting the technical requirements imposed by the law while paying little attention to the deeper purposes of the law within society. In a very real sense, managers literally papered over the spirit of the law.

In the context of dismissals and transfers, management consistently went through the proper motions. More specifically, it petitioned the *profkom* in a timely fashion and, upon receiving its consent, prepared a written dismissal order that specified the statutory basis for the dismissal. When necessary, management also offered redundant workers other jobs within the enterprise. For the most part, its actions represented form without substance. The jobs offered in cases of redundancy often turned out to be completely unsuited to the worker's qualifications, yet *profkom* consent was rarely denied. To be sure, enterprise management modified its behavior slightly in response to the dictates of the law. It did, after all, go to the trouble of creating the sort of documentary record required by the statute. At the same time, management continued to fire workers at will, thereby thwarting the basic purpose of the law, which was to eliminate (or at least minimize) arbitrary dismissals by management.

In a very real sense, management had triumphed over the law. Yet one would be hard-pressed to find a group that felt less like winners. The frustration felt by managers over the way in which law undermined their ability to deal effectively with their labor force emerged as a constant theme in my interviews. They always cited the unreasonable prerequisites imposed by the law as one of the primary reasons they had not rationalized their workforce. Indeed, to a person, they complained about the paperwork burden, claiming that the documentation demanded by law was so onerous that they often had no choice but to keep incompetent workers on the payroll. Such tales were most frequently spun about workers who had been drunk on the job.[89]

This feeling of being put upon is, of course, relative and difficult for an outsider to judge. Furthermore, it is not unique to Soviet managers. Similar sentiments are often voiced by Western managers who have to deal with administrative regulations. What are the sources of this ambivalence about the law on the part of Soviet managers? A definitive answer to this question is not possible, but we can suggest several contributory factors.

For some, the complaints may not reflect actual experience but principled objections to the system. Managers who believe they should have carte blanche in resolving manpower issues would chafe under any kind of regulatory regime, regardless of how reasonable. This generalized dislike of the system can be fueled by the experiences (real or rumored) of colleagues in which various worst-case scenarios are played out. This probably explains the popularity among Soviet managers of stories about drunk workers who supposedly could not be legally fired. These stories rarely drew on the personal experience of the interviewees but were rather cases they had heard or read about and believed to be true. Along the same lines, American managers routinely cite the difficulty of firing civil service workers as evidence of the dangers of over-regulation by the federal government. Yet the fact is that civil service workers can be fired if the reasons are properly documented. As in the Soviet Union, the law is intended not as a blanket prohibition on dismissals but as an incentive for management to behave in a fair and nonarbitrary fashion.

For other managers, complaints about the law may come from concrete experience. If management does have a worker reinstated over its objections, it may assume its experience is the norm. In the Soviet Union, for example, reliable statistical data about such matters were not readily available, and the rumor mill supported the notion that it was virtually impossible to fire workers. Soviet managers, already overwhelmed with paperwork generated by the planning system, might have shrunk from yet another potential hassle.

Management's interactions with the Soviet legal system were deeply conflicted. Although management routinely prevailed, it persisted in believing that the system was biased against it. Changing these beliefs, which were largely based on perceptions rather than actual experience, will not be easy.

Workers' Attitudes toward Law. The relationship of workers to the law is inherently different from that of management. Management is forced to interact with the legal system in its day-to-day activities; it then decides whether to disregard legal norms, obey them, or follow some intermediate course of action. Workers, on the other hand, can easily go through life without having much contact with the legal system.

Even when they are dismissed or have some other dispute with management, they have to make an affirmative choice to mobilize the law. Their decision is complicated by the fact they are well acquainted with the representative of management. As Black notes, "the greater the relational distance between the parties to a dispute, the more likely is law to be used to settle the dispute."[90] Litigation often forces parties into adversarial positions that make working together difficult or even impossible. Law, therefore, is used most often when relationships are ending. Consequently, in European labor tribunals, workers are more likely to sue management for severance pay than for reinstatement to their old job.[91]

The value of these generally accepted propositions about workers' propensity to mobilize the law in making sense of the Soviet case is not entirely clear. For one thing, the Russian Labor Code permitted only two weeks of severance pay, which provided little material incentive to sue management.[92] The only reason to initiate legal action was if the worker wanted to be reinstated. Thus, while Soviet workers seem to fit the general pattern in that they tended not to pursue legal remedies when fired, the reasons why they hung back are somewhat unique.

The empirical evidence—limited though it is—clearly indicates that the vast majority of Soviet workers dismissed at the initiative of management did not pursue the matter to court. A 1983 study indicates that only 2 percent of dismissed workers appealed.[93] Three alternative explanations for this suggest themselves. First, the dismissals may have been legally justified. Second, the employment opportunities may have been so plentiful and attractive that leaving the enterprise posed no hardship to the dismissed worker. Third, workers may have believed (rightly or wrongly) that the legal system was biased against them, making it pointless to pursue legal remedies.

The first explanation is not terribly persuasive. While many dismissals were no doubt completely within the law, I have shown that Soviet managers tended merely to go through the motions of obeying the law. In chapter 4, I presented numerous examples in which they complied with its formal prerequisites but skirted its more substantive elements. Moreover, I have argued that the economic incentive system—with its overriding emphasis on fulfilling the plan—tended to encourage and even reward such behavior.

The second explanation is also problematic. Dismissed workers may well have been able to obtain employment at another enterprise, but that would not have adequately compensated them for what they lost by leaving a long-term position. The enterprise controlled social benefits (including housing) and allocated them on the basis of seniority. When a worker left one enterprise for another, he or she forfeited his or her place in line. The absence of the market in the Soviet Union meant that no alternative source existed for these goods and services. Logically, these factors should have made workers eager to retain their jobs. They should also have served as sufficient incentives to push them into the legal system to petition for reinstatement and overcome the bias against the remedy of reinstatement.

It is the nature of the Soviet legal system that most compellingly explains why workers were so reluctant to mobilize the law. In many ways, the procedural deck was stacked against them both within the enterprise and in the court system. The *profkomy* were unable to stand up to management in personnel matters, leaving the way clear for management to push through any dismissal it wanted.

The dismissed worker then had to decide whether to appeal to the court for reinstatement. For most, this was their first exposure to the judicial system. Making their way through the process was made even more intimidating by the fact that they usually had to do it on their own. Defense counsel were reluctant to take labor cases because they were not very lucrative and could be time consuming due to the typical management strategy of wearing down the other side through endless continuances. As I noted in chapter 5, workers were greatly disadvantaged by the lack of legal counsel and by the lack of an independent bar in the Soviet Union. They could not possibly compete with the enterprise's in-house counsel, who typically had tried many similar cases.

Workers' lack of respect for the institution of courts also contributed to their unwillingness to pursue their legal remedies. The Party's manipulation of the courts (both institutionally and in specific cases) tainted the courts. The reforms of the late 1980s, while promising, could not obliterate the culture of dependency that prevailed within the Soviet judiciary. Consequently, workers did not see themselves as "rights-bearing citizens," in the sense of having expectations that the courts would enforce their legal rights.

Conclusion

I began this chapter by questioning why Soviet managers had so little regard for the law—why they just went through the motions of complying and failed in any meaningful way to respect workers' rights. The foregoing review of the economic system these managers operated within makes it clear that their behavior was entirely rational. To put it bluntly, managers had little incentive to obey the law. What was missing was (1) the disciplining force of the market, (2) pressure from labor unions, and (3) a surrounding legal culture that condemned and threatened punishment of managers who neglected the spirit of the law and that provided meaningful remedies to complainants.

The hierarchical nature of the Soviet administrative-command system meant that managers were understandably concerned primarily with pleasing their superiors—the officials of the industrial ministries—who were solely interested in whether the enterprise fulfilled its obligations under the plan. As a rule, the ministries did not inquire into how these output targets were met or whether managers contravened the law in the process. The absence of pressure on management to obey the law from below by workers or trade unions (their nominal representatives) caused the behavioral patterns to become ever more deeply ingrained. All concerned became accustomed to the marginalized role of law, and nobody pressed to make it more meaningful. In a very real sense, in the Soviet case the law atrophied from disuse.[94]

Part 4
Theoretical Implications

CHAPTER 7

Summary and Speculations

The Marginalization of Soviet Law

During the 74 years of Soviet rule, law evolved into an instrument that was available to, and regularly used by, the state to maintain its version of social order and ensure widespread compliance with its policy objectives. In the Soviet Union, law was not an interactive and ongoing process in which state and society cooperated to work out legal norms that reflected the shared values of society. As a result, citizens did not view law as a means of protecting themselves from encroachments by the state or its agents.

This vision of law as a mechanism of control emasculated Soviet society. Thus, while law certainly mattered under the Soviet regime because ordinary citizens changed their behavior in response to its dictates, it mattered primarily in a coercive sense. Compliance stemmed from fear, not from respect for the law. In the Soviet Union, law rarely mattered in a reciprocal sense; that is, citizens did not generally perceive it to be a means for achieving justice or even solving problems.

The Soviet Union was not the first or the only state in which law was simply an instrument of social control and social engineering in the hands of political elites. Even in democratic polities, those in positions of power endeavor to use law instrumentally—as a means for reshaping society in the desired image. Indeed, law, is an instrument of social control exercised by political authorities; but in accordance with the ideal of the rule of law, law also constrains these authorities. The tension between these two functions of law is inescapable. In fact, as societal forces, instrumentalism and the rule of law tend to displace one another. When there is a high degree of procedural regularity and of the other indicia of the rule of law,[1] the ability of political authorities to manipulate law to serve their ends tends to be curtailed. Nonet and Selznick argue that a "historic bargain" has been struck in the Western liberal democracies:

> *Legal institutions purchase procedural autonomy at the price of substantive subordination.* The political community delegates to the jurists a limited authority to be exercised free of political intrusion, but the condition of that immunity is that they remove themselves from the formation of public policy. (emphasis in original)[2]

A limited sphere of autonomy for law is carved out in the procedural realm, and the judiciary is granted a limited degree of institutional independence.[3] This, in turn, contributes to the understanding of law as universal and as a stabilizing force within society. But this is only half of the bargain.

Democracy also requires that a bargain be struck between state and society with regard to the substance of the law. Periodic multiparty (and multicandidate) elections force political authorities to answer to the citizens. If the laws adopted are too far out of line with a substantial portion of the citizens' notions of fundamental fairness, then the responsible legislators or executive authorities will not be returned to office.

In the Soviet Union, by contrast, the state eschewed such bargains. Law (both substantively and procedurally) was penetrable and consequently manipulable by political authorities, even on a case-by-case basis. Soviet courts enjoyed no institutional independence. The Party kept a tight rein on the selection, tenure and promotion of judges, and individual Party officials were able to dictate the outcome of politically (or even personally) sensitive cases. The courts became irrevocably tainted in the eyes of ordinary citizens.

To a certain degree, law became marginalized within Soviet society. While attempting to live within the boundaries established by law, people recognized that these boundaries were changeable at a moment's notice. They further understood that the law applied differently depending on one's status and political connections and, from that, grasped that law had no meaningful ability to constrain the behavior of the politically powerful. As a result, they did not embrace law as a mechanism for achieving justice. This unwillingness to mobilize the law to defend or advance legal interests constitutes a barrier to constructing a legal system in which law matters reciprocally.

In order for law to come to matter reciprocally in Russian society, it is not necessary that everyone endorse the notion of law as a potent defensive mechanism against official misconduct and as an offensive weapon for advancing individual or group interests. Nor is it necessary that everyone make use of the law every time it is possible to do so. All societies, even the Western liberal democracies that are notable for a high degree of mobilization of the law, have large numbers of alienated, cynical, apathetic, or legally incompetent people, unwilling or unable to use the law to their advantage. The key is that *enough* people be willing and able to use the law. "Enough" has been achieved when the state and private entities and individuals are concerned that they will be called to account if they violate the legal rights of others.

The Historical Legacy

The reshaping of Russian law into Soviet law began immediately after the 1917 October Revolution. Lenin (a trained lawyer) and his cohort distrusted law, regarding it as one of many tools historically used by the ruling class to oppress the proletariat.[4] Consequently, much of the tsarist legal system was dismantled, amid talk of the eventual "withering away" of law as administrative commands supplanted market capitalism and, more specifically, as private property was eliminated.[5] The remaining statutory law was subject to being overriden whenever it was deemed to contradict the spirit of the revolution.[6] This concept of "revolutionary justice" laid the groundwork for a legal system that was permeable by extralegal forces.

This vision of law as the handmaiden of politics was further amplified under Stalin. In contrast to his predecessors, Stalin wanted a strong state and embraced law, at least formalistically, as a means of protecting it.[7] As a result, law did not "wither away" under Soviet power. Just the opposite occurred. The 1920s and 1930s witnessed a tremendous flurry of legislative activity, as the basic codes were redrafted to take account of the postrevolutionary reality. Yet law was not permitted to become autonomous; both procedurally and substantively, it was consistently bent to the will of the rulers. "Revolutionary justice" lived on, remaining among the prominent purposes served by law.

The Duality of Soviet Law

The persistence of "revolutionary justice" gave rise to a dual legal culture in which law operated (or appeared to operate) with regularity much of the time but in which the dictates of the law were always subject to being countermanded by more urgent political needs. Such intervention was most common in cases with clear political implications but was not unheard of in ordinary civil or criminal cases.[8] This duality provided the appearance of legality—the color of law—for the mass repression of ordinary citizens that characterized the Stalinist period and for the more selective repression of political dissidents during the Brezhnev period. It also undermined whatever trust people might have had in the law and had a chilling effect as well on the judicial corps insofar as no one could be sure when the legal system would be allowed to function unimpeded.

Throughout the life of the Soviet Union, law continued to be conceptualized as a one-way projection of state authority. The close identification of the Party with the state allowed political elites to manipulate law and legal process to further their own agendas.[9] The decrease in the level of state-sponsored coercion following Stalin's death in 1953 brought a corresponding decrease in levels of compliance with the law because the willingness to obey the law had never been grounded in a sense of reciprocity or voluntarism. The technical shortcomings of the law, that is, statutory language that was vague and overbroad and provisions that were internally contradictory or that contradicted other laws, also prompted evasive behavior.

Thus, duality of law represented a more or less permanent feature of Soviet law. Political authorities went through the motions of complying with the law but consistently bent it to serve their interests, often to the point of unrecognizability. In time, ordinary citizens adopted this practice of going through the motions. What resulted was a profound disparity between the law as it appeared on the books and as it was implemented on a day-to-day basis. That such a gap existed in the Soviet context is not surprising. After all, in no country, regardless of the underlying economic and governmental structure, does the law in action fully live up to the hopes of its drafters. However, the more interesting questions are (1) how this gap expressed itself in Soviet society, (2) how it became ingrained in Soviet legal culture, and (3) what sort of institutional and cultural changes will be needed to break the cycle and bring post-Soviet legal practice more in line with the aspirations of the law.

The Case Study

The nature of the gap between the statutory law and its implementation can be grasped through a detailed case study of the law governing dismissals and transfers of Soviet workers at the initiative of management during the 1980s. This case study will begin with an examination of the statutory law and related published materials. I will then expand the sphere of inquiry to include the reality of its implementation, which I uncovered during my year of fieldwork (1989–90) in Moscow's lower courts and industrial enterprises. This methodology allows me to document the inconsonance between Soviet labor law in the form it takes in the published materials and the way it operates on a day-to-day basis.

The Law on the Books. Soviet labor law and the ancillary published material suggest that Soviet workers' rights under the law were well protected in instances of illegal dismissals or transfers. According to the letter of the law, a worker could not be transferred unilaterally and could not be laid off unless there were no comparable positions within the enterprise to which he or she could be reallocated. Under no circumstances could a worker be fired without the consent of the factory trade union committee *(profkom)*.

When workers were laid off or transferred illegally, and were willing to press their rights through the legal system, the published cases suggest that the Soviet courts bent over backward to protect workers' rights. This impression stems not only from the fact that workers usually prevailed in the published case decisions—though they did—but from the way in which they prevailed. The higher courts routinely held management to a significantly higher burden of proof than workers. To a certain extent, this imbalance is to be expected. After all, management has greater access to enterprise records and typically has the advantage of being a repeat player in the judicial game. But the published case decisions went beyond merely trying to even the contest between unmatched opponents.

While the plaintiff-worker's burden of proof could be sustained by unsubstantiated allegations of impropriety on the part of management, management was consistently required to answer with documentary evidence conclusively disproving the worker's charges. Moreover, the documents produced had to be from a list of evidence considered relevant, as specified in the official commentary to the labor code. A picture emerges from these published appellate case decisions of a management incapable of satisfying the courts. Often when it met the statutory requirements, the courts would respond by raising the ante, invoking standards of fundamental fairness in order to sustain the worker's claim.

The Law in Practice. The published materials suggest that labor law was a force that could be mobilized by Soviet workers to protect their rights and interests. My field research in Moscow revealed the illusory nature of this image. At every step of the process—from the *profkom*'s in-house review to the judicial procedure in lower courts—those charged with carrying out the law did the absolute bare minimum.

The law required management to obtain the consent of the *profkom* before dismissing a worker. In the factories I studied, managers were well aware of this duty and typically requested consent in a timely fashion. The propensity of the *profkomy* simply to rubber-stamp such requests blunted the impact of the law. Management requests for consent were rarely declined and, furthermore, rarely sparked any debate. When confronted about their apparent failure to defend workers' rights, trade union officials defended themselves on the grounds that the dismissals were carried out with rigorous attention to the statutory requirements. When reminded that their duty under the law called for more—that dismissals should be tolerated only when there was no other alternative—these trade unionists became visibly uncomfortable with the idea that they should openly challenge management.

This willingness to rubber-stamp management decisions to dismiss or transfer a worker was also reflected in the unpublished records I analyzed in Moscow trial court archives. The courts' willingness to accept evidence submitted by management at face value rendered the heavier burden of proof, seen so consistently in the published case decisions of appellate courts, largely meaningless. My observations of trials and my review of records for the 1980s in two Moscow trial courts strongly suggested that workers engendered little sympathy among judicial personnel. Through their courtroom demeanor and actions, trial judges made it clear that they regarded workers petitioning for reinstatement as nuisances. Since only 15 percent of workers were represented by counsel, this attitude on the part of judges left workers with no advocate. Most plaintiff-workers were first-timers and were not well versed in the rules of the game. Often they undermined their cases by failing to challenge patently problematic evidence or to point out that they had been singled out for special treatment by management.

Like management and the trade unions, the courts were just going through the motions with respect to their legal duties. The sort of rigorous attention to detail and concern for workers' rights found in the published case decisions was strikingly absent in trial court records. Under these circumstances, the workers' tendency not to mobilize their rights when laid off or transferred in violation of the statutory law was entirely rational.[10] The presence of the seemingly attractive remedy of reinstatement to one's prior position (and to the collateral social benefits that were based on seniority) did not serve as a sufficient incentive in the face of workers' distrust of the integrity of the legal system.

Explaining the Duality of Soviet Law

Why did this perfunctory attitude toward law develop and persist in the Soviet Union, even after the Gorbachev-era calls for legal reform? Why did law not matter to workers or to management? There is no simple answer to these questions. The answer must instead be pieced together through an examination of the underlying institutional structure and the incentives it created for each of the interest groups involved. In this way, the logic of the behavior of the Soviet judiciary, enterprise management, trade unions, and workers becomes apparent.

The Economic Incentive System. During the Soviet period, enterprise managers operated within the constraints of the rigidly hierarchical administrative-command system.[11] Profitability and other indicia of efficiency on the part of management were largely irrelevant. Soviet managers did not have to worry about their market position or about bad publicity that might result from an inquisitive press publicizing legal violations such as the failure to implement environmental regulations or workplace safety rules.[12] Most importantly, the Soviet system did not allow for bankruptcy.

The hierarchical nature of the system dictated that the key to success was to please one's superiors. The one fail-safe way to do this was to meet all of the production targets established by the centrally generated economic plan. With plan fulfillment came assurances of job security, advancement, and substantial financial rewards in the form of bonuses.[13] Consequently, managers on all levels went to extraordinary lengths to satisfy the plan. No one paid much attention to how this was done—whether it required cutting some legal corners or engaging in patently inefficient behavior such as the hoarding of supplies or labor. The nature of the incentive system drove managers and their superiors in the planning bureaus and the industrial ministries to be primarily concerned with quantitative ends rather than with qualitative means. The end result was not open disobedience of the law but a formalistic attitude toward law. Managers protected themselves by going through the motions of complying with the law. In most cases, however, the mountains of paperwork certifying compliance turned out to be a house of cards, giving only the outward appearance of legality, which collapsed upon closer scrutiny.

The general absence of differentiation within the Soviet economy meant that enterprise management experienced relatively little pressure from other economic actors to comply more fully with the law. This stands in contrast to the situation within most Western market economies, in which management has to answer to contractual trading partners, banks, trade unions, workers (including potential whistle-blowers) and a wide variety of regulatory agencies, all of which can haul the company into court.

Soviet trade unions existed, but they were sweetheart unions, thoroughly coopted by enterprise management.[14] Technically, workers elected the members of their trade union committees, but management assembled the slates of candidates. As a result, the "winners" owed more to their management sponsors than to their coworkers. Soviet trade unions ultimately evolved into a quasi-branch of management, charged with allocating certain social welfare benefits, such as housing, day care, vacations, and big ticket consumer goods. Furthermore, like other Soviet workers, the bonuses paid to union leaders were tied to plan fulfillment. As a result, *profkomy* were more concerned with stimulating labor productivity than with protecting workers' rights. None of this was lost on the workers; unions enjoyed very little legitimacy among their membership. The recognition of this fact caused enterprise trade union organizations to edge ever closer to management, thereby increasing their dependence and their passivity. The dynamic was circular and self-perpetuating, resulting in deep alienation between workers and unions.

The Soviet Judicial System. If the Soviet Union had had a more autonomous judiciary perhaps the judicial process would have acted to level the playing field between management and workers. In theory, the impartiality of the judge allows him or her to consider each case on the merits without any outside interference. Decisions are rendered dispassionately and in accord with the dictates of the law and, when the law is vague or silent, in accord with prevailing community standards. In the Soviet case, however, the impartiality of the judiciary was seriously compromised, both institutionally and individually.

Despite constitutional claims to the contrary, the Soviet judicial system was not independent.[15] Its institutional impartiality was undermined in large part by the political control exercised by the Communist Party.[16] The Party controlled the selection process, and most judges had only five-year terms, which left them at the mercy of the Party for continued employment. Political reliability, that is, adhering to the Party line, became the key to initial selection and long-term tenure. The Party's control over the operating budgets of the courts and the salaries paid to judges gave it additional leverage over the institution itself. The minimal level of financial support provided to courts along with their shabby facilities (when compared to Party buildings) vividly demonstrated the marginal role of courts within Soviet society.

The bureaucratic structure, which placed the courts within the Soviet Ministry of Justice, also undermined judicial independence.[17] This sort of arrangement is standard in Western Europe and does not necessarily compromise the institutional integrity of the courts. It did so in the Soviet case because the jurisdiction of the ministry was not limited to administrative supervision but extended to matters of substance. Indeed, the ministry became a sort of intermediary between the Party and the courts, riding herd on judges to ensure compliance with policy pronouncements.

The individual impartiality of judges—their objectivity, incorruptibility, and commitment to basic principles of justice—was likewise problematic in the Soviet context. Once again, the Communist Party was the proximate cause. While the Party certainly did not micromanage all trials, Party officials were able to dictate the outcome of specific cases and, on occasion, were even able to use the courts as vehicles for pursuing private vendettas. Although outside interference was not the norm, its specter had an insidiously corrosive effect as judges learned to censor themselves in order to avoid incurring the wrath of the Party.

But the Party was not solely to blame for the passivity of the Soviet judiciary. Judges were socialized to be dependent and were regarded as political hacks, not sages. There was an absence of cohesion within the ranks that might have allowed them to stand up to outside interference. The system of legal education was geared to rote memorization, not critical analysis. Low pay and poor working conditions meant that the best and brightest among law faculty graduates shied away from judicial careers. Merely removing Party influence from the judicial process was not sufficient to change the behavior of judges.

All of the factors discussed thus far—the formalistic approach to law of enterprise management, the cooptation and impotence of trade unions, and the passivity of courts—unwittingly worked in tandem to convince Soviet workers that mobilizing the law in an effort to protect their rights was pointless. The limited statistical data available as well as my own observations leave little doubt that workers had opted out of the system, at least in the realm of labor law. This was particularly telling in the context of dismissals because the remedy of reinstatement should have provided a powerful incentive for mobilizing the law. It was this unwillingness to use the law that caused its marginalization.

Making Law Matter in Russia

Although law did not matter in a reciprocal sense in the Soviet Union, can the cycle now be broken in post-Soviet Russia? Can law now be transformed into a potent force that average citizens are willing to mobilize to protect themselves from the arbitrariness of the state? These are difficult questions. They require a reconsideration of the role of law in Soviet society and how it might be reconceptualized if law is to come to matter reciprocally. Only then can the question of how that new vision of law might evolve in the post-Leninist context be pursued, that is, which emerging social and political forces might push legal development in that direction or might deter such development. The argument is intended to be speculative, not deterministic. The vitalization of law in Russia is certainly not inevitable. It is therefore necessary to consider other possibilities for the future of Russian society in the short run. Each of the developmental scenarios, with its implicit political and economic bargains, has different implications for the role of law.

Law as an Interactive Enterprise

Merely creating new laws and reformulating old laws to meet the needs of the nascent market economy, while necessary, is not sufficient to make law matter in a reciprocal sense. More profound changes are required. In essence, substantial numbers of people have to be convinced to change the way they think about law. They have to stop thinking of law as an exclusive instrument of the state and begin to consider it as a tool potentially available to all members of society. They have to trust that law will serve their interests and not just those of the political elite. Building trust is never an easy process.[18] In the Russian context, it is complicated by the legacy of the past.[19] The dualistic Soviet legal culture, in which highly prescriptive law coexisted with a lax enforcement regime, left residual feelings of contempt and disdain for law. Law was imposed from above; it did not come from within society and made no pretense at reflecting the values of the community at large.

Legitimizing law under these conditions requires a break with past ways of creating and implementating law. The law-making process has to become more interactive, with society playing a role in working out rules and regulations.[20] The goal is for law to be understood as an evolving process that reflects and responds to the interests and needs of society more generally rather than simply reflecting the desires of the rulers. Making the process of creating law more inclusive enhances the likelihood that the resulting law will embody (or be perceived as embodying) the values of the community. In theory, the reciprocal nature of this process acts over time to increase the willingness of citizens to use the law.[21]

Procedural Regularity

But the degree of mobilization is not only a function of the substantive legitimacy of the law, that is, whether on its face it is considered basically fair. Equally important is the perception that the law is implemented in a fair and even-handed way. One key institutional prerequisite is an independent judiciary with the power to review and reverse official decisions. The political neutrality of judges is critical; they must be free to interpret and enforce the law with no danger of interference from those with political power.[22] As the Soviet case demonstrates, people do not bother with the law if they believe the decision makers are biased in favor of the powerful or are susceptible to outside pressure.

The overall legitimacy of law is also strengthened when the statutes and regulations are imbued with the qualities that Fuller describes as constituting an "inner morality."[23] More specifically, law should be openly promulgated and available to all at a minimum of expense and effort. The substance of a given law should not be subject to constant revision. The level of vagueness and internal contradiction should be kept to an absolute minimum. Finally, law should not impose duties that are impossible to fulfill.

Efficacy of Law

As the previous section suggests, people in large part are motivated to mobilize the law by the attractiveness of the potential remedy. Ideally, law responds to the needs of those at whom it is targeted.[24] Judges must have sufficient political muscle to follow through on such remedies.

Inga Markovits's inquiry into why West Germans mobilized their legal rights with more regularity than their East German counterparts is helpful in understanding the Soviet case.[25] She identifies several reasons why law mattered less under Leninism than under liberal capitalism. The first is the lack of relational distance between potential plaintiffs and defendants under state socialism. People tended to make do with what they had rather than seeking to change it through the courts. As Markovits notes: "In West Germany, plaintiffs sue to alter the status quo. . . . In many East German situations, nobody can change the status quo. . . . So why sue?"[26]

The unsatisfactory nature of the available remedies only further undermined citizens' motivation to sue. The typical remedy was money damages. But in the absence of a market money rarely served as adequate compensation for the losses suffered. In a contractual dispute, for example, the petitioner could not mitigate his or her losses by purchasing from an alternative source. Even in post-Soviet Russia, the opportunities for doing so are greatly limited by the prevalence of monopoly producers and the immaturity of emerging market institutions.[27] What is needed is injunctive relief, but that does not fall within the purview of the economic courts *(arbitrazhnyi sud)* as currently empowered.

To summarize, a number of necessary characteristics of a law that matters reciprocally have been identified. Principal among these are a general societal trust in the basic fairness of the law, both in its substance and its application; a remedial structure that addresses the needs of citizens; a judiciary with sufficient political capital to stand up to legislative and executive power; and a conceptualization of law as an interactive process in which both state and society participate on a more or less equal basis.

But thus far the picture remains a still life—a static image of the end result desired by Russian policymakers. The task now is to breathe life into that picture—to explore how law might come to matter reciprocally in post-Leninist Russia.

How Does the "Rule of Law" Evolve?

The Legacy of Weber. What is needed is an evolutionary model of legal development. The scholarship of Max Weber provides a useful starting point.[28] Weber was primarily concerned with understanding and explaining the emergence of market capitalism in Western Europe (and its failure to emerge elsewhere). Law is central to his theory. He argued that the specific features of Western legal systems—the autonomous role of law, the belief in natural law, the emphasis on general theory in the training of legal professionals, the rejection of particularistic rules—are all critical to the development of capitalism.

But Weber did not accept Western law as a given. He viewed Western law and legal systems as highly rational and recognized this as being unique. For Weber, rationality is akin to what I defined in chapter 2 as the rule of law in that it encompasses elements of both procedural regularity and substantive legitimacy. In his sociology of law, Weber sought to explain how law becomes "rationalized."

Weber identifies a number of factors critical to the process of rationalization but fails to specify their relative importance. First is the existence of a fragmented and nontraditional society in which no single group can claim a monopoly on political or economic power and all are forced to compromise with one another concerning the substance of the law. In Western Europe, the increased differentiation of society was accompanied by the rise of market capitalism, with attendant calls by the nascent bourgeoisie for greater regularity in trading relationships. Under such circumstances, law gradually emerged as a relatively neutral mediating force because it was in everyone's interest—the crown, the aristocracy, and the merchants alike—that there be preexisting rules that were enforced in an evenhanded manner.

Buttressing this was the underlying belief system of society. The commitment to the principles of natural law that grew out of the Judeo-Christian tradition of Western Europe facilitated the transcendence of particularism in law.[29] Furthermore, the European system of legal education, with its emphasis on legal theory rather than mundane statutory law, reflected a universalistic view of law and inculcated it in successive generations of legal professionals.

Also contributing to the development of autonomy within the procedural realm was the emergence of a bureaucracy composed of salaried officials appointed on the basis of educational and other nonstatus qualifications, who make careers within an established hierarchy of offices and have predefined spheres of competence. The distinctive mode of operation within a bureaucracy, as conceived by Weber, is the application of preexisting abstract rules to particular cases.

The final factor militating in favor of the rationalization of law is a clear separation of legal institutions along functional lines. For the most part, legislators make the rules, while the task of applying the law in specific instances is left to judges and other apolitical decision makers. In this way, law becomes endowed with considerable procedural autonomy while its substance remains within the control of political elites.

Rationalizing Russian Law. As this brief summary indicates, Weber's theory of the rationalization of law is remarkably rich and ambitious in its scope, weaving cultural, structural, and economic factors together into a cohesive whole.[30] But its applicability to the Russian case is not immediately apparent. The factors Weber identifies as necessary were strikingly absent for much of the Soviet period. The relevance of certain of these factors to the Soviet case, however, began to change as a result of reforms introduced during the later Gorbachev years and the post-Soviet era. Other aspects of Weber's theory are specific to the West European experience.[31] This is particularly true of the cultural elements, for example, a societal commitment to natural law and a European-style approach to legal education. Functional equivalents may exist in post-Soviet Russia, though the fit can never be exact.

Official Soviet legal doctrine rejected natural law as hopelessly bourgeois. The positivistic conceptualization of Soviet law as coterminous with the state left little room for appeals to higher authorities as the true source of law. Moreover, the principle that positive (statutory) law should yield to natural law, which is basic to natural law theory, directly contradicts the Soviet idea of law as an instrument to be used at the discretion of the political elite.

While natural law has yet to be embraced by the post-Soviet leadership of Russia, there is a burgeoning interest in human rights. Russian legislators and legal scholars have looked to principles of international human rights as guidelines when criticizing and reformulating positive law and administrative rules.[32] As with natural law, human rights law embodies abstract and humanistic values and reflects a universalistic approach to law. Assuming the commitment to human rights is genuine, it constitutes grounds for guarded optimism regarding the chances for the development of universalistic standards in Russia.

Similarly, Weber's emphasis on the continental system of legal education (with its conceptual and abstract approach to the study of law) in explaining the rationalization of law is problematic in the Russian context. While the logic of his argument is undeniable—teaching law students to think about law in terms of abstract principles encourages them to view law as autonomous, principled, and of universal applicability—its underlying premise flies in the face of the Russian reality. During the Soviet period, lawyers were taught to memorize statutory law not to think critically about law. Efforts are being made in post-Soviet Russia to reshape the institutions of legal education more in the Western image. In many cases, however, these efforts are being stymied by the older generation of scholars, who are unsettled by the prospect of reform. In the short term, the socialization of Russian lawyers as activists who mobilize the law on behalf of their clients is taking place in the new private law firms, not in the law schools. The influx of Western businessmen and their lawyers looking for business opportunities has had a profound impact on how law is practiced in Russia. Whether this on-the-job training can serve as an adequate substitute for a rigorous university-based program of legal education is unclear. Perhaps over time, a more Western approach will gradually be filtered back into the formal legal education system as Russian lawyers return to teach and to share their experiences.

Following the 1917 October Revolution, the sort of governmental structures that Weber viewed as essential to the rationalization of law was rejected. In the place of liberal democratic institutions, such as the separation of powers, the Soviet authorities introduced a dictatorship of the proletariat, under which the Communist Party assumed a virtual monopoly on political power. These were hardly the conditions under which the rule of law could be expected to take root.

Little changed until Gorbachev came to power and began his effort to revitalize the country politically and economically. Gorbachev and his cohort spoke frequently about the need for separation of powers within the government and for the professionalization of the administrative staff (both in the executive and legislative branches).[33] The rhetoric of their successors in the Russian government is similar. Symbolically, this represents a critical step away from the Soviet past, in which the Communist Party effectively dominated all governmental functions and politicized the bureaucracy. At the same time, these must be recognized as reforms that go to the very essence of the old system. Such profound changes cannot be realized by merely passing a law but require many years to be fully absorbed. The argument made in chapter 5 with regard to the structural reforms to the judicial system introduced in the late 1980s and early 1990s applies to the reforms more generally—they represent a move in the right direction but in practice remain largely changes in form rather than substance.

The final element in Weber's sociology of law is tied to the process of societal fragmentation or differentiation. He argues that a desire for law as a means of neutral arbitration is created as traditional society breaks down and competing groups emerge. In the West European context, the growth in size and power of the middle class, which coincided with, and to some extent caused, the breakdown of autocratic power, generated a new set of demands for predictability within society. The decisions of the ruler were no longer satisfactory. Instead, abstract rules were demanded that would bind both the nascent middle class and the former aristocracy by their terms.

It is this final theoretical insight of Weber's that provides the germ for my hypothesis regarding legal development in contemporary Russia. The argument is that law will come to matter when society demands it and that the single most important factor in generating that demand is the rise of market-based economic activity.

The unraveling of the Soviet administrative-command system and the introduction of market forces have given rise to a whole new set of pressures within the Russian economy and Russian society more generally. The incentive system has changed fundamentally. Profitability has replaced plan fulfillment as the key to success. With that change comes a new definition of what constitutes efficient and rational behavior. The emphasis has shifted from quantity to quality. Hoarding labor or raw materials and integrating vertically in order to be able to produce spare parts in house may no longer make economic sense.[34] In order to produce goods at the lowest possible cost and thereby generate income, such redundancies have to be eliminated or at least minimized.

At the same time as this sea change is proceeding in the Russian economy, a similar transformation is underway within the Russian power structure. The control of the Communist Party was effectively broken by the abortive coup of August 1991 (if not before), but who now holds the reins of power remains unclear. Thanks to the introduction of market forces and the loosening of controls over Soviet society during the Gorbachev years, new interest groups and nascent political parties have arisen and have gained some measure of political influence. These are the precise conditions—namely, the rapid differentiation of society and the emergence of a middle class—that Weber suggests provide fertile ground for the growth of rational law. He argues that as it becomes clear to all that no single group is going to triumph and that they will have to learn to live together, law as a means of arbitrating among them will emerge as a second-best solution for all concerned.[35] This scenario, of course, assumes a conceptualization of law as embodying abstract rules that are applied universalistically by a politically neutral judiciary and are backed by the coercive power of the state.

How this dynamic will play itself out in the Russian case remains uncertain. But an argument can be made that the demand for more meaningful law is present, if not yet openly acknowledged. Within the economy, for example, managers can no longer look to the industrial ministries for help when contractual obligations are breached. In theory, this should generate a desire for the contract itself to be enforceable. This, in turn, should stimulate a need for a workable contractual regime, that is, a substantive statutory law that meets the needs of economic actors and creates an impartial mechanism for resolving disputes. Similarly, ordinary citizens can no longer appeal to local Communist Party officials to solve problems. The predictability and security (for some) that previously stemmed from connections to the power elite now has to be sought through some alternative source.

But a demand for law, while necessary, is not sufficient on its own to vitalize law within Russian society. Indeed, this demand, if left unsatisfied, may have the effect of further diminishing the overall legitimacy of law due to dashed expectations. Thus, to make a difference the demand must be met by an adequate supply of law.

The state in the form of the legislature and the administrative agencies is the traditional supplier of law, and, while this is unlikely to change, the nature of the law-making process must be changed. For law to matter reciprocally, it must cease to be an exclusively top-down process; it must be reconceptualized as a collaborative effort in which both state and society participate. The abandonment of single-candidate elections and the opening up of the legislative process through television coverage would seem to represent steps in the right direction. At the same time, the road to political pluralism in Russia has been rocky in the post-Soviet period, and what shape the political system will take in the final analysis remains unclear.

Visions of the Russian Future

Whether law can be transformed in Russia remains an open question. There is no inevitable outcome to the overall transformation process currently underway in post-Soviet Russia. Yet the possibilities are not entirely limitless but depend rather on a number of contributory factors that are still evolving. Of these, perhaps the two most critical are the relationship between the state and the market and the institutional structure that underlies this relationship. Law and its role within Russian society represents one aspect of the interrelationship between politics and economics. At this point, three potential scenarios can be suggested.

The Fragmented State

The first possibility is that Russia will continue to muddle along much as it has since the breakup of the Soviet Union. During this period, the state has steadily withdrawn from the economy, as evidenced by the lifting of most price controls in early 1992, the opening of the economy to foreign investors, and the loosening of restrictions on foreign currency transactions by Russian nationals. The privatization of state enterprises, begun under the Soviet regime, has continued but in a remarkably haphazard fashion. Laws and regulations exist that ostensibly govern the privatization process, but they are riddled with inconsistencies and loop-holes that the managers of many state enterprises are using to their advantage. As a result, those with good connections to the Moscow government are able to set their own terms for privatization, while others are hamstrung by the law. Notwithstanding these shortcomings in the process, the fact remains that a significant percentage of industrial enterprises is now in private hands, at least nominally.[36]

In the post-Soviet period, the power of the state has been fractionalized. In fact, even arriving at a workable definition of the state is problematic. During the initial Yel'tsin period (January 1992–October 1993), political gridlock developed because of the inability of the authorities in Moscow to agree on Russia's political structure. While there was general agreement on the need for a division of power among the legislative, executive, and judicial branches, no one (either individually or institutionally) was eager to give up or even share power. The central authorities also had to face increasingly strident demands for greater autonomy on the part of regional officials and representatives of non-Russian ethnic minorities.[37] Consequently, the process of adopting a new constitution was tortuous.

In the realm of economics, the executive authorities favored a rapid transition to Western-style market capitalism during this initial period.[38] In contrast, the Russian legislature, admittedly a fractious body, generally favored a slower pace for economic reform and blocked numerous efforts to introduce private ownership of land and other market-related institutions.

Yel'tsin attempted to break the stalemate in October 1993 by dissolving the parliament. The legislators, however, did not go quietly into the night. Tensions escalated and, ultimately, Yel'tsin responded militarily.[39] These events vividly symbolize the absence of tolerance in Russian politics. The December 1993 elections that followed produced a parliament (the Duma) that, like its predecessor, had profound misgivings about market reforms. Although the ratification of the constitution by referendum as part of these elections meant that the basic structure of the government was now in place, disagreements between the executive and legislative branches continued.

In some cases, regional authorities responded to the gridlock in Moscow by taking matters into their own hands, that is, creating the institutional structure and passing the laws needed to allow the market to work.[40] While these tendencies toward decentralization may turn out to be positive in the long run in that they may give rise to a vibrant federalist system of government in Russia, in the short run they have only further undermined the people's trust in law as a stable force within society.

The old state structures, premised on the monopolistic control of the Communist Party, disintegrated (or were consciously destroyed) before new ones could develop to take their place. In this power vacuum, private groups have emerged and have taken on quasi-governmental functions such as maintaining social order and contractual compliance. Typically, their services are costly and nonvoluntary, and their enforcement tactics are brutally violent.[41] Further complicating matters is the widespread corruption among governmental officials.[42] The weakness of the Russian state makes it incapable of stemming the tide of corruption (both public and private) and has effectively rendered meaningless the laws that declared such activities illegal.

The prospects for Russian society seem rather dangerous. In the absence of a state capable of supplying abstract rules, applying them universalistically, and possessing the power to enforce social order, corruption is running rampant.[43] Despite the high-minded rhetoric about the need for a law-based state, the chances for evolution toward the rule of law in Russia have only grown more remote in the years since the breakup of the Soviet Union. Thus, not only does Russian law seem to be evolving away from mattering in a reciprocal sense, it seems to be retreating even from mattering in the coercive sense it did during the Soviet period. The state is unwilling or unable to stem the tide, and the short-term result is a society marked by instability, at times verging on chaos.

The Developmental State

A second more speculative scenario for the future of Russia is premised on the reemergence of a strong state. While such a state would undoubtedly assume an interventionist role vis-à-vis the economy, its model would not be the now discredited Soviet administrative-command system but the industrial capitalism found in Japan and the newly industrialized countries of East Asia. This model calls for a "developmental state" that manages economic policy through controlled competition.[44] The state pursues aggressive trade export policies while nurturing fledgling industries in strategic sectors and protecting them from domestic competition from imports. These policies are implemented by a professional (Weberian) bureaucracy with broad authority and freedom from political controls. Johnson argues that legislative and judicial authorities should have only "safety valve" functions, that is, they should be ready to step in if the bureaucracy oversteps its authority but should not control economic policy on a day-to-day basis.[45]

In the developmental state, law plays a primarily instrumental role, a tool of the state's efforts to facilitate economic development. Flexibility is essential to its success, which leads to a greater dependence on administrative regulations than on statutory law. This, in turn, undermines the idea of law as a societal touchstone, one of the central tenets of a legal culture based on the rule of law. Indeed, it is worth recalling the complementary nature of instrumentalism and the rule of law as societal forces. On the other hand, the developmental state model does not contemplate instrumentalism run rampant. The discretion of the state is held in check by the legislative and judicial branches of government, which possess sufficient independence and authority to declare acts of the state bureaucracy invalid and enforce such decisions.

As my discussion of the role of law suggests, the model of the developmental state appears to share many of the characteristics of the Soviet model. Both envision an activist state, operating administratively, that controls economic policy and the behavior of enterprises. But as with the role of law, closer examination reveals the similarities to be only skin deep. In contrast to the Soviet state, which was all encompassing and took responsibility for reshaping society and its citizens in the image of Leninism, the developmental state is concerned first and foremost with economic development. This defining task is pursued by focusing on certain sectors determined to be of strategic importance. A second difference lies in attitudes toward the market. The Soviet model denied the importance of market forces in stimulating efficient behavior among economic actors and replaced the market with its own indicators of success, which were set forth in the plan. The developmental state model seeks market-conforming methods of state intervention. Competition is not outlawed but is embraced, and this requires a certain degree of autonomy for law, at least in the realms of property and contract. Finally, the two models diverge with respect to the nature of their bureaucracies. The Soviet model required an administrative apparatus that served the Communist Party, not a professional staff that applied preexisting abstract rules to particular problems. In contrast, a Weberian bureaucracy is a sine qua non of the developmental state.

Although the differences between the developmental state and the

Soviet state models can be clearly documented in conceptual terms, in real life their apparent similarities make for a slippery slope in which the former could well slide into the latter. Having been socialized within the Soviet state, the Russian authorities, by deciding to pursue the developmental model, would seem to be raising the real danger of drifting, perhaps unintentionally, into familiar behavioral patterns of the past.

The Liberal State

The final scenario, also speculative, envisions a state that takes a relatively hands-off approach to the economy. To be sure, the state takes affirmative steps to create the institutional underpinnings of the market and, in some cases, it assumes the role of regulator or monitor.[46] But the state does not control the economy—there is no mandatory economic plan—nor is it the primary force shaping the economy. Instead, the state acts as a facilitator: it establishes the framework within which the economy develops through its policies on such matters as antitrust, the environment, and labor relations. Naturally, the state must be strong enough to enforce the law vigorously. But economic actors make their decisions independently, taking into account the dictates of the law and the likely responses of competitors and consumers.

Under this scenario, the law is available to both state and society as an instrument to further its interests. The courts serve as neutral decision makers, sufficiently independent to rule against the politically powerful when warranted and sufficiently powerful to enforce such rulings. In terms of working out substantive law, the state must become responsive to the needs of society, reflecting an understanding of law as a collaborative enterprise, and giving rise to a feeling among citizens that law grows out of society rather than being imposed upon it. The laws so developed must be applied universalistically. This scenario posits a relationship between political and economic forces that will allow law to matter in a reciprocal fashion.

The tensions within post-Soviet Russian society that militate in favor of this outcome have previously been alluded to but merit restating. As the transition to the market (including privatization of state enterprises) continues and as managers struggle to cope in a world marked by uncertainty, logic suggests that they will demand the introduction of generally applicable rules that will govern their relationships with other economic actors. Initially, these demands will most likely be concentrated in the contractual realm because this is where the need is most acute. If and when contractual law becomes a reliable resource, providing meaningful and enforceable remedies, managers will use it to defend and advance their interests. Furthermore, as citizens become accustomed to law mattering in economic transactions, they may well extend their demands to other sectors. Mobilizing law may become a habit among significant portions of the population, thereby providing the cultural base for the institutionalization of the rule of law.

Two central lessons emerge from these reflections on what the future holds for Russia. The first is that a demand on the part of ordinary citizens for law that matters in a reciprocal sense will not necessarily be answered by the state. Thus, societal demand is a necessary but not sufficient condition for the evolution of the rule of law. The second lesson is that there are many different factors that influence the capacity of the state to meet such demands. Primary among them is an ability on the part of the state to maintain some minimal level of cohesion and authority within society. While the Soviet past demonstrated that an overly strong state is inherently incompatible with a reciprocal notion of law, the Russian present demonstrates just as compellingly that an overly weak state is equally problematic. The state's ability to fulfill the supply side of the equation is also profoundly affected by the nature of the political and economic structures that develop.

Conclusion: Final Theoretical Speculations

We have now come full circle and return to the questions with which we began this study. Under what conditions does law come to matter in a reciprocal fashion? How does law become a stable and effective force within society, capable of restraining official arbitrariness?

At the most basic level, the role played by law in a given society depends on how law is defined by the political elite and the citizenry. If law is narrowly conceived and understood as a tool of social control to be exercised by the state, ordinary citizens will be unlikely to mobilize it to advance their interests or to protect themselves from intrusive state action. By the same token, legal institutions will be unlikely to encourage this sort of activist behavior by nonstate actors. On the other hand, a more inclusive conception of law as an interactive process in which state and society participate on relatively equal footing provides an opening for law to be used by a wider spectrum of society.

But the broad acceptance of a reciprocal notion of law does not in and of itself guarantee that law will matter in a reciprocal fashion—that the rule of law will flourish. Also important is the character of the society and of the state. The development of the rule of law requires that society be sufficiently differentiated—both politically and economically—so that no single group or class can fully dominate.

Political differentiation or pluralism brings a tolerance of dissent that is essential to reciprocal law. Nongovernmental groups of all kinds (whose power stems from their potential impact on the political process) are able to criticize existing law and affect its evolution, thereby ensuring that it is not allowed to stagnate. These groups are also able to monitor the implementation of law and disclose to the public the extent to which the government's actions live up to the promises embodied in the law. Naturally, a free press also helps to keep government honest—thanks not only to its day-to-day reporting but also to the implicit threat of exposure posed by an inquisitive press.

Political differentation can, however, be taken too far and can actually undermine the evolution of reciprocal law. If society becomes fragmented (whether due to political, economic, or ethnic pressures) to the extent that chaos ensues, a hue and cry is likely to go up for a "strong hand." The need for a strong state that can maintain order and eliminate social strife will drive the rule of law off the political agenda.

Economic differentiation within society gives rise to a desire for regularity in trading relationships. This is the dynamic that Weber described so vividly of merchants demanding rules of general applicability to govern market relationships. There are at least two ways in which their demands can be answered. One possibility is the emergence of a relatively strong state that makes economic development its raison d'être. This is the developmental state option outlined in the preceding section. It does not allow much autonomy for law in the economic realm; the state prefers the flexibility of administrative acts to the predictability of legislation. This does not mean that law cannot matter reciprocally but that the degree of stability of law will be less (at least in the economy). The other possibility assumes a state that is weaker or that does not define itself in terms of economic development. In such a case, the law becomes more important. By establishing a relatively immutable framework for economic transactions, the law embodies the rules of the game. At the same time, the pluralistic nature of society ensures that these rules do not outlive their usefulness.

It is important to recognize that economic development in the contemporary age is subject to pressure from the international financial community, on both an institutional and individual level.[47] International financial institutions, such as the World Bank and the International Monetary Fund, influence the course of economic development (and ultimately the nature of the state) by making specific demands and then tying the delivery of desperately needed loans and credits to the accomplishment of these goals. Individual businessmen can have an impact by refusing to invest without certain legal guarantees, thereby providing an incentive for local economic actors to pressure the government for the creation of a Western-style legal regime.

While the pressure exerted by outsiders can act as a catalyst, it may not be entirely positive in the long run. If laws are passed as a result of pressure from the international community before the target society is ready for them, these laws will lie dormant. In the case of Russia, this will only deepen the cynicism of ordinary citizens about law. Periodic efforts to solve problems by passing high-profile laws to which no one paid attention in reality was symptomatic of the Soviet period. The emergence of a similar pattern under Gorbachev and Yel'tsin leads people to assume it is just more of the same.

In addition to a politically and economically differentiated society, there are certain characteristics of the state that tend to facilitate the evolution of reciprocal law. In essence, the state must be (1) sufficiently strong to maintain social control and to collect taxes in order to sustain at least a minimal level of public services and (2) sufficiently secure to permit dissent. Both aspects are relevant to the sort of legal institutions needed to support reciprocal law. On the one hand, the courts must be perceived as institutionally independent from the political elite, and judges must be perceived as honest and impartial. On the other hand, the courts must have the power and authority to enforce their decisions, particularly when they go against the state. Ordinary citizens will appeal to the courts only if they believe that the courts are not irrevocably biased in favor of the state or other powerful interest groups.

The foregoing discussion, with its emphasis on the need for a legitimate state and for pluralism in the political and economic arenas, raises the question of democracy. Is a democratic form of government necessary for the evolution of law that matters in a reciprocal fashion? Probably not, if what we are talking about is not necessarily American-style free-for-all democracy. As the outline of possible scenarios of the Russian future demonstrates, there is no single path to law that matters. Basically, reciprocal law requires a tolerance of dissent. This, in turn, requires a public willing to criticize the government and a government willing to listen carefully to such criticism and not bring down the coercive machinery of the state on those who originated the criticism.

But it is important to recognize that it is not just an overly strong state that dooms the evolution of law that matters in a reciprocal fashion. Certainly the history of the Soviet Union demonstrates that the two cannot coexist peacefully. In many ways, however, an overly weak state poses just as many dangers for the development of reciprocal law. After all, if the state is incapable of enforcing legislation, the fact that this legislation emerged through some kind of negotiation between state and society will be irrelevant because no one will pay attention to it. Striking a balance between a state that is too strong and one that is too weak is certainly not easy. Whether Russia will be able to do so remains an open question.

Notes

Chapter 1: Introduction

1. See Max Weber, *Economy and Society,* eds. Guenther Roth and Claus Wittich (Berkeley: University of California Press, 1978), 1:31–36. Note that, under this definition, law may or may not be written.

2. See E. Adamson Hoebel, *The Law of Primitive Man: A Study in Comparative Legal Dynamics* (Cambridge, MA: Harvard University Press, 1954), chap. 2; compare Donald Black, *The Behavior of Law* (New York: Academic Press, 1976), 2–10.

3. See Harold J. Berman, *Justice in the U.S.S.R.: An Interpretation of Soviet Law,* rev. ed. (Cambridge, MA: Harvard University Press, 1963); Ingo Muller, *Hitler's Justice: The Courts of the Third Reich,* trans. Deborah Lucas Schneider (Cambridge, MA: Harvard University Press, 1991).

4. See, generally, Lon L. Fuller, *The Morality of Law,* rev. ed. (New Haven: Yale University Press, 1969); Philip Selznick, *Law, Society, and Industrial Justice* (New York: Russell Sage Foundation, 1969).

5. For a definition of "autonomous law," see Philippe Nonet and Philip Selznick, *Law and Society in Transition: Toward Responsive Law* (New York: Octagon Books, 1978), 29–52.

6. Gorbachev was the first person with legal education since Lenin to lead the Soviet Union. Robert G. Kaiser (*Why Gorbachev Happened: His Triumphs, His Failure, and His Fall* [New York: Simon and Schuster, 1991], 226) comments that Gorbachev's calls for a "socialist legal state" were "the fruits of Gorbachev's legal education thirty years earlier." The doctrinaire nature of Soviet legal education makes such a link unlikely. See Dusko Doder and Louise Branson, *Gorbachev: Heretic in the Kremlin* (New York: Viking Penguin, 1990), 8–9; and Zhores A. Medvedev, *Gorbachev* (New York: W. W. Norton, 1986), 35–43.

7. The Communist Party of the Soviet Union approved political and legal reforms designed to create a socialist law-based state at the Nineteenth Party Conference in July 1988 (*Pravda,* [5 July 1988]: 3). See, generally, V. N. Kudriavtsev and E. A. Lukasheva, "Sotsialisticheskoe pravovoe gosudarstvo," *Kommunist,* no. 11 (1988): 44–55; G. N. Manov, "Sotsialisticheskoe pravovoe gusodarstvo: problemy i perspektivy," *Sovetskoe gosudarstvo i pravo,* no. 6 (1989): 3–10; and I. L.

Petrukhin, "Pravovoe gosudarstvo i pravosudie," *Sovetskoe gosudarstvo i pravo,* no. 1 (1991): 19–29. For a helpful discussion of the meaning of *pravovoe gosudarstvo,* which places the term in theoretical perspective, see Harold J. Berman, "The Rule of Law and the Law-Based State (*Rechtsstaat*)," *The Harriman Institute Forum* 4, no. 5 (1991).

8. For example, N. G. Aleksandrov, *Soviet Labour Law* (Delhi, India: University Book House, 1961); O. S. Ioffe, *Sovetskoe grazhdanskoe pravo,* 3 vols. (Leningrad: Izdatel'stvo Leningradskogo Universiteta, 1958–65); V. V. Laptev, "Zakon o predpriiatii i kodifikatsiia khoziastvennogo zakonodatel'stva," *Sovetskoe gosudarstvo i pravo,* no. 12 (1987): 67–74; V. A. Maslennikov, "Zakon o trudovykh kollektivakh," *Sovetskoe gosudarstvo i pravo,* no. 10 (1983): 3–9; and K. A. Shaibekov, "Pravo sel'skokhoziaistvennogo zemlenopol'zovaniia v SSSR," *Sovetskoe gosudarstvo i pravo,* no. 3 (1977): 50–57.

9. For example, V. I. Nikitinskii, *Effektivnost' norm trudovogo prava* (Moscow: Iuridicheskaia literatura, 1971).

10. See Louise Shelley, "Soviet Courts as Vehicles for Political Maneuver," *Soviet Union* 13, no. 2 (1986): 163–86.

11. For example, Olympiad S. Ioffe and Peter B. Maggs, *Soviet Law in Theory and Practice* (New York: Oceana Publications, 1983); Olympiad S. Ioffe, *Soviet Law and Soviet Reality* (Dordrecht, the Netherlands: Martinus Nijhoff, 1985); Dina Kaminskaya, *Final Judgment: My Life as a Soviet Defense Attorney,* trans. Michael Glenny (New York: Simon and Schuster, 1982); and Konstantin M. Simis, *USSR: The Corrupt Society,* trans. Jacqueline Edwards and Mitchell Schneider (New York: Simon and Schuster, 1982).

12. My difficulties in gaining access to industrial enterprises and trial courts when carrying out my field research for this study in Moscow from 1989–90 are discussed in chapter 4. It is worth noting that the suspicion of foreigners has not disappeared with the demise of the Soviet Union. While doing research in an aircraft factory in Saratov in 1993 and 1994, local state security officers questioned factory employees about their contacts with me.

13. For example, George M. Armstrong, *The Soviet Law of Property* (The Hague: Martinus Nijhoff, 1983); Donald D. Barry, "The Soviet Union," in *Governmental Tort Liability,* ed. Donald D. Barry (Leyden, the Netherlands: A. W. Sijthoff, 1970), 21–78; George Ginsburgs, *The Citizenship Law of the USSR* (Boston: Martinus Nijhoff, 1983); Serge L. Levitsky, *Copyright, Defamation, and Privacy in Soviet Civil Law* (Alphen aan den Rijn, the Netherlands: Sijthoff & Noordhoff, 1979); Michael A. Newcity, *Taxation in the Soviet Union* (New York: Praeger, 1986); and Gordon B. Smith, *The Soviet Procuracy and the Supervision of Administration* (Alphen aan den Rijn, the Netherlands: Sijthoff & Noordhoff, 1978).

14. Mary McAuley, *Labour Disputes in Soviet Russia, 1957–65* (Oxford: Clarendon Press, 1969).

15. Similarly helpful are the studies of Soviet enterprises conducted by Western economists, which are based primarily on written sources but are augmented by interviews with émigrés and some first-hand observations. For example, Joseph S. Berliner, *Factory and Manager in the USSR* (Cambridge, MA: Harvard University

Press, 1957); and David Granick, *The Red Executive: A Study of the Organization Man in Russian Industry* (Garden City, NY: Doubleday, 1960).

16. Nicholas Lampert, *Whistleblowing in the Soviet Union: Complaints and Abuses under State Socialism* (London: Macmillan, 1985).

17. Louise I. Shelley's monograph on the role of lawyers in the Soviet workplace, *Lawyers in Soviet Work Life* (New Brunswick: Rutgers University Press, 1984), a valuable source, was also based largely on interviews with emigres in Israel.

18. Whistle-blowers would not seem to be the most appropriate test case insofar as their supervisors usually have a strong personal interest in their dismissal and so become highly motivated to find a way around the law. This is not unique to the Soviet case but is an inescapable fact of economic life everywhere. See Myron P. Glazer and Penina M. Glazer, *The Whistleblowers: Exposing Corruption in Government and Industry* (New York: Basic Books, 1989), chap. 5.

19. George Feifer, *Justice in Moscow* (New York: Simon and Schuster, 1964).

20. Robert Rand, *Comrade Lawyer* (Boulder, CO: Westview Press, 1991). Rand's research focused primarily on the defense bar (*advokatura*) in Moscow, but following these lawyers took him frequently to local trial courts.

21. See, generally, David Remnick, *Lenin's Tomb: The Last Days of the Soviet Empire* (New York: Random House, 1993).

22. See Kenneth Jowitt, *New World Disorder: The Leninist Extinction* (Berkeley and Los Angeles: University of California Press, 1992), 284–305; and David Stark, "Path Dependence and Privatization Strategies in East Central Europe," *Eastern European Politics and Societies,* 6, no. 1 (1992): 48–54.

23. For example, Harold J. Berman, *Law and Revolution: The Formation of the Western Legal Tradition* (Cambridge, MA: Harvard University Press, 1983); Roberto M. Unger, *Law in Modern Society: Toward a Criticism of Social Theory* (New York: Free Press, 1976); and Max Weber, *Max Weber on Law in Economy and Society,* ed. Max Rheinstein (Cambridge, MA: Harvard University Press, 1967).

24. For a thoughtful discussion of the difficulty of applying Weber's theory in a non-Western context, see Daniel S. Lev, "Judicial Authority and the Struggle for an Indonesian Rechtsstaat," *Law & Society Review* 13, no. 1 (1978): 37–43.

25. In the wake of the breakup of the Soviet Union, there has been much debate within the scholarly community as to why Sovietologists were unable to predict the demise. For example, George W. Breslauer, "In Defense of Sovietology," *Post-Soviet Affairs* 8, no. 3 (1992): 197–238; Michael Burawoy, "The End of Sovietology and the Renaissance of Modernization Theory," *Contemporary Sociology* 21, no. 6 (1992): 774–85; and Theodore Draper, "Who Killed Soviet Communism?" *New York Review of Books* 39, no. 11 (June 11, 1992): 7–14.

26. For example, Guillermo O'Donnell, Philippe C. Schmitter, and Laurence Whitehead, eds., *Transitions from Authoritarian Rule: Prospects for Democracy* (Baltimore: Johns Hopkins University Press, 1986); Giuseppe Di Palma, *To Craft Democracies: An Essay on Democratic Transitions* (Berkeley and Los Angeles: University of California Press, 1990). For a debate on the usefulness of the transi-

tions literature in the post-Leninist context, compare Philippe C. Schmitter and Terry Lynn Karl, "The Conceptual Travels of Transitologists and Consolidologists: How Far East Should They Attempt to Go?" *Slavic Review* 53, no. 1 (1994): 173–85; Valerie Bunce, "Should Transitologists Be Grounded?" *Slavic Review* 54, no. 1 (1995): 111–27.

27. Logic suggests that such demands will not be limited to the contractual arena but will extend to legal protection of property rights, protection against fraud, and so on. See Kathryn Hendley, "The Spillover Effects of Privatization on Russian Legal Culture," *Transnational Law & Contemporary Problems* 5, no. 1 (1995): 39–64.

Chapter 2: Law under Capitalism and Leninism

1. Martin Krygier, "Marxism and the Rule of Law: Reflections after the Collapse of Communism," *Law & Social Inquiry* 15, no. 4 (1990): 639.

2. See, generally, Milovan Djilas, *The New Class: An Analysis of the Communist System* (New York: Praeger, 1957); and Michael S. Voslenskii, *Nomenklatura,* trans. Eric Mosbacher (Garden City, NJ: Doubleday, 1984).

3. Jane Henderson, "Law of the USSR: On the Status of Judges in the USSR," *Review of Socialist Law* 16, no. 3 (1990): 314–16; and George Ginsburgs, "The Soviet Judicial Elite: Is It?" *Review of Socialist Law* 11, no. 4 (1985): 300–304.

4. Inga Markovits, "Law and *Glasnost':* Some Thoughts about the Future of Judicial Review under Socialism," *Law & Society Review* 23, no. 3 (1989): 400.

5. Ibid., 406.

6. John Henry Merryman sets forth the criteria for distinguishing between legal systems in *The Civil Law Tradition: An Introduction to the Legal Systems of Western Europe and Latin America,* 2d ed. (Stanford: Stanford University Press, 1985), 1–5. The less than satisfying nature of this categorization scheme has been recognized by many scholars. For example, Martin M. Shapiro, *Courts: A Comparative and Political Analysis* (Chicago: University of Chicago Press, 1981), 1–64, 126–56; and Alan Watson, *The Making of the Civil Law* (Cambridge, MA: Harvard University Press, 1981), 1–13.

7. Unger, *Law in Modern Society,* 56–57, 176. Unger goes on (192–223) to argue that certain characteristics of the present-day welfare state tend to undermine the rule of law.

8. Selznick, *Law, Society, and Industrial Justice,* 11.

9. Krygier ("Marxism and the Rule of Law," 645) notes that the "elements [of the rule of law] are nowhere fully or uniformly realized but are approximated to greater or lesser degree in different societies." See also John Hasnas, "The Myth of the Rule of Law," *Wisconsin Law Review,* no. 1 (1995), 199–233.

10. Ronald Dworkin, *Law's Empire* (Cambridge, MA: Harvard University Press, 1986), 92–95, 217–19, 224–76.

11. Selznick, *Industrial Justice,* 8.

12. Unger, *Law in Modern Society,* 57, 176–79.

13. For a survey of the various roles played by law, see Steve D. Smith, "Reductionism in Legal Thought," *Columbia Law Review* 91, no. 1 (1991): 68–109; and

Charles G. Howard and Robert S. Summers, *Law: Its Nature, Functions, and Limits* (Englewood Cliffs, NJ: Prentice-Hall, 1965).

14. For a critical legal scholar's catalog of the shortcomings of Western legal systems, see Richard L. Abel, "Capitalism and the Rule of Law: Precondition or Contradiction?" *Law & Social Inquiry* 15, no. 4 (1990): 685–97.

15. See, generally, Hans Kelsen, *Pure Theory of Law,* trans. Max Knight (Berkeley and Los Angeles: University of California Press, 1967); compare Joseph Raz, "The Purity of the Pure Theory," in *Essays on Kelsen,* eds. Richard Tur and William Twining (Oxford: Clarendon Press, 1986), 79–97.

16. Lon L. Fuller, *The Morality of Law,* 106.

17. Unger, *Law in Modern Society,* 144–45, 166–73, 178.

18. Tom R. Tyler, *Why People Obey the Law* (New Haven: Yale University Press, 1990), 57–68.

19. See, generally, Max Weber, *Law* ; and Unger, *Law in Modern Society,* 75–80.

20. Ed Rubin, "Law and Legislation in the Administrative State," *Columbia Law Review* 89, no. 2 (1989): 369–427.

21. There is a wide-ranging literature on how the "rule of law" should be defined. For example, Fuller, *The Morality of the Law;* Franz Neumann, *The Rule of Law: Political Theory and the Legal System in Modern Society* (Dover, NH: Berg Publishers, 1986); Joseph Raz, "The Rule of Law and Its Virture," in *The Authority of Law: Essays on Law and Morality* (Oxford: Clarendon Press, 1979), 210–29.

22. For example, Unger, *Law in Modern Society,* 177.

23. Selznick, *Industrial Justice,* 11.

24. While agreeing that law in liberal democracies is generally thought to constrain power, Unger (*Law in Modern Society,* 179–81) questions whether this is actually possible. This echoes Weber, *Law,* 228.

25. Fuller, *The Morality of Law,* 39–40.

26. For a discussion of what constitutes judicial independence, see chap. 5. See, generally, Shapiro, *Courts,* 19–35.

27. Compare Judith Resnik, "Managerial Judges," *Harvard Law Review* 96, no. 2 (1986): 376–448; and Abram Chayes, "The Role of the Judge in Public Law Litigation," *Harvard Law Review* 89, no. 7 (1976): 1281–316.

28. Nonet and Selznick, *Law and Society in Transition,* 58.

29. The heavy reliance upon judicial precedent in common law systems means that judges within such systems are more often called upon to "make" law than are their Romanist counterparts. In recent years in the United States, the question of how and when judges should "make" law has become highly charged politically. John Hart Ely (*Democracy and Distrust: A Theory of Judicial Review* [Cambridge, MA: Harvard University Press, 1980], 1–72) provides a useful analysis of the battle between interpretivists (strict constructionists) and noninterpretivists (lawmakers). For a harsher view of judicial lawmaking, see Robert H. Bork, *The Tempting of America: The Political Seduction of the Law* (New York: Free Press, 1990).

30. Fuller, *The Morality of Law,* 33–94.

31. Selznick (*Industrial Justice,* 13–14) notes the danger of procedural regularity degenerating into "legalism."

32. Weber, *Law,* 61–64, 224–55.

33. Edmond N. Cahn, *The Sense of Injustice: An Anthropocentric View of Law* (New York: New York University Press, 1949), 13.

34. Ibid.; Fuller, *The Morality of Law,* 12.

35. Cahn, *The Sense of Injustice,* 13–14.

36. Judith N. Shklar, *The Faces of Injustice* (New Haven: Yale University Press, 1990), 83. She goes on to discuss the intellectual history of the sense of injustice, 84–101.

37. See William L. F. Felstiner, Richard L. Abel and Austin Sarat, "The Emergence and Transformation of Disputes: Naming, Blaming, Claiming . . . ," *Law & Society Review* 15, nos. 3–4 (1980–81): 631–54; Marc Galanter, "Reading the Landscape of Disputes: What We Know and Don't Know (and Think We Know) About Our Allegedly Contentious and Litigious Society," *UCLA Law Review* 31, no. 4 (1983): 5 ff.

38. Compare Clyde Summers, "Effective Remedies for Employment Rights: Preliminary Guidelines and Proposals," *University of Pennsylvania Law Review* 141, no. 2 (1992): 457–546; and Inga Markovits, "Pursuing One's Rights under Socialism," *Stanford Law Review* 38, no. 3 (1986): 689–761.

39. See Donald J. Black, "The Mobilization of Law," *The Journal of Legal Studies* 2, no. 1 (1973): 132–44.

40. See, generally, David Remnick, *Lenin's Tomb;* Martin Malia, "A New Russian Revolution?" *New York Review of Books* 38, no. 13 (July 18, 1991): 29–31; and Timothy Garton Ash, *The Uses of Adversity: Essays on the Fate of Central Europe* (New York: Random House, 1989), 218–73.

41. See Stark, "Path Dependence," 17–54.

42. See Jowitt, *New World Disorder,* 284–305.

43. See, generally, Zbigniew K. Brzezinski, *The Soviet Bloc: Unity and Conflict,* rev. ed. (Cambridge, MA: Harvard University Press, 1967), 67–138.

44. For example, John Quigley, "Socialist Law and the Civil Law Tradition," *American Journal of Comparative Law* 37, no. 4 (fall 1989): 781–808; and Harold J. Berman, "What Makes 'Socialist Law' Socialist?" *Problems of Communism* 20, no. 5 (1977): 24–30. A more subtle approach is suggested by Rodolfo Sacco, "The Romanist Substratum in the Civil Law of the Socialist Countries," *Review of Socialist Law* 14, no. 1 (1988): 65–86.

45. Nonet and Selznick, *Law and Society in Transition,* 29–52. Unger (*Law in Modern Society,* 67) uses the label "bureaucratic law" to capture the same phenomenon.

46. For example, the five-year and annual economic plans had the force of law.

47. The Soviet system presupposed the close identification of the state with the Communist Party. See John N. Hazard, *The Soviet System of Government,* 3d ed. (Chicago: University of Chicago Press, 1964), 44–48.

48. See, generally, Hugh Collins, *Marxism and Law* (Oxford: Oxford University Press, 1982).

49. Nonet and Selznick, *Law and Society in Transition,* 39–40, suggest that this tendency for rulers to identify their interests with those of the community is com-

mon to regimes operating under repressive law. See also Unger, *Law in Modern Society,* 53, 67.

50. On the development of democratic centralism, see Leonard Shapiro, *The Communist Party of the Soviet Union,* 2d ed. (New York: Vintage Books, 1971), 201–34.

51. Quoted in Nonet and Selznick, *Law and Society in Transition,* 32.

52. Collins, *Marxism and Law,* 100–108. See, generally, Jane Burbank, "Lenin and the Law," *Slavic Review* 54, no. 1 (1995), 23–44.

53. Robert Tucker, ed., "State and Revolution," in *The Lenin Anthology* (New York: W. W. Norton, 1975), 314–15, 369–84.

54. John N. Hazard, *Settling Disputes in Soviet Society: The Formative Years of Legal Institutions* (New York: Columbia University Press, 1960), 1–9; and Shapiro, *The Communist Party of the Soviet Union,* 265–70.

55. Berman, *Justice in the U.S.S.R.,* 29–33.

56. See ibid., 31–46; Gregory J. Massell, *The Surrogate Proletariat: Moslem Women and Revolutionary Strategies in Soviet Central Asia* (Princeton: Princeton University Press, 1974), 185–212.

57. For a general overview of Pashukanis's theory, see Piers Beirne and Robert Sharlet, "Toward a General Theory of Law and Marxism: E. B. Pashukanis," in *Revolution in Law: Contributions to the Development of Soviet Legal Theory, 1917–1938,* ed. Piers Beirne (Armonk, NY: M. E. Sharpe, 1990), 17–44; and Robert Sharlet, "Pashukanis and the Rise of Soviet Marxist Jurisprudence, 1924–1930," *Soviet Union* 1, no. 2 (1974): 103–21.

58. Robert Sharlet, "Pashukanis and the Withering Away of the Law in the USSR," in *Cultural Revolution in Russia, 1928–1931,* ed. Sheila Fitzpatrick (Bloomington: Indiana University Press, 1984), 171.

59. Ibid., 170.

60. Arkady Vaksberg details the tragic fate of Pashukanis under Stalin in *Stalin's Prosecutor: The Life of Andrei Vyshinsky,* trans. Jan Butler (New York: Grove Weidenfeld, 1991), 127–30.

61. Robert Sharlet, "Stalinism and Soviet Legal Culture," in *Stalinism: Essays in Historical Interpretation,* ed. Robert C. Tucker (New York: W. W. Norton, 1977), 168–78.

62. Ibid., 155.

63. For example, Aleksandr I. Solzhenitsyn, *The Gulag Archipelago: 1918–1956, I–II,* trans. Thomas P. Whitney (New York: Harper & Row, 1973), 299–455; and Robert Conquest, *The Great Terror: A Reassessment* (New York: Oxford University Press, 1990), 261–90.

64. See Sharlet, "Stalinism," 178–79.

65. Hazard, *Settling Disputes,* 4, 17.

66. Ibid., 17.

67. Certain administrative penalties were theoretically possible, but such in-house remedies were not terribly effective.

68. See, generally, Barry, "The Soviet Union," 21–78; and Christopher

Osakwe, "An Examination of the Modern Soviet Law of Torts," *Tulane Law Review* 84, no. 1 (1979): 1–79.

69. Article 58 of the 1977 Constitution purported to give citizens the right to sue officials when harmed by their misconduct, but this right proved illusory due to the failure to enact enabling legislation. See Donald D. Barry, "Compensation for Damages Caused by the Acts of Soviet Criminal Justice Organs: The 1981 Legislation," *Review of Socialist Law* 8, no. 4 (1982): 331–40.

70. See chapter 5 for a more detailed discussion of what factors are relevent in determining the relative independence of the judiciary.

71. Hazard, *Settling Disputes,* 3–5.

72. Shapiro, *The Communist Party of the Soviet Union,* 265–70. Nonet and Selznick (*Law and Society in Transition,* 51) argue that "the direct subordination of legal institutions to public and private governing elites" is one of the cardinal features of repressive law.

73. Hazard, *Settling Disputes.*

74. Ibid., 47–50.

75. Though the courts of general jurisdiction were not always involved in political cases during and after the Stalin period, the fact remains that the proceedings carried the color of law. The impact over time was to tarnish law and legal institutions in the eyes of ordinary citizens.

76. I am grateful to Peter Solomon for drawing this to my attention.

77. For example, Joseph E. Davies, *Mission to Moscow* (New York: Simon and Schuster, 1941), 261–62, 268–80. Davies was the American ambassador to the USSR from 1936 to 1938 and attended many of the high-profile purge trials.

78. Vaksberg (*Stalin's Prosecutor,* 97) notes that, had their roles not been identified, he would have been unable to tell the difference between prosecutors and defense counsel by the trial transcript.

79. Ibid., 170, 189. Evgenia Ginzburg (*Journey into the Whirlwind,* trans. Paul Stevenson and Max Hayward [New York, Harcourt, Brace & World, 1967], 62) reports that her trial lasted only seven minutes and that the court returned its verdict of guilty after only two minutes of deliberation. Yet she estimates that the decision must have taken twenty minutes to type, clearly indicating that it had been prepared in advance.

80. See, generally, Robert C. Tucker, "Stalin, Bukharin, and History as Conspiracy," in *The Soviet Political Mind: Stalinism and Post-Stalin Change* (New York: W. W. Norton, 1971), 49–86.

81. For example, Lydia Chukovskaya, *Sofia Petrovna,* trans. Aline Werth (Evanston, IL: Northwestern University Press, 1967).

82. A translation of the "secret speech" is set forth as an appendix to Khrushchev's memoirs. Strobe Talbott, trans. and ed., *Khrushchev Remembers* (Boston: Little, Brown, 1970), 559–618.

83. Berman, *Justice in the U.S.S.R.,* 70–72.

84. The failure to replace politically tainted judges does not inevitably undermine citizens' trust in the legal system, as the history of post-Nazi Germany demonstrates. See Muller, *Hitler's Justice,* 201–30.

85. For example, Simis, *USSR: The Corrupt Society*, 23–29, 100–107.

86. See, generally, Joshua Rubenstein, *Soviet Dissidents: Their Struggle for Human Rights* (Boston: Beacon Press, 1980). Transcripts of several of the major dissident trials of the Brezhnev period have been translated. Pavel Litvinov, comp., *The Trial of the Four: A Collection of Materials on the Case of Galanskov, Ginzburg, Dobrovolsky, and Lashkova (1967–68)*, trans. Janis Sapiets, Hilary Sternberg, and Daniel Weissbort (New York: Viking Press, 1972), 41–224; and Natalia Gorbanevskaia, *Red Square at Noon*, trans. Alexander Lieven (London: Andre Deutsch, 1972), 75–264.

87. Kaminskaya, *Final Judgment*, 31–33.

88. See, generally, Shelley, "Soviet Courts as Vehicles ," 163–86. On the issue of corruption more generally, see Kenneth Jowitt, "Soviet Neotraditionalism: The Political Corruption of a Leninist Regime," *Soviet Studies* 35, no. 3 (1983): 275–97.

89. See William E. Butler, "Toward a *Svod zakonov* in the USSR," in *Codification in the Communist World*, eds. Donald D. Barry, F. J. M. Feldbrugge, and Dominik Lasok (Leiden, the Netherlands: A. W. Sijthoff, 1975), 89–111.

90. See Gianmaria Ajani, "The Soviet Experience with Codification: Theoretical and Comparative Perspectives," in *The Soviet* Sobranie *of Laws: Problems of Codification and Non-Publication*, eds. Richard M. Buxbaum and Kathryn Hendley (Berkeley: International and Area Studies, University of California, 1991), 184–96.

91. Fuller, *The Morality of the Law*, 37.

92. For an overview of the frequency of changes in major legislation, see the table of Soviet legislative acts in William E. Butler, *Soviet Law* (London: Butterworths, 1983), xi–xviii.

93. Dietrich Andre Loeber, "Statutes of the Agencies of State Administration in the Soviet Union—An Unexplored Area of Codification," in *Codification in the Communist World*, 221–38.

94. Berman, *Justice in the U.S.S.R.*, 31.

95. Vaksberg, *Stalin's Prosecutor*, 105.

96. Ibid.

97. Andrei Sakharov, *Memoirs*, trans. Richard Lourie (New York: Vintage Books, 1992), 509–23; and Kevin Klose, *Russia and the Russians: Inside the Closed Society* (New York: W. W. Norton & Company, 1984), 128–39.

98. See, generally, Shapiro, *Courts*, 126–56; and John P. Dawson, *The Oracles of the Law* (Ann Arbor: University of Michigan Press, 1969).

99. Kathryn Hendley, "Does Law Matter in the Soviet Economic Reform Process? A Case Study of the Law Governing Internal Transfers," *Review of Central and East European Law* 18, no. 2 (1992): 101–34.

100. Bernard Rudden, "The Role of the Courts and Judicial Style Under the Soviet Civil Codes," in *Codification in the Communist World*, 317–31.

101. Moshe Lewin, *Russian Peasants and Soviet Power: A Study of Collectivization*, trans. Irene Nove (New York: W. W. Norton, 1968), 280–88, 482–509.

102. Ibid., 505.

103. For example, Solzhenitsyn, *The Gulag Archipelago;* and Conquest, *The Great Terror,* 283–85.

104. Fuller, *The Morality of the Law,* 37.

105. On the symbiotic relationship that developed between plan and contract, see Stanislaw Pomorski, "State Arbitrazh in the U.S.S.R.: Development, Functions, Organization," *Rutgers-Camden Law Journal* 9, no. 1 (1977): 67–70.

106. Paul R. Gregory and Robert C. Stuart, *Soviet Economic Structure and Performance,* 2d ed. (New York: Harper & Row, 1981), 82.

107. George M. Armstrong, "The Evolution of the Concept of Fault and Impossibility of Performance in the Soviet Law of Contracts between Enterprises," *Review of Socialist Law* 7, no. 4 (1981): 388.

108. Roy A. Medvedev (*Let History Judge: The Origins and Consequences of Stalinism,* trans. Colleen Taylor [New York: Alfred A. Knopf, 1972], 111–28, 137) provides a thorough discussion of trials involving "wrecking" and notes that the first and most notorious of these trials, the "Shakhty Affair" (1928), resulted in five executions. Moshe Lewin (*The Making of the Soviet System: Essays in the Social History of Interwar Russia* [New York: Pantheon Books, 1985], 232, 241–43) contends that thousands were arrested and sent to camps as part of this assault on the "bourgeois intelligentsia."

109. See John Clark and Aaron Wildavsky, *The Moral Collapse of Communism: Poland as a Cautionary Tale* (San Francisco: Institute for Contemporary Studies Press, 1990), 171–73 (hereafter cited as *The Moral Collapse of Communism*); and Martin Krygier's review of it, "A Morality Tale," *The National Interest,* no. 23 (1991): 96–100.

110. We need only recall the U.S. Supreme Court's struggle to define unfair conduct or conduct that shocked the conscience. See Laurence H. Tribe, *American Constitutional Law,* 2d ed. (Mineola, NY: Foundation Press, 1988), 777–80.

111. See Robert C. Tucker, *Stalin in Power: The Revolution From Above, 1928–1941* (New York: W. W. Norton, 1990), 69–145; Adam B. Ulam, *Stalin: The Man and His Era* (New York: Viking Press, 1973), 289–357.

112. Compare J. Arch Getty, *Origins of the Great Purges: The Soviet Communist Party Reconsidered, 1933–1938* (New York: Cambridge University Press, 1985); with Isaac Deutscher, *Stalin: A Political Biography,* 2d ed. (New York: Oxford University Press, 1966).

113. See Lewin, *Russian Peasants and Soviet Power.*

114. Ibid., 216–30.

115. Lynn Viola, "The Campaign to Eliminate the Kulak as a Class, Winter 1929–1930: A Reevaluation of the Legislation," *Slavic Review* 45, no. 3 (1986): 503–24.

116. Lewin, *Russian Peasants and Soviet Power,* 482–509.

117. Ibid., 284.

118. Alec Nove, *An Economic History of the U.S.S.R.* (New York: Penguin Books, 1969), 209–10. See, generally, Solomon M. Schwarz, *Labor in the Soviet Union* (New York: Praeger, 1952), 86–129.

119. Nove, *An Economic History of the U.S.S.R.,* 262.

120. Ibid., 261–64. See also Schwarz, *Labor in the Soviet Union,* 106–15.

121. Massell, *The Surrogate Proletariat,* 185–212.

122. Butler, *Soviet Law,* 274–76.

123. See Robert Sharlet, *Soviet Constitutional Crisis: From De-Stalinization to Disintegration* (Armonk, NY: M. E. Sharpe, 1992), 15–54.

124. See Sakharov, *Memoirs,* 466–69, 482–85, 492–500.

125. Compare Weber, *Law,* 228 ff.

126. See, generally, Armstrong, "The Evolution of the Concept of Fault," 287; and Heidi Kroll, "Breach of Contract in the Soviet Economy," *Journal of Legal Studies* 16, no. 1 (1987): 119–48.

127. Pomorski, "State Arbitrazh in the U.S.S.R.," 61–116.

128. For example, George W. Breslauer, "Evaluating Gorbachev as Leader," *Soviet Economy* 5, no. 4 (1989): 299–340. Compare Jerry F. Hough, "Understanding Gorbachev: The Importance of Politics," *Soviet Economy* 7, no. 2 (1991): 89–109. See, generally, Moshe Lewin, *The Gorbachev Phenomenon: A Historical Interpretation* (Berkeley and Los Angeles: University of California Press, 1988).

129. For example, Kudriavstev and Lukasheva, "Sotsialisticheskoe pravovoe gosudarstvo," 44 ff; Iu. M. Baturin, R. Z. Livshits, *Sotsialisticheskoe pravovoe gosudarstvo: ot ideiu k osuchshestvleniiu* (Moscow: Nauka, 1989); Berman, "The Rule of Law"; and Eugene Huskey, "From Legal Nihilism to *Pravovoe Gosudarstvo:* Soviet Legal Development," in *Toward the "Rule of Law" in Russia? Political and Legal Reform in the Transition Period,* ed. Donald D. Barry (Armonk, NY: M. E. Sharpe, 1992), 23–42.

130. See Anders Aslund, *Gorbachev's Struggle for Economic Reform: The Soviet Reform Process* (Ithaca: Cornell University Press, 1989), 104–5.

131. For example, R. Z. Livshits, "Pravo i zakon v sotsialisticheskom pravovom gosudarstve," *Sovetskoe gosudarstvo i pravo,* no. 3 (1989): 17.

132. See Kaiser, *Why Gorbachev Happened,* 309–10, 450–51.

133. Like Krygier ("Marxism, Communism, and Narcissism," *Law & Social Inquiry* 15, no. 4 [1990]: 723, see also 724–30), I use the concept of "normality" to refer to a baseline. He notes that "[t]here are certain achievements which are taken for granted in 'normal' societies, not universally but 'with a generality simply unknown—let alone presumed—east of the Elbe.'" Compare Abel's ("Capitalism and the Rule of Law," 692–94) strong criticism of the normative implications of the concept.

134. Anatoly Sobchak, *For a New Russia* (New York: Free Press, 1992), 21. Sobchak was a law professor at Leningrad State University who became a prominent member of the USSR Supreme Soviet during the Gorbachev years, when he associated with the democratic factions. He later won election as the mayor of St. Petersburg.

135. Boris Yeltsin, *Against the Grain,* trans. Michael Glenny (New York: Summit Books, 1990), 156–72.

136. Hiroshi Oda, "Judicial Review of Administration in the USSR," in *The Impact of Perestroika on Soviet Law,* ed. Albert J. Schmidt (Boston: Martinus Nijhoff, 1990), 157–73. In one Moscow trial court, I had to sift through all of the filed civil cases in order to find the labor cases. In doing so, I came across a num-

ber of complaints filed under this new statute. I was struck by the reluctance of the trial court judges to hear these cases on the merits. The majority of the cases were dismissed on jurisdictional grounds, even though the law clearly grants courts the right to resolve such cases.

137. See Doder and Branson, *Gorbachev,* 168–69.

138. See Anthony Jones and William Moskoff, *Ko-ops: The Rebirth of Entrepreneurship in the Soviet Union* (Bloomington: Indiana University Press, 1991), 87–91.

139. See Sharlet, *Soviet Constitutional Crisis,* 107; and V. M. Savitskii, "Aspects of Judicial Reform in the USSR," *Coexistence,* no. 28 (1991): 119–31.

140. In a February 1991 interview in Moscow, a member of the USSR Supreme Court reported that deputies in the newly-reincarnated legislature actively lobbied for their friends and constituents who had matters pending before the Court. See also Henderson, "Law of the USSR," 314–16.

141. See Donald D. Barry, "The Quest for Judicial Independence: Soviet Courts in a *Pravovoe Gosudarstvo,*" in *Toward the "Rule of Law" in Russia?,* 257–76.

142. See Eugene Huskey, "Government Rulemaking as a Brake on Perestroika," *Law & Social Inquiry* 15, no. 3 (1990): 419–32.

143. Law of the USSR on State Enterprise (Association), *Vedomosti SSSR,* no. 26, item 385 (1987).

144. Law on Property in the USSR, *Vedomosti SND SSSR,* no. 11, item 164 (1990); and Statute on Joint-Stock Companies and Limited Liability Companies, *Sobranie Postanovlenii Pravitel'stva SSSR,* no. 15, item 82 (1990). In some instances, enterprise management compensated for the inadequacies of the written law by constructing its own internal legal regime. See Kathryn Hendley, "Legal Development and Privatization in Russia: A Case Study," *Soviet Economy* 8, no. 2 (1992): 130–57.

145. On the "war of laws," see Peter Reddaway, "The End of the Empire," *New York Review of Books* 38, no. 18 (November 7, 1991): 53–59.

146. For a thoughtful analysis of the role to be played by federal and republican legislation in the context of labor under these new conditions, see R. Z. Livshits, "Trudovoe zakonodatel'stvo: poisk kontseptsii," *Sovetskoe gosudarstvo i pravo,* no. 7 (1990): 52; and V. I. Nikitinskii, "Perestroika fundamenta sistemy zakonodatel'stva o trude," *Sovetskoe gosudarstvo i pravo,* no. 7 (1990): 56–64.

147. See Michael Burawoy and Kathryn Hendley, "Between Perestroika and Privatization: Divided Strategies and Political Crisis in a Soviet Enterprise," *Soviet Studies* 44, no. 3 (1992): 371–402.

148. Remnick, *Lenin's Tomb,* 162–67, 220–21.

149. Frances H. Foster, "Procedure as a Guarantee of Democracy: The Legacy of the Perestroika Parliament," *Vanderbilt Journal of Transnational Law* 26, no. 1 (1993): 1–109.

150. Sobchak, *For a New Russia,* 2.

151. "On Urgent Measures for the Stabilization of Economic Ties in the Fourth Quarter of 1990 and During 1991," *Izvestiia,* (28 September 1990): 1.

152. Fuller, *Morality of the Law,* 71.

153. On predictions of unemployment see, V. Shcherbakov, "Unemployment: Search for Work Abroad," (interview) *Izvestiia,* 13 October 1990, trans. in *BBC Summary of World Broadcasts,* SU/0898 (2 November 1990): A7; and A. Kotliar, "Nuzhno li nam polnaia zaniatost'," *Pravda,* (21 November 1989), 2. In February 1988, a chapter dealing with laid-off workers was added to the labor code (*Vedomosti SSSR,* no. 6, item 95 [1988]; *Vedomosti RSFSR,* no. 6, item 168 [1988]).

154. See Alan M. Ball, *Russia's Last Capitalists: The NEPmen, 1921–1929* (Berkeley and Los Angeles: University of California Press, 1987).

155. The law was adopted in July 1987 but did not become effective until January 1988 (*Vedomosti SSSR,* no. 26, item 385 [1987]).

156. Stanislaw Pomorski, "The Future of the State Enterprise and the 'Restructuring' of the National Economy in the USSR," *Tulane Law Review* 61, no. 6 (1987): 1395.

157. Clark and Wildavsky, *The Moral Collapse of Communism,* 189.

158. For example, Stewart Macaulay, "Non-Contractual Relations in Business: A Preliminary Study," *American Sociological Review* 28, no. 1 (1963): 55–67.

159. See, generally, Michael Burrage, "*Advokatura:* In Search of Professionalism and Pluralism in Moscow and Leningrad," *Law & Social Inquiry* 15, no. 3 (1990): 433–72.

160. Black, "Mobilization of Law," 132.

Chapter 3: The Law on the Books

1. Fuller, *Morality of Law,* 71.

2. See Ioffe and Maggs, *Soviet Law in Theory and Practice;* and Ioffe, *Soviet Law and Soviet Reality.*

3. When I speak of "law on the books," I am referring not merely to legislation but also to the published materials that provide guidance to practitioners and judges as to how the legislation should be interpreted and implemented.

4. Compare Markovits, "Pursuing One's Rights," 689–761.

5. "Unemployment: Search for Work Abroad" (an interview with V. Shcherbakov, chairman of the USSR State Committee on Labor and Social Questions [*Goskomtrud*]), *Izvestiia,* 13 October 1990, trans. in *BBC Summary of World Broadcasts,* SU/0898 (2 November 1990): A7. Other specialists argued that the number would be considerably lower, around 16 million. See A. Kotliar, "Nuzhno li nam polnaia zaniatost'," *Pravda,* (21 November 1988): 2.

6. For example, Butler, *Soviet Law,* 39–68.

7. The Fundamentals are translated in *The Soviet Union through Its Laws,* ed. and trans. Leo Hecht (New York: Praeger Publishers, 1983), 93–130. Since this English translation was published, however, the Fundamentals have been amended several times. See *Svod zakonov SSSR,* 2:184–213, and *Trud,* 21 May 1991, 1, 3.

8. These codes were adopted at a time when only one organizational form, that of the state enterprise, was available. In the late 1980s, there was a virtual explosion in organizational forms, including cooperatives, leased enterprises, small

businesses *(maloe predpriiatie)*, joint-stock companies *(aktsionnernoe obshchestvo)*, and individual labor activities. See Philip Hanson, "Property Rights in the New Phase of Reforms," in *Milestones in Glasnost and Perestroyka: The Economy*, eds. Ed A. Hewett and Victor H. Winston (Washington, D.C.: Brookings Institution, 1991), 420–25; and Aslund, *Gorbachev's Struggle*, 150–76. Several prominent Soviet labor law experts questioned the applicability of existing labor legislation to these new organizational forms. V. I. Nikitinskii and V. Vaipan, "Pravovoe regulirovanie truda v usloviiakh mnogoobraziia form sobstvennosti," *Sotsialisticheskii trud*, no. 1 (1991), 80–88. They advocated expanding the scope of labor legislation to include these new property forms. However, the May 1991 amendments to the Fundamentals left these issues unaddressed (*Trud*, 21 May 1991, 1, 3). My research centers on state enterprises, to which the existing labor legislation clearly applies.

9. R. Z. Livshits ("Trudovoe zakonodatel'stvo," 52) argued that this system of having the republic-level codes copy the substance of the Fundamentals ought to be abandoned. He argued that the Fundamentals should be relatively short and should contain only the most basic principles of the legal regulation of labor and a list of the general social rights of workers. All remaining questions should be left to the discretion of the republic legislatures. There have been a series of similar articles in journals attempting to lay the theoretical foundation for new labor legislation. See, generally, V. I. Nikitinskii, "Perestroika fundamenta," 56–64; Livshits and Nikitinskii, "Reforma trudovogo zakonodatel'stva: voprosy teorii," *Sotsialisticheskii trud*, no. 1 (1989): 80–85; and Iu. Volegov, "Neobkhodimy radikal'nye izmeneniia," *Sotsialisticheskii trud*, no. 8 (1989): 91–96. The process of drafting new labor legislation is underway but is being conducted behind closed doors. The USSR Supreme Soviet passed certain amendments to the Fundamentals in the spring of 1991, (*Trud*, 21 May 1991, 1, 3), but these fell far short of the fundamental reworking of the legislation called for by these scholars.

10. The RSFSR Labor Code has been translated by Preston M. Torbert in *The Soviet Codes of Law*, ed. William B. Simons (Alphen aan den Rijn, the Netherlands: Sijtnoff & Noordhoff, 1980), 681–760. The RSFSR Labor Code was amended several times during the 1980s. For the most up-to-date version, see *Svod zakonov RSFSR*, 2:123–189.

11. *Iuridicheskii entsiklopedicheskii slovar'*, 1984 ed., s.v. "Rukovodiashchie Raz"iasneniia," by Kh. B. Sheinin.

12. The importance of guiding explanations as a source of law is well accepted among Western scholars of Soviet law. For example, Peter H. Solomon, Jr. "The U.S.S.R. Supreme Court: History, Role, and Future Prospects," *American Journal of Comparative Law* 38, no. 1 (winter 1990), 136; and Donald D. Barry, "The USSR Supreme Court: Recent Developments," *Soviet Studies* 20, no. 4 (April 1969), 511.

13. "Guiding explanations" of the USSR Supreme Court: "O primenenii v sudebnoi praktike osnov zakonodatel'stva soiuza SSR i soiuznikh respublik o trude," *Biulleten' Verkhovnogo Suda SSSR*, no. 3 (1974): 19–21 (hereafter cited as *BVS SSSR*); "O vipolnenii sudami postanovlenii plenuma Verkhovnogo Suda

SSSR ot 18 oktiabria 1971," *BVS SSSR*, no. 3 (1980): 9–14; "O primenenii sudami zakonodatel'stva, reguliruiushchego zakliuchenie, izmenenie i prekrashchenie trudovogo dogovora," *BVS SSSR*, no. 3 (1984): 24–33; "O primenenii sudami zakonodatel'stva o truduvom dogovore i povishenii ikh roli v ukreplenii trudovoi distsiplini," *BVS SSSR*, no. 6 (1986): 8–11; and "O vnesenii izmenenii i dopolnenii v postanovlenie plenuma Verkhovnogo Suda SSSR ot 26 aprelia 1984," *BVS SSSR*, no. 3 (1988): 7–12.

"Guiding explanations" of the RSFSR Supreme Court: "O nekotorykh voprosakh primeneniia norm kodeksa zakonov a trude RSFSR o perevodakh o peremeshcheniiakh raboshikh i sluzhishchikh na druguiu rabotu," *Biulleten' Verkhovnogo Suda RSFSR*, no. 3 (1973): 6–8 (hereinafter cited as *BVS RSFSR*); "O nekotorykh voprosakh primineniia sudami RSFSR zakonodatel'stva pri razreshenii trudovikh sporov," *BVS RSFSR*, no. 3 (1987): 12–16; "O vnesenii izmenenii i dopolnenii v postanovlenie Plenuma Verkhovnogo Suda RSFSR ot 16 dekabria 1986," *BVS RSFSR*, no. 10 (1988): 8–9; and "O nekotorykh voprosakh primeneniia sudami RSFSR zakonodatel'stva pri razreshenii trudovykh sporov," *BVS RSFSR*, no. 7 (1989): 9–15.

14. Interview with N. Iu. Sergeevna, member of RSFSR Supreme Court, Moscow, February 1991. See also Kh. B. Sheinin, "Rukovodiashchie raz"iasneniia plenuma Verkhovnogo suda SSSR," *Sovetskoe gosudarstvo i pravo*, no. 9 (1980): 70–78.

15. For example, Blair A. Ruble, "The Soviet-American Comparison: A High-Risk Venture," *Comparative Labor Law* 2, no. 4 (winter 1977): 252.

16. For example, Yuri Luryi, "The Scientific-Technical Revolution and Soviet Labor Legislation," in *Soviet and East European Law and the Scientific-Technical Revolution*, eds. Gordon B. Smith, Peter B. Maggs, George Ginsburgs (New York: Pergamon, 1981), 217.

17. For example, V. Ershov, "Rassmotrenie sporov, sviazannykh s perevodami na druguiu rabotu," *Sovetskaia iustitsiia*, no. 12 (1989): 21–22 (author is chairman of the Zheleznodorozhnyi district people's court of Moscow); V. Kovalev and S. Ryzhkov, "Sudebnaia praktika primeneniia zakonodatel'stva o trude (obzor)," *Sovetskaia iustitsiia*, no. 15 (1989): 7–9 (authors are members of the Rostov oblast' court); V. Gliantsev, "Spornye voprosy rassmotreniia del, sviazannykh s perevodom i peremeshcheniem rabotnikov," *Sovetskaia iustitsiia*, no. 18 (1989): 5–7 (author is a member of the RSFSR Supreme Court); and G. Shabalina, "Spory o vosstanovlenii na rabote (obzor kassatsionnoi i nadzornoi praktiki)," *Sovetskaia iustitsiia*, no. 13 (1990): 19–21 (author is a member of the Kirov oblast' court).

18. For example, A. I. Stavtseva, "Kommentarii sudebnoi praktike po trudovym sporam," in *Kommentarii sudebnoi praktiki za 1979 god*, eds. E. V. Voldyreva and A. I. Pergament, (Moscow: Iuridicheskaia literatura, 1980): 3–35; R. Z. Livshits, "Izmenenie trudovogo dogovora," *Sotsialisticheskii trud*, no. 8 (1988): 55–60; and I. Orlo and Kh. Siigur, "Primenenie v sudebnoi praktike zakonodatel'stva, reguliruiushchego trudovoi dogovor," *Sovetskoe pravo*, no. 5 (1988): 333–41.

19. For example, John N. Hazard, "Is Russian Case Law Becoming Significant

as a Source of Law? *Parker School Journal of East European Law* 1, no. 1 (1994): 23–26; and Blair A. Ruble, "Full Employment Legislation in the U.S.S.R.," *Comparative Labor Law* 2, no. 3 (fall 1977): 181–82.

20. For example, Quigley, "Socialist Law and the Civil Law Tradition," 781–808; and Harold J. Berman, "What Makes 'Socialist Law' Socialist?" *Problems of Communism* 20, no. 5 (September–October 1977): 24–30.

21. Ibid. Given the unraveling of the Soviet bloc and the collapse of the Soviet Union in December 1991, scholars may well abandon the category of "socialist law" and return the former Soviet Union and the countries of Eastern Europe to the "civil law" fold.

22. Merryman, *Civil Law Tradition,* 34–38; and Shapiro, *Courts,* 126–56. See, generally, Dawson, *Oracles of the Law.*

23. *Kommentarii k zakonodatel'stvu o trude* (Moscow: Iuridicheskaia literatura, 1988). Previous editions of the *Komentarii* were published in 1976, 1981, 1984, and 1986. Unfortunately, no edition has taken into account the February 1988 amendments to the Fundamentals and the RSFSR Labor Code.

24. The commentator for the sections dealing with internal transfers is V. I. Nikitinskii, who was a well-respected authority on Soviet labor law with the Institute of Soviet Legislation.

25. Article 17, Fundamentals; and Article 33, RSFSR Labor Code.

26. Livshits, *Trudovoe zakonodatel'stvo,* 51.

27. Z. K. Simorot, "Trade Union Protection of Labour Rights in Cases of Dimissal," in *Comparative Labour Law,* eds. W. E. Butler, B. A. Hepple, and Alan C. Neal (Hants, England: Gower Publishing, 1987), 88. For a thorough discussion of at-will employment in the American context, see Paul C. Weiler, *Governing the Workplace: The Future of Labor and Employment Law* (Cambridge, MA: Harvard University Press, 1990).

28. Legal scholars played an important role in drafting laws in the Soviet Union. They worked together with government and Party officials. Legislators were largely extraneous to the process.

29. See, generally R. Z. Livshits and V. I. Nikitinskii, "Gde neobkhodimy novye resheniia," *Sotsialisticheskii trud,* no. 3 (1989): 96–97; and Livshits, *Trudovoe zakonodatel'stvo,* 60–61.

30. Article 17, point 1, Fundamentals; and Article 33, point 1, RSFSR Labor Code.

31. For a discussion of mobilization, see Felstiner, Abel, and Sarat, "Emergence and Transformation of Disputes," 631–54; and Black, "Mobilization of the Law," 125–50. On the question of how often Soviet workers challenge their dismissals, see, generally, Nicholas Lampert, "Job Security and the Law in the USSR," in *Labour and Employment in the USSR,* ed. David Lane (Brighton, United Kingdom: Wheatsheaf Books, 1986), 265; and Ger P. van den Berg, "Judicial Settlement of Individual Labor Disputes in the Soviet Union," *Review of Socialist Law* 9, no. 2 (1983): 148–52.

32. *BVS RSFSR* no. 8 (1990): 1–2.

33. For example, A. I. Stavtseva, "Kommentarii sudebnoi praktike," 22–23.

34. M. Pankin, "Novoe v zakonodatel'stve o trude," *Sotsialisticheskii trud,* no. 4 (1988): 67.

35. Article 213, RSFSR Labor Code. See, generally, *BVS SSSR,* no. 3 (1988): 7–12 (post-February 1988 USSR Supreme Court plenum outlining new procedure to be followed by the lower courts when *profkom* consent was lacking); *BVS RSFSR,* no. 7 (1989): 9–15 (plenum of RSFSR Supreme Court to same effect); and A. Pavlov, "Bez soglasiia profkoma," *Sovetskie profsoiuzy,* nos. 1–2 (1990): 56–57.

36. The amended law raised the political stakes for the *profkom.* No longer is its denial of consent merely part of the dismissal process. Instead, the *profkom* must now take responsibility for an affirmative decision to reinstate the worker, a decision that might rise the ire of management. Some labor law scholars argued that this change had an undesired deterrent effect on *profkomy.* Interview with A. I. Stavtseva, Institute for State Construction and Legislation, February 1991, Moscow.

37. *Trud,* 21 May 1991, 1.

38. For example, A. I. Stavtseva and A. K. Gavrilina, "Sudebnaia praktika po trudovym delam," in *Sudebnaia praktika za 1987–88 gg.* (Moscow: Iuridicheskaia literatura, 1989), 31.

39. Article 34 of the RSFSR Labor Code sets forth certain criteria to be used by management when deciding the order in which workers are to be let go.

40. For example, "Obzor sudebnoi praktiki Verkhovnogo suda RSFSR po nekotorym voprosam voznikshim pri rassmotrenii grazhdanskikh del v kassitsionnom i nadzorom poriadke," *BVS RSFSR,* no. 8 (1989): 10; "Primenenie sudami zakonodatel'stva pri rassmotrenii trudovikh sporov: Obzor sudebnoi praktiki," *BVS SSSR,* no. 6 (1980): 9; and R. Z. Livshits, *Spravochnik pravovogo inspektora truda* (Moscow: Profizdat, 1979), 82.

41. For example, Livshits, *Trudovoe zakonodatel'stvo,* 61; and Lampert, "Job Security," 256–77.

42. *Kommentarii k zakonodatel'stvu o trude* 64; and Postanovlenie No. 12 Plenuma Verkhovnogo Suda SSSR, "O primenenii sudami zakonodatel'stva o trudovom dogovore i povyshenii ikh v ukreplenii trudovoi distsiplinii," *BVS SSSR,* no. 6 (1986): 9.

43. This list includes the annual labor plan, the personnel schedule *(shtatnoe raspisanie),* materials indicating a pending reduction in the wage fund, and documents showing that, due to a change in the character or volume of work, fewer workers would be needed (*Kommentarii* [1986], nn. 25, 56).

44. Stavsteva and Gavrilina, "Sudebnaia praktika," 12.

45. For example, *BVS RSFSR,* no. 9 (1977): 8–9.

46. *BVS RSFSR,* no. 3 (1985): 12–13.

47. *BVS RSFSR,* no. 4 (1986): 4; see also Stavtseva and Gavrilina, "Sudebnaia praktika," 7–8.

48. *BVS RSFSR,* no. 5 (1983): 8.

49. In Russian, this process is known as *attestatsiia.*

50. For example, *BVS RSFSR,* no. 2 (1986): 11–12; *BVS RSFSR,* no. 12

(1986): 9; *BVS RSFSR,* no. 5 (1988): 1–2; and A. I. Stavtseva, "Kommentarii sudebnoi praktike," 10–11.

51. For example, *BVS SSSR,* no. 2 (1988): 42–43; *BVS RSFSR,* no. 2 (1986): 11–12; *BVS RSFSR,* no. 9 (1990): 12–16.

52. *BVS SSSR,* no. 2 (1988): 42–43. (The worker's request for reinstatement and back pay was satisfied at the new hearing.)

53. *BVS RSFSR,* no. 1 (1990): 1–2.

54. *Kommentarii* (1986), nn. 25, 56; and *Kommentarii k zakonodatel'stve o trude,* 73.

55. Compare *Sovetskoe pravo,* no. 1 (1981): 141–42. (The judicial panel for civil cases of the Estonian Supreme Court accepted at face value management's claim that the newly created position ["senior engineer"] differed materially from the position the petitioner had previously held ["leading designer"].)

56. *BVS RSFSR,* no. 6 (1975): 8–9. See also *BVS SSSR,* no. 5 (1961): 13–14. (The USSR Supreme Court imposed a duty on management to prove the dismissed worker was unable to perform the duties of his replacement even though the replacement was performing different duties and was paid at a different rate.)

57. Stavtseva and Gavrilina, "Sudebnaia praktika," 9.

58. Merely hiring other workers of any type was sufficient to shift the burden back to management. In these cases, the courts looked to be convinced that management could not have transferred the dismissed worker to the position occupied by the replacement. The basic question was whether management could have avoided having to dismiss anyone (*BVS SSSR,* no. 6 [1984]: 12–14).

59. See Iu. P. Orlovskii, "Trudoustroistvo v novykh usloviiakh upravleniia ekonomikoi," *Sotsialisticheskii trud,* no. 1 (1988): 55–56.

60. "Nekotorye voprosy sudebnoi praktiki po grazhdanskim delam (obzor sudebnoi praktiki)," *BVS RSFSR,* no. 7 (1978): 10; and *Kommentarii* (1986), nn. 25, 65.

61. The work of E. A. Golovanova (*Prekrashchenie trudovogo dogovora* [Moscow: Iuridicheskaia literatura, 1966], 53–54) indicates that this duty predates the enactment of the Fundamentals and the RSFSR Labor Code.

62. *BVS RSFSR,* no. 7 (1978): 10–11. See also E. A. Golovanova, *Perevody rabochikh i sluzhashchikh na druguiu rabotu* (Moscow: Iuridichskaia literatura, 1986), 76.

63. *BVS RSFSR,* no. 4 (1990): 9.

64. "Obzor sudevnoi praktiki Verkhovnogo suda RSFSR po nekotorym voprosam, voznikshim pri rassmotrenii grazhdanskikh del v kassatsionnom poriadke i v poriadke nadzora," *BVS RSFSR,* no. 2 (1987): 12. See also *BVS RSFSR,* no. 11 (1982): 12.

65. See, generally, Stavtseva and Gavrilina, "Sudebnaia praktika," 11–13.

66. *BVS SSSR,* no. 3 (1988): 7–12.

67. *BVS RSFSR,* no. 6 (1974): 7.

68. For example, "Nekotorye voprosy sudebnoi praktiki po grazhdanskim delam," *BVS RSFSR,* no. 7 (1978): 10; and *BVS RSFSR,* no. 4 (1979): 12–13. See, generally, Golovanova, *Prekrashchenie trudovogo,* 68.

69. *BVS RSFSR*, no. 2 (1975): 1.

70. *BVS SSSR*, no. 3 (1980): 12. All translations from Russian to English have been made by the author. See, generally, Orlovskii, "Trudoustroistvo," 55–56.

71. *BVS SSSR*, no. 3 (1990): 7–12. The RSFSR Supreme Court reaffirmed the principle in a 1989 survey of the work of the lower courts. "Obzor sudebnoi praktiki Verkhovnogo suda RSFSR po nekotorym voprosam voznikshim pri rassmotrenii grazhdanskikh del v kassitsionnom i nadzorom poriadke," *BVS RSFSR*, no. 8 (1989): 10–16. See also "Obzor sudebnoi praktiki Verkhovnogo suda RSFSR," *BVS RSFSR*, no. 2 (1987): 12–13.

72. *BVS RSFSR*, no. 3 (1990): 15; and *BVS RSFSR*, no. 9 (1990): 1–2.

73. For example, "Problemy ratsional'nogo i ekonomnogo ispol'zovaniia trudovykh resursov" (kruglyi stol), *Sovetskoe gosudarstvo i pravo*, no. 8 (1987): 36–52 (especially comments of Maslova and Ivanov); L. Iu. Bugrov, "Perestroika i razvitie sovetskogo zakonodatel'stva o perevodakh na druguiu rabotu," *Sovetskoe gosudarstvo i pravo*, no. 12 (1988): 42–43; and O. Antonova, "Upravlenie protsessom vysvobozhdeniia i pereraspredeleniia rabochei sily v GDR," *Sotsialisticheskii trud*, no. 1 (1988), 134; and Orlovskii, "Trudoustroistvo," 54–56.

74. See Peter A. Hauslohner, "Managing the Soviet Labor Market: Politics and Policymaking under Brezhnev" (Ph.D. diss., University of Michigan, 1984), 487–540.

75. Indeed, many were still not computerized by 1993, despite the tremendous rise in unemployment.

76. See N. Gorelko, "Obespechenie zaniatosti vysvobozhdaemykh rabotnikov," *Sovetskaia iustitsiia*, no. 20 (1989): 19–21; I. I. Gladkii, "Intensivnoi ekonomike—effektivnuiu zaniatost'," *Sotsialisticheskii trud*, no. 5 (1988): 3–9; S. Blazhevich, "Sluzhba trudoustroistva v nobykh usloviiakh: Problemy, perspektivy, razvitiia," *Sotsialisticheskii trud*, no. 12 (1988): 27–29; and M. Solntsev, "Sluzhba trudoustroistva v novykh usloviiakh: Raionnoe zveno," *Sotsialisticheskii trud*, no. 12 (1988): 29–31.

77. Article 34, RSFSR Labor Code.

78. For example, *BVS RSFSR*, no. 9 (1990): 1–2; *BVS RSFSR*, no. 4 (1986): 4; and *BVS RSFSR*, no. 1 (1985): 3.

79. *BVS RSFSR*, no. 1 (1989): 1–2.

80. This sort of strict constructionist view of the labor contract has never been accepted in the United States (nor does it enjoy widespread acceptance elsewhere in the West). Indeed, the at-will nature of the employment contract afforded management considerable flexibility in reallocating its labor force. Workers who disagreed were fired and had no legal recourse. In recent years, the relationship between workers and management has been somewhat leveled, as state legislatures pass statutes requiring "just cause" for dismissals. See, generally, Weiler, *Governing the Workplace;* and Terri A. Zall, "Unfair Dismissal in the United States and the United Kingdom: A Procedural Comparison of Remedies," *Comparative Labor Law Journal* 9, no. 3 (1988): 433–49.

81. Article 13, Fundamentals; and Article 25, RSFSR Labor Code.

82. R. Z. Livshits and V. I. Nikitinskii, *An Outline of Soviet Labour Law* (Moscow: Progress Publishers, 1977), 47.

83. For a helpful analysis of the difference between "place of work" *(mesto raboty)* and "workplace" *(rabochee mesto),* see V. I. Krivoi, "Mesto raboty po sovetskomu trudovomu pravu," *Sovetskoe gosudarstvo i pravo,* no. 11 (1989): 56–58.

84. For a discussion of how this definitional issue has developed over time, see Bugrov, "Perestroika i razvitie," 38–39.

85. Article 13, Fundamentals; and Article 25, RSFSR Labor Code.

86. *BVS RSFSR,* no. 3 (1974): 6. Similar language can be found in the 1974 decree of the USSR Supreme Court (*BVS SSSR,* no. 3 [1974]: 20). This language was reprinted in the 1976 edition of the *Kommentarii k zakonodatel'stvu o trude,* 51. Interestingly, it is not contained in the 1986 edition of the *Kommentarii* (39) perhaps indicating a more restrictive view.

87. For example, Golovanova, *Perevody rabochikh,* 6; and V. K. Kolosov, *Trudovye spory* (Moscow: Profizdat, 1986), 28–29.

88. "Primenenie sudami zakonodatel'stva pri rassmotrenii trudovikh sporov: Obzor sudebnoi praktiki," *BVS SSSR,* no. 6 (1980): 7.

89. A. Kniazev, "Razreshenie sudami sporov o vosstanovlenii na rabote (obzor nadzornoi praktiki)," *Sovetskaia iustitsiia,* no. 12 (1983): 11 (author is a procurator).

90. *BVS RSFSR,* no. 10 (1976): 2.

91. *BVS RSFSR,* no. 2 (1984): 1.

92. Livshits and Nikitinskii, *An Outline of Soviet Labour Law,* 48.

93. *BVS RSFSR,* no. 2 (1974): 1–2.

94. Livshits, *Spravochnik,* 58–60.

95. A group of Soviet labor law experts argued that "[t]he consent of an employee is a sine qua non of any transfer to other permanent work. It is even necessary when the new job is better paid or carries a higher status" (V. Glazyrin, V. Nikitinskii, N. Maksimova, A. Yarno, *Soviet Employee's Rights in Law,* trans. James Riordan [Moscow: Progress Publishers, 1987], 30). A worker could convey his or her consent to a transfer in written or oral form or by voluntarily complying with the demands of management. However, if a worker filed a complaint but followed management's orders, this was not considered evidence of consent. For example, Ershov, "Rassmotrenie sporov," 21; and *BVS RSFSR,* no. 1 (1973): 3.

96. For example, Krivoi, "Mesto raboty po sovetskomu trudovomu pravu," 58; and Orlo and Siigur, "Primenenie v sudebnoi praktike zakonodatel'stva," 335.

97. *BVS SSSR,* no. 4 (1977): 41; *BVS SSSR,* no. 3 (1974): 20; and *BVS RSFSR,* no. 3 (1974): 6. See Livshits, *Spravochnik,* 67.

98. *Kommentarii* (1976), 53; *Kommentarii* (1986), 39–40; *Kommentarii* (1988), 43–44.

99. L. Iu. Bugrov, *Sovetskoe zakonodatel'stvo o perevodakh na druguiu rabotu* (Krasnoiarsk: Izdatel'stvo krasnoiarskogo universiteta, 1987), 55–56.

100. In 1980, the USSR Supreme Court reported that the lower courts had found 69.9 percent of transfers to other work to be illegal and attributed this to the

lack of clarity in the law and the need for case-by-case analysis (*BVS SSSR,* no. 6 [1980]: 7). Iu. A. Dmitriev (*Poniatiia "normal'nye," "vrednye," "opasnye," "tiazhelye," "sushchestvennye" usloviia truda i ikh pravovoe znachenie* [Leningrad, 1984], 19–21) has also criticized the law on these grounds.

101. Article 17, part 4, Fundamentals; and Article 33, part 4, RSFSR Labor Code.

102. "Obzor sudebnoi praktiki po grazhdanskim delam," *BVS RSFSR,* no. 7 (1981): 10–11.

103. *BVS SSSR,* no. 2 (1987): 11–12.

104. Ironically, such a recommendation would have been more appropriate in the Kosmos cafe case since the cafe where the petitioner originally worked had been closed (*BVS RSFSR,* no. 7 [1981]: 10–11). In contrast, the technical design bureau headed by the plaintiff in the 1987 case continued to exist (*BVS SSSR,* no. 2 [1987]: 11–12).

105. Work brigades have existed for much of Soviet history, but only in the late 1970s and early 1980s did they begin to be organized on a formal basis and used as a tool to increase productivity. See, generally, Peter Rutland, "Productivity Campaigns in Soviet Industry," in *Labour and Employment in the USSR,* ed. David Lane (Brighton, United Kingdom: Wheatsheaf Books, 1986), 200–202.

106. See, generally, Walter D. Connor, *The Accidental Proletariat: Workers, Politics, and Crisis in Gorbachev's Russia* (Princeton: Princeton University Press, 1991), 179–84; and Darrell Slider, "The Brigade System in Soviet Industry: An Effort to Restructure the Labor Force," *Soviet Studies* 29, no. 3 (1987): 388–405.

107. The rules governing the creation of, and the exclusion of members from, production brigades are set forth in "Tipovoe polozhenie o proizvodstvennoi brigade, brigadire, sovete brigady i sovete brigadirov," *Biulleten' Goskomtrud,* no. 7 (1984).

108. *BVS RSFSR,* no. 7 (1984): 12–13.

109. The Court was able to conclude that the plaintiff's place of work *(mesto raboty)* had not changed because its analysis stopped at the level of the shop *(tsekh)*. A shop is composed of several subunits *(uchastki)* and, while the plaintiff continued to work in the same shop, she was moved to another subunit following her ejection from the brigade. Before she had worked in the decorating subunit, whereas afterward she was assigned to the subunit that polishes samovars before nickel-plating. Thus, the Court had to work very hard to come to the conclusion that a transfer had not occurred.

110. *Kommentarii* (1986), 40–41.

111. For example, Bugrov, *Sovetskoe zakonodatel'stvo,* 55–57.

112. "O primenenii sudami zakonodatel'stva o trudovom dogovore i povishenii ikh roli v ukreplenii trudovoi distsiplini," *BVS SSSR,* no. 6 (1986): 10–11. The 1988 edition of the *Kommentarii* (45) refers to this decree rather than to the 1984 decision of the RSFSR Supreme Court.

113. *BVS SSSR,* no. 6 (1986): 11.

114. "Primenenie sudami zakonodatel'stva o trudovom dogovore: obzor sudebnoi praktiki," *BVS SSSR,* no. 2 (1987): 40.

115. Vedomosti SSSR, no. 6, item 95 (1988); and *Vedomosti RSFSR,* no. 6, item 168 (1988).

116. See Aslund, *Gorbachev's Struggle,* 104–5.

117. Livshits and Nikitinskii, "Reforma trudovogo," 78.

118. For example, A. Fatuev and E. Chezhina, "Stat'ia 25 KZoT RSFSR: problemy i suzhdenia," *Sotsialisticheskii trud,* no. 7 (1990): 90–93; Krivoi, "Mesto raboty," 59–61; and Bugrov, "Perestroika i razvitie," 41–42.

119. S. A. Ivanov, "Labor Law in Socialist Countries: Three Issues of General Theory," *Comparative Labor Law Journal* 11, no. 1 (1989): 84.

120. A. S. Pashkov, "O kontseptsii obnovleniia trudovogo zakonodatel'stva," *Pravovedenie,* no. 2 (1990): 20–22. For a discussion of the concept of *pravovoe gosudarstvo* in the Soviet context, see Berman, "Rule of Law"; and Mark R. Beissinger, "The Party and the Rule of Law," *Columbia Journal of Transnational Law* 28, no. 1 (1990): 41–50.

121. In the late 1980s, this institute was known as the Institute for Soviet State Structure and Legislation and was affiliated with the Ministry of Justice. It later changed its affiliation to the Russian Supreme Soviet. In 1995, it was known as the Institute for Comparative Law and Legislation and was affiliated with the office of the president.

122. *Trud,* 21 May 1991, 1, 3.

123. A good example of this is the provision dealing with the consent of the enterprise trade union committee to dismissals. In February 1988, the law was changed such that the consent no longer had to be preliminary. In May 1991, the work "preliminary" *(predvaritel'no)* was reinserted into the statute (*Trud,* 21 May 1991, 1).

124. Quoted in Livshits and Nikitinskii, "Reforma trudovogo," 79.

125. For a helpful discussion of the implications of these changes, see Krivoi, "Mesto raboty," 53–60.

126. See Livshits, "Izmenenie trudovogo dogovora," 56–58; and V. Kovolev and S. Ryzhov, "Sudebnaia praktika primeneniia zakonodatel'stva o trude (obzor)," *Sovetskaia iustitsiia,* no. 15 (1989): 8.

127. Livshits, "Izmenenie trudovogo dogovora," 56.

128. Ibid., 58.

129. Kovolev and Ryzhov, "Sudebnaia praktika," 7–8.

130. See, for example, Livshits, "Izmenenie trudovogo dogovora," 56; and V. Gliantsev, "Spornye voprosy," 130.

131. Gliantsev, "Spornye voprosy," 5.

132. As a part of my field research, I examined the minutes of trade union committee *(profkom)* meetings at three Moscow enterprises. At only one of these enterprises did I find instances of changes in the official job descriptions being submitted to the *profkom* for approval.

133. For example, Livshits, "Izmenenie trudovogo dogovora," 59; and Bugrov, "Perestroika i razvitie," 38.

134. Livshits and Nikitinskii ("Reforma trudovogo zakonodatel'stva," 80) have

been critical of the fact that the law seems to allow management to reassign a worker to another shop even where the labor contract specifies the original shop.

135. Article 13, part 3, Fundamentals; and Article 25, part 3, RSFSR Labor Code.

136. Krivoi, "Mesto raboty," 58, n. 21.

137. Kh. Siigur and I. Orlo, "Ob izmeneniiakh v kodekse zakonov o trude Estonskoi SSR," *Sovetskoe pravo,* no. 5 (1988): 337.

138. Gliantsev, "Spornye voprosy," 6.

139. *BVS SSSR,* 1988: 3, 11. Gliantsev ("Spornye voprosy," 6), a member of the RSFSR Supreme Court, describes a case in which the Court overturned a trial court decision on the grounds that the court failed to verify management's motives in light of evidence that its action had been prompted not by the production interests but by the personal interests of the institute director. Along similar lines, Livshits ("Izmenenie trudovogo dogovora," 58) describes a case of truck drivers being "shifted" from one type of truck to another with less horsepower, resulting in lower wages. Management argued that its action was linked to efforts to improve production. The workers contended that it had been prompted by ill will between the parties. The court sided with the workers and ordered their prior conditions reinstated.

140. This contradicts the usual tendency of Soviet courts to be very formalistic when it comes to procedural requirements imposed by statutory law. A good example of this is the requirement that the *profkom* consent to all dismissals. If this consent were absent, the court would automatically reinstate the worker, leading it to be criticized on the grounds of formalism. See, generally, Pavlov, "Bez soglasiia profkoma," 56–57; and Livshits, *Trudovoe zakonodatel'stvo,* 58–60.

141. *BVS RSFSR,* no. 7 (1989), pp. 12–13.

142. Ibid., 58–59.

143. Fatuev and Chezhina, "Stat'ia 25," 86; and Kh. Siigur, "O trudovom dogovore v usloviiakh intensivnogo razvitiia ekonomiki i polnogo khozrascheta," *Sovetskoe pravo,* no. 4 (1988): 261.

144. See, generally, Fatuev and Chezhina, "Stat'ia 25," 89.

145. For example, Gliantsev, "Spornye voprosy," 5, 7.

146. For a general overview of the procedure, see Livshits and Nikitinskii, *An Outline of Soviet Labour Law,* 196–207.

147. For example, *BVS RSFSR,* no. 5 (1989): 1–2; Shabalina, "Spory o vosstanovlenii," 19.

148. Livshits ("Trudovoe zakonodatel'stvo," 51) has been highly critical of the *KTS.* In a February 1991 interview in Moscow, he advocated the complete elimination of the *KTS,* thereby allowing all labor disputes to be heard immediately by the courts. In May 1991, the law governing the resolution of individual labor disputes was changed, but the basic procedural structure was retained (*Trud,* 17 May 1991, 1, 3).

149. A number of Soviet labor law experts have argued that *profkom* consent should be required for all transfer-related dismissals. For example, Krivoi, "Mesto raboty," 60; and Siigur and Orgo, "Ob izmeneniiakh v kodekse," 338.

150. Kathryn Hendley, "The Ideals of the *Pravovoe Gosudarstvo* and the Soviet Workplace: A Case Study of Layoffs" in *Toward the "Rule of Law" in Russia?* 315–36.

151. Ibid.

152. See, generally, "Problemy ratsional'nogo i ekonomnogo ispol'zovaniia," 36–52.

153. See, generally, V. G. Kostakov, "Zaniatost': defitsit ili izbytok?" *Kommunist,* no. 2 (1987): 78–82; and I. Iakovets, "Trudovoi potentsial obshchestva: tendentsii i perspektivy," *Sotsialisticheskii trud,* no. 8 (1988): 46–48.

Chapter 4: The Law in Practice

1. The following is a partial list of the scholars with whom I spoke and their institutional affiliation. At the Institute of State and Law of the Academy of Sciences, I spoke with R. Z. Livshits, S. A. Ivanov, A. A. Shugaev, and M. I. Piskotin. At the Institute of Soviet Legislation of the Soviet Supreme Soviet, I spoke with A. I. Stavtseva, E. A. Pavelodskii, V. V. Glazyrin, V. I. Nikitinskii, and Iu. P. Orlovskii. At the Institute of the International Labor Movement of the Academy of Sciences, I spoke with M. N. Nochevnik, V. Gimpelson, L. L. Gordon, and T. T. Timofeev. At the Institute of Sociology of the Academy of Sciences, I spoke with N. A. Andreenkova.

2. S. A. Ivanov ("Krizis sovetskogo trudovogo prava," *Sovetskoe gosudarstvo i pravo,* no. 7 [1990]: 44), head of the labor law sector of the Institute of State and Law, claims that 40 percent of all Soviet industrial workers are engaged in manual labor (55 percent in construction). However, E. Kotliar ("Metodicheskie voprosy sovershenstvovaniia ucheta ruchnogo truda," *Sotsialisticheskii trud,* no. 12 [1988]: 55–57), a prominent labor economist, while not disputing that the level of manual labor acts as a brake on economic development, argues that the imprecise method of calculating it leads to misstated and perhaps overestimated.

3. I was unable to examine all of the cases for 1989 because some of the cases were still active and so the records had not yet been sent to the archives.

4. The following table outlines the incidence of labor cases in the trial court for the *Proletarskii* region of Moscow between 1983 and 1990.

Year	*Dismissals*	*Labor Cases*	*Total Civil Cases*
1983	28	52	3,652
1984	28	54	3,728
1985	25	76	3,862
1986	24	46	3,476
1987	29	55	3,183
1988	28	50	3,440
1989	39	54	2,877
1990	N/A	58	2,579

5. The Russian phrase for resigning *(uvolnenie po sobstvennomu zhenaliiu),* which translated literally means "a dismissal pursuant to your own wish," captures

the dynamic well. The same word *(uvolnenie)* is used for all cases when a worker leaves the enterprise. Depending on the context, it can refer to a resignation, a lay-off, or a firing.

At a textile factor in the heart of Moscow, in excess of 90 percent of all departures during the 1980s were recorded as "resignations." Conversations with the in-house counsel and the personnel director confirm that many left under duress. The actual numbers are set forth below:

Year	*Departures*	*Resignations*	*Management-Initiated Firings*
1980	50	47	3
1981	45	43	2
1982	50	48	2
1983	45	44	1
1984	45	44	1
1985	50	46	4
1986	50	48	2
1987	45	42	3
1988	45	43	2
1989	50	47	3

6. The review of trial court records reveals that such cases were regularly filed. Most often workers sued to have the reason changed from one that implied they had behaved improperly, for example, absenteeism, disciplinary violations, embezzlement, to a notation that they had resigned voluntarily.

7. V. I. Nikitinskii (*Effektivnost' norm trudovogo prava,* 5–7), a prominent Soviet labor law scholar associated with the Institute of Soviet Legislation, decried the slackness in record keeping in Soviet enterprises. He also criticized the failure to collect statistical data on a systematic basis.

8. A joint decree of the USSR Council of Ministers, the Central Committee of the Communist Party, and the All-Union Central Council of Trade Unions, issued in early 1988, formalized this policy. A number of the changes made to the Fundamentals and the Russian Labor Code in February 1988, including the expansion of unemployment benefits for those dismissed on grounds of redundancy *(sokrashchenie shtata),* can be traced back to this decree (*Pravda,* 19 January 1988, 1–2).

9. Interview with A. A. Shugaev, associate director, Institute of State and Law, Moscow, November 1989.

10. Ivanov, "Labor Law in Socialist Countries," 84.

11. Pashkov, "O kontseptsii obnovleniia trudovogo zakonodatel'stva," 20–22.

12. For a more thorough discussion of the conditions at Rezina, see Burawoy and Hendley, "Between Perestroika and Privatization," 371–402.

13. These findings would seem to be somewhat at odds with the claim of S. A. Ivanov ("Krizis sovetskogo trudovogo prava," 39–47), the head of the labor law sector at the Institute of State and Law of the Russian Academy of Sciences, that 46 percent of all dismissed workers are reinstated by the courts on the grounds that *profkom* consent had not been obtained. On the other hand, when I questioned

Professor Ivanov about the source of that particular statistic during an interview, he was unable to back it up with any hard data.

14. The total number of management-initiated dismissals in 1986 and 1987 was eight and seven, respectively.

15. Fourteen workers were dismissed at the initiative of management in 1989.

16. The number of management-initiated dismissals during 1986 and 1987 was 14 and 40, respectively.

17. See note 4 for a summary of the number of cases reviewed.

18. Hendley, "The Ideals of the *Pravovoe Gosudarstvo,*" 315–36.

19. This factory, as with all of the factories whose records I examined, had a higher than normal number of disputes being considered by the *KTS.* Livshits ("Trudovoe zakonodatel'stvo," 52) claims that, on average, 1.3 or 1.4 disputes are heard per year. He contrasts this with the hundreds of thousands of complaints sent to the "central organs" on labor.

20. The *KTS* does not have the right to consider claims brought by certain categories of management personnel. Instead, such claims must be pursued through the ministry. See, generally, V. V. Shkuro, "O rasshirenii sudebnoi zashchity trudovykh prav grazhdan," *Sovetskoe gosudarstvo i pravo,* no. 8 (1989): 48–49.

21. Testimony regarding the plaintiff's work performance would have been relevant if management had dismissed her for failure to perform her expected duties. Soviet law did not permit the court to pick and choose among the statutory bases for dismissal. Instead, the defendant-management was required to prove that the reason cited in the dismissal order was legally justified.

22. I was able to review only 18 of the 54 labor-related cases brought in 1989 because many of the files had still not been transferred to the archives.

Chapter 5: The Courts

1. See, generally, P. S. Atiyah and Robert S. Summers, *Form and Substance in Anglo-American Law: A Comparative Study of Legal Reasoning, Legal Theory, and Legal Institutions* (Oxford: Clarendon Press, 1987); and Mirjan R. Damaska, *The Faces of Justice and State Authority: A Comparative Approach to the Legal Process* (New Haven: Yale University Press, 1986).

2. See Lawrence M. Friedman, *Total Justice* (Boston: Beacon Press, 1985), 28–29.

3. See, generally, Robert Satter, *Doing Justice: A Trial Judge at Work* (New York: Simon & Schuster, 1990).

4. Shapiro, *Courts,* 20, 27, 66–67, 151–56.

5. Benjamin N. Cardozo, *The Nature of the Judicial Process* (New Haven: Yale University Press, 1921), 108.

6. Shapiro (*Courts,* 67) makes a similar argument with regard to the contemporary English bench.

7. Nonet and Selznick, *Law and Society in Transition,* 58.

8. For example, Shapiro (*Courts,* 65; see also 19–34, 65–69) speaks of "the functional utility of the myth of judicial independence . . ."; and Theodore L.

Becker, *Comparative Judicial Politics: The Political Functioning of Courts* (Lanham, MD: University Press of America, 1987), 146–67.

9. Becker, *Comparative Judicial Politics,* 141.

10. Luis Muniz-Arguelles and Migdalia Fraticelli-Torres, "Selection and Training of Judges in Spain, France, West Germany, and England," *Boston College International and Comparative Law Review* 8, no. 1 (1985): 1–37. There are certain exceptions, but the end result is the same—a career civil service-style judiciary. Judges in Switzerland, for example, are chosen by elections. The judicial posts are divided on a voluntary basis among the political parties, and they control who is selected. Commentators find that judicial independence flourishes. See Walther J. Habscheid, "Election, Status and Responsibility of the Judiciary in Switzerland," in *The Role of Courts in Society,* ed. Shimon Shetreet (Dordrecht, the Netherlands: Martinus Nijhoff, 1988), 131–32; and Fred L. Morrison, "The Swiss Federal Court: Judicial Decision Making and Recruitment," in *Frontiers of Judicial Research,* eds. Joel B. Grossman and Joseph Tanenhaus (New York: John Wiley and Sons, 1969), 151. In Norway, by contrast, judges are culled from the private bar and the civil service. See Torstein Eckhoff, "Impartiality, Separation of Powers, and Judicial Independence," *Scandinavian Studies in Law* 9 (1965): 35.

11. Peter J. van Koppen, "The Dutch Supreme Court and Parliament: Political Decisionmaking versus Nonpolitical Appointments," *Law & Society Review* 24, no. 3 (1990): 746–51. The extent of political interference in such appointments varies widely among European countries, being quite significant in Germany and Italy and relatively unimportant in Holland (ibid., 762–63)

12. See Jacqueline Lucienne Lafon, "The Judicial Career in France: Theory and Practice under the Fifth Republic," *Judicature* 75, no. 2 (1991): 97–106.

13. See, generally, Mauro Cappelletti, *The Judicial Process in Comparative Perspective* (Oxford: Clarendon Press, 1989), 51, 104; and Arthur von Mehren, "The Judicial Process: A Comparative Analysis," *American Journal of Comparative Law* 5, no. 2 (1956): 216.

14. Merryman, *Civil Law Tradition,* 25. See also Donald P. Kommers, "The Federal Constitutional Court in the West German Political System," in *Frontiers of Judicial Research,* eds. Joel B. Grossman and Joseph Tanenhaus (New York: John Wiley and Sons, 1969), 93–95; and von Mehren, "Judicial Process," 216.

15. For example, Shapiro, *Courts,* 156; and Henry W. Ehrmann, *Comparative Legal Cultures* (Englewood Cliffs, NJ: Prentice-Hall, 1976), 77.

16. von Mehren, "Judicial Process," 211. The tradition of recruiting judges from the practicing lawyers dates back to the fourteenth century in England. See Dawson, *Oracles of the Law,* 11; and Theodore F. T. Plucknett, "The Place of the Legal Profession in the History of English Law," *Law Quarterly Review* 48, no. 191 (1932): 333.

17. Atiyah and Summers, *Form and Substance in Anglo-American Law,* 339–40.

18. See Robert A. Kagan, Bobby D. Infelise, and Robert R. Detlefsen, "American State Supreme Court Justices, 1900–1970," *American Bar Foundation Research Journal,* no. 2 (1984): 375. Some have argued that partisan elections for

judges often create the appearance of impropriety as well as the occasional reality. See Donald W. Jackson and James W. Riddlesperger Jr., "Money and Politics in Judicial Elections: The 1988 Election of the Chief Justice of the Texas Supreme Court," *Judicature* 74, no. 4 (1991): 184–89.

19. Joseph R. Grodin, *In Pursuit of Justice: Reflections of a State Supreme Court Justice* (Berkeley and Los Angeles: University of California Press, 1989), 3–4.

20. Research suggests that presidential appointments have had a significant political impact on the federal courts. For example, Sheldon Goldman, "The Bush Imprint on the Judiciary: Carrying on a Tradition," *Judicature* 74, no. 6 (1991): 294–306; Sheldon Goldman, "Reagan's Judicial Legacy: Completing the Puzzle and Summing Up," *Judicature* 72, no. 8 (1989): 318–25; and Sheldon Goldman, "Carter's Judicial Appointments: A Lasting Legacy," *Judicature* 64, no. 8 (1981): 344–55.

21. For example, Muller, *Hitler's Justice,* part II. Jose J. Toharia's research ("Judicial Independence in an Authoritarian Regime: The Case of Contemporary Spain," *Law & Society Review* 9, no. 3 [1975] 475–96) on Franco Spain suggests that one method of preserving some measure of judicial independence under an authoritarian regime is to scale back the jurisdiction of ordinary courts to exclude all cases with political overtones.

22. American history is marked by periodic confrontations between the executive and judicial branches. For example, *Youngstown Sheet & Tube Co. v. Sawyer,* 343 U.S. 579 (1952) (U.S. Supreme Court invalidates President Truman's seizure of steel mills in order to avoid steel strike during Korean War); and *U.S. v. Nixon,* 418 U.S. 683 (1974) (U.S. Supreme Court orders President Nixon to produce evidence demanded by special prosecutor). See, generally, Tribe, *American Constitutional Law,* chap. 4.

23. In Bangladesh, the legislature lowered the retirement age from 65 to 62, which immediately caused the retirement of two distinguished judges. See Shimon Shetreet, "Judicial Independence: New Conceptual Dimensions and Contemporary Challenges," in *Judicial Independence: The Contemporary Debate,* eds. Shimon Shetreet and Jules Deschenes (Dordrecht, the Netherlands: Martinus Nijhoff, 1985), 607. In Great Britain, in contrast, a 1959 statute introducing a mandatory retirement age was not applied to judges serving at the time it was passed (ibid.).

24. Following a military coup in Uruguay in 1973, a statute was passed giving the executive branch the power to dismiss a judge peremptorily after four years (ibid., 606). More insidious was Nazi legislation that abolished the security of judicial tenure by permitting the removal of judges on such grounds as political undesirability and ethnic heritage. See Muller, *Hitler's Justice,* 72.

25. See, generally, Anthony F. Mason, "Judicial Independence and the Separation of Powers—Some Problems Old and New," *University of British Columbia Law Review* 24, no. 2 (1990): 346–52.

26. Ehrmann, *Comparative Legal Cultures,* 92.

27. As Judith Resnik ("Managerial Judges," 376, 382–83, 446–48) argues, the

imagery of a blindfolded Justice plays directly into this myth of judges as passive decision makers.

28. Abram Chayes, "The Role of the Judge in Public Law Litigation," *Harvard Law Review* 89, no. 7 (1976): 1281–304.

29. Resnik, "Managerial Judges," 377. Resnik is critical of the tendency of this more activist style to undermine traditional due process safeguards. She notes that "[m]anagerial judges frequently work beyond the public view, off the record, with no obligation to provide written, reasoned opinions, and out of reach of appellate review" (ibid., 378; see also 425–31).

30. In India, the erosion of salaries has resulted in judges receiving less in real terms in 1981 than their predecessors received one hundred years earlier. Shetreet, "Judicial Independence," 608; see also Mason, "Judicial Independence," 351 (on the situation in Australia).

31. Logically, as law begins to matter reciprocally (rather than having only coercive functions within society), judges' desire to "do justice" should become stronger.

32. When judicial impartiality is defined in this sort of narrow, positivistic fashion, it tends to legitimate a system like South Africa's. While judges apply the laws unquestioningly and so can be considered impartial, they certainly cannot be considered to be "doing justice." According to observers, South African judges consistently interpret the statutes in a proadministration fashion, thereby granting color of law to the repressive security laws. See Christopher Forsyth, "The South African Judiciary in Time of Crisis," in *The Role of Courts in Society,* ed. Shimon Shetreet (Dordrecht, the Netherlands: Martinus Nijhoff, 1988), 26–33. Shapiro (*Courts,* 156) has also been highly critical of defining impartiality in this sort of narrow fashion.

33. See Oliver Wendell Holmes, *The Common Law* (Boston: Little, Brown, 1923); and Cardozo, *The Nature of the Judicial Process.*

34. Although the concept of reciprocal law as I present it here bears some resemblance to that of "responsive law" advocated by Nonet and Selznick, this should not be read as a wholehearted embrace of their view. Nonet and Selznick's "responsive law" (*Law and Society in Transition,* 78, 73–113) is unapologetically instrumental in its "search for *implicit values* in rules and policies" (emphasis in original) and in its focus on consequences of legal decision making. It consciously assumes a high degree of participation in the legal system, which, in turn, presupposes conditions of political pluralism (Ibid., 95–103). I am uncomfortable with its potential implications for societies without a stable liberal democracy.

35. Muller, *Hitler's Justice,* 220. Muller argues quite persuasively that the claim that Nazi judges' hands were tied by the letter of the law and their training in legal positivism is a myth that grew up after the war as part of the effort to whitewash the past (ibid., 220–221).

36. Becker, *Comparative Judicial Politics,* 165–67.

37. Ibid., 146–151.

38. Kommers ("Federal Constitutional Court," 94) has argued that the German legal education system (which is similar to that of the rest of Europe) "is sed-

imented in a long tradition of idealism and positivism." Derek Bok ("A Flawed System," *Harvard Magazine* [May–June 1983], 44–45, 70) has voiced strong criticism of the American legal educational system's tendency to socialize students toward system maintenance rather than improving the status quo.

39. For example, Eckhoff, "Impartiality, Separation of Powers, and Judicial Independence," 32–33; and Morrison, "Swiss Federal Court," 150–61.

40. On the other hand, basing promotions on a judge's record on appeal, which is the typical practice in the European civil service style judiciary, has been widely criticized for stifling initiative. As Ehrmann comments, "[c]autiousness, self-restraint, and possibly professional sycophancy appear to most judges as useful attitudes if they wish to move into more rewarding posts" (*Comparative Legal Cultures,* 78). See also Becker, *Comparative Judicial Politics,* 88–89; and von Mehren, "Judicial Process," 216.

41. Most judges prevail in retention elections, allowing the structure to serve the dual purpose of promoting an experienced judiciary and ensuring public accountability. See Susan B. Carbon, "Judicial Retention Elections: Are They Serving Their Intended Purpose?" *Judicature* 64, no. 5 (1980): 210–33. For a detailed account of a politically charged retention election, see John T. Wold and John H. Culver, "The Defeat of the California Justices: The Campaign, the Electorate, and the Issue of Judicial Accountability," *Judicature* 70, no. 6 (1987): 348–55. For a more personal view, see Grodin, *In Pursuit of Justice,* 168–86.

42. The American Constitution permits the impeachment of federal judges if they do not exhibit "good behavior." Cases of impeachment are, however, relatively rare. See, generally, Philip B. Kurland, "The Constitution and the Tenure of Federal Judges: Some Notes from History," *University of Chicago Law Review* 36, no. 3 (1969): 665–98.

43. Various solutions have been adopted in Western Europe and the United States. For example, Michele Graziadei and Ugo Mattei, "Judicial Responsibility in Italy: A New Statute," *American Journal of Comparative Law* 38, no. 1 (1990): 103–26; and Habscheid, "Election, Status and Responsibility," 135.

44. Quoted in Cappelletti, *Judicial Process,* 83.

45. Max Rheinstein, "Who Watches the Watchmen?" in *Interpretations of Modern Legal Philosophies: Essays in Honor of Roscoe Pound,* ed. Paul Sayre (New York: Oxford University Press, 1947), 596–97.

46. Cappelletti, *Judicial Process,* 83.

47. The relative institutionalization and relevance of the remedies provided for by law also affect the rate at which grievances are transformed into claims that are pursued in court. See Markovits, "Pursuing One's Rights under Socialism," 744–61; and Richard E. Miller and Austin Sarat, "Grievances, Claims, and Disputes: Assessing the Adversary Culture," *Law & Society Review* 15, nos. 3–4 (1980–81): 545, 561–65.

48. See David M. Trubek, Austin Sarat, William L. F. Felstiner, Herbert M. Kritzer, and Joel B. Grossman, "The Costs of Ordinary Litigation," *UCLA Law Review* 31, no. 1 (1983): 72–123.

49. Felstiner, Abel and Sarat, "Emergence and Transformation of Disputes," 645–46.

50. The state and those with means would be characterized as "repeat players" in Marc Galanter's ("Why the 'Haves' Come Out Ahead: Speculations on the Limits of Legal Change," *Law & Society Review* 9, no. 1 [1974]: 97–106) typology of parties and, as such, are better able to strategize and to manipulate the system to their advantage. See, generally, Grodin, *In Pursuit of Justice,* 33–36.

51. Black, "Mobilization of Law," 132, 137–38.

52. Robert A. Dahl, *Polyarchy: Participation and Opposition* (New Haven: Yale University Press, 1971), 48–61.

53. See Berman, *Law and Revolution,* 204–15.

54. See Shapiro, *Courts,* 65–125.

55. See Unger, *Law in Modern Society,* 67–76.

56. *Pravda,* 16 July 1989, 2.

57. Ginsburgs ("Soviet Judicial Elite," 305) contends that "the judicial hierarchy serves as a loyal mouthpiece of the political leadership."

58. See, generally, Feifer, *Justice in Moscow,* 247–50; Kaminskaya, *Final Judgment,* 57; and Otto Ulc, *The Judge in a Communist State: A View From Within* (Columbus: Ohio University Press, 1972), 62–63.

59. Feifer, *Justice in Moscow,* 250.

60. This stands in contrast to the typical Western practice of changing sentencing policy legislatively, thereby affording an opportunity for opponents to criticize the change publicly and work to forestall it. The attitude of the judges also differed markedly. While Western judges might follow the new sentencing policies, they would feel free to criticize the changes openly, whereas their Soviet counterparts feared the consequences of such disobedience.

61. These campaigns did not always require judges to impose stricter sentences. Sometimes they called for leniency, often as part of a holiday celebration (ibid.). See also Kaminskaya, *Final Judgment,* 56–58.

62. See, generally, Peter Juviler, "Secret Justice and Personal Rights," in *The Soviet* Sobranie *of Laws,* 156–72. Markovits ("Last Days," *California Law Review* 80, no. 1 [1992]: 83–85) describes how the East German judges unquestioningly implemented secret policy directives regarding citizens who applied to leave the country. To these judges, this did not represent undue interference nor did it smack of injustice because the party/government was not interfering in individual cases. They failed to recognize the corrosive effect of blanket policy orders on the institutional integrity of the judiciary.

63. These policies also acted to undermine the individual impartiality of judges.

64. Ginsburgs, "Soviet Judicial Elite," 300–301.

65. John Quigley, "Law Reform and the Soviet Courts," *Columbia Journal of Transnational Law* 28, no. 1 (1990): 71.

66. Kaminskaya, *Final Judgment,* 57; Louise I. Shelley, "The Political Function of Soviet Courts: A Model for One-Party States," *Review of Socialist Law* 13, no. 3 (1987): 266; and Ginsburgs, "Soviet Judicial Elite," 300. This high percentage of Party membership among the judiciary was also found in other socialist legal systems. For example, Markovits, "Last Days," 31; and Leonard J. Cohen, "Judicial Elites in Yugoslavia: The Professionalization of Political Justice," *Review of Socialist Law* 11, no. 4 (1985): 336.

67. Simis, *USSR: The Corrupt Society,* 101; and Kaminskaya, *Final Judgment,* 57.

68. Kaminskaya, *Final Judgment,* 57.

69. A 1985 survey revealed that one third of all Serbian judges viewed periodic elections as a barrier to the autonomous exercise of their judicial functions. In Yugoslavia, elections were held every eight years (Cohen, "Judicial Elites in Yugoslavia," 340).

70. Kaminskaya, *Final Judgment,* 57.

71. Peter H. Solomon Jr., "The U.S.S.R. Supreme Court: History, Role, and Future Prospects," *The American Journal of Comparative Law* 38, no. 1 (1990): 134, n. 21.

72. Feifer, *Justice in Moscow,* 84. See also Burrage, *"Advokatura,"* 468.

73. Otto Ulc, who worked as a judge in postcommunist Czechoslovakia reveals that the Ministry of Justice fixed a production quota for each court. His approach was similar to that adopted by factory workers, namely, to overfulfill the plan but not to be too zealous for fear of attracting unwanted attention from the ministry (*The Judge in a Communist State,* 42–43).

74. Feifer, *Justice in Moscow,* 84.

75. Markovits, "Last Days," 80.

76. Donald D. Barry, "The Quest for Judicial Independence: Soviet Courts in a *Pravovoe Gosudarstvo,*" in *Toward the "Rule of Law" in Russia?* 257–73.

77. That court buildings are hard to find I can attest to from the personal experience of wandering around in circles the first time I visited any district court. The people on the street—even the old women who usually knew everything about an area—had no idea there was a court nearby. See, generally, Feifer, *Justice in Moscow,* 48; Henderson, "Law of the USSR," 312–13; and Ginsburgs, "Soviet Judicial Elite," 310.

78. One of the most basic conventions of Soviet society is that one never goes into an appointment wearing or even carrying one's overcoat. It is considered a sign of disrespect to do so. Thus, the fact that there was no cloakroom can be taken as an indication of the low esteem in which the courts were held. Defense lawyers told me privately that they viewed it as a sign of disrespect to them as well.

79. Henderson, "Law of the USSR," 313.

80. One trial court judge gave these administrative duties as the principle reason why the majority of Soviet judges were women. She contended that men were less capable of keeping track of all the paperwork necessary to build a record.

81. As Robert Rand (*Comrade Lawyer* [Boulder: Westview Press, 1991], 41–42) notes, "[the secretary's] attention wavers. Material is passed over." When describing East German court proceedings, Markovits ("Last Days," 61, 66) comments on the general absence of modern technical equipment but later notes the presence of a tape recorder, which would suggest that fairly accurate trial transcripts could be produced.

82. Henderson, "Law of the USSR," 312. For background information on wage policy during the Brezhnev period (both for judges and others), see Ger P.

van den Berg, "Soviet Labor Laws in the Collection of USSR Laws," in *The Soviet* Sobranie *of Laws,* 68–102.

83. See, generally, Feifer, *Justice in Moscow,* 234–35; and Rand, *Comrade Lawyer,* 11–13. Until 1988, the Ministry of Justice set the fees that lawyers could charge. Rand notes that with the liberalization of the fee structure in 1988, the incentive for under-the-table payments *(maksimal'noe ispolzovanie klienta sverkh taksi* or *MIKS)* had been eliminated (ibid., 13).

84. Henderson, "Law of the USSR," 312.

85. Quigley, "Law Reform," 68.

86. Ibid., 66; and Barry, "Quest for Judicial Independence."

87. *Vedomosti SSSR,* no. 9, item 223 (1989), translated in Henderson, "Law of the USSR," 327–38.

88. See, generally, Barry, "Quest for Judicial Independence"; Henderson, "Law of the USSR," 305–24; and Quigley, "Law Reform," 71–72.

89. Henderson reports that this aspect was changed between the draft and final version submitted to the legislature. Originally, the local legislative bodies were to elect trial court judges. The motivation for the change was a fear that local officials would not respect the institutional integrity of the trial courts ("Law of the USSR," 308).

90. See Brendan Kiernan and Joseph Aistrup, "The 1989 Elections to the Congress of People's Deputies in Moscow," *Soviet Studies* 43, no. 6 (1991): 1049–64.

91. These qualifications panels existed on each level of the judicial system. The members were elected at the conference of judges (attended by all judges) for a term of five years. The panels' function was to review the qualifications of potential nominees and to make recommendations (Articles 15, 16, USSR Law on the Status of Judges).

92. Article 16, USSR Law on the Status of Judges.

93. Henderson, "Law of the USSR," 323.

94. Ibid., 313.

95. Ibid. See also Quigley, "Law Reform," 67.

96. See Barry, "Quest for Judicial Independence."

97. Feifer, *Justice in Moscow,* 18.

98. In the labor-related cases I reviewed at the *Proletarskii* region people's court of Moscow, an average of 18 percent of worker-petitioners was represented by counsel. Trial lawyers *(advokaty)* explained that they avoided labor cases because the government-set fee for such cases was quite small, if fees were allowed at all. In contrast, procurators participated in an average of 77 percent of cases.

99. For example, Barry, "Quest for Judicial Independence;" Simis, *USSR: The Corrupt Society,* 101.

100. Shelley, "Soviet Courts as Vehicles," 163–86.

101. Ulc (*The Judge in a Communist State,* 61) notes that, despite the lack of interference in 90 percent of all cases, "the awareness that someone might at any time inflict his 'suggestion' upon us, conditioned *all* our adjudication" (emphasis in the original).

102. See, generally, Barry, "Quest for Judicial Independence"; and Simis, *USSR: The Corrupt Society,* 101.

103. Kaminskaya, *Final Judgment,* 58.

104. Shelley, "Soviet Courts as Vehicles," 184.

105. Quoted in Quigley, "Law Reform," 67.

106. Ibid., 66. See, generally, Henderson, "Law of the USSR," 314–15.

107. Markovits, "Last Days," 67.

108. Quoted in Barry, "Quest for Judicial Independence."

109. Markovits, "Last Days," 111.

110. For example, as late as 1990, when I attended Soviet court sessions, judges still routinely asked parties in both civil and criminal actions about their Party affiliation.

111. Feifer, *Justice in Moscow,* 145. Markovits ("Last Days," 80) comes to a similar conclusion in her work on the East German judicial system. She notes that "it is the metaphor of the family that best conveys the intentions of socialist law."

112. Feifer (*Justice in Moscow,* 162) comments that "most of the civil cases I watched were handled with dispatch and a kind of rough reason, and without the complicated legal maneuvering that sours good citizens on the value of the courts as an arbiter of their private conflicts."

113. Markovits, "Last Days," 65.

114. Ginsburgs, "Soviet Judicial Elite," 303.

115. See Simis, *USSR: The Corrupt Society,* 97–125.

116. Ibid., 309; and Feifer, *Justice in Moscow,* 49.

117. See Robert A. Kagan, *Regulatory Justice: Implementing a Wage-Price Freeze* (New York: Russell Sage Foundation, 1978), chap. 8.

118. For example, Litvinov, comp., *The Trial of the Four;* and Gorbanevskaia, *Red Square at Noon.*

119. See Feifer, *Justice in Moscow,* 83.

120. Shelley, "Soviet Courts as Vehicles."

121. Quoted in Burrage, *"Advokatura,"* 455.

122. See Eugene Huskey, "Between Citizen and State: The Soviet Bar (Advokatura) under Gorbachev," *Columbia Journal of Transnational Law* 28, no. 1 (1990): 111.

123. Rand, *Comrade Lawyer,* 9–12.

124. Ibid., 32.

125. Ibid., 108.

126. Feifer, *Justice in Moscow,* 245.

127. Burrage (*"Advokatura,"* 466–70) argues that the rise in the status of *advokaty* can be linked directly to Gorbachev and his emphasis on the importance of law and legal institutions.

128. See, generally, Rand, *Comrade Lawyer,* 13, 25–26.

129. Huskey, "Between Citizen and State." In the years that followed, other professional associations were created.

130. See, generally, Henderson, "Law of the USSR," 308–9, 321–24.

131. See Henderson, "Law of the USSR."

132. Feifer, *Justice in Moscow,* 78–79.

133. Compare Joel B. Grossman, Herbert M. Kritzer, Kristen Bumiller, and Stephen McDougal, "Measuring the Pace of Civil Litigation in Federal and State Trial Courts," *Judicature* 65, no. 2 (1981): 86–113.

134. This is another instance in which worker-petitioners were hampered by their lack of knowledge and experience. They rarely made demands on the judge, and, when they did, they did not take full advantage of the material (or witness) produced, relying on the judge to ferret out the truth.

135. See Feifer, *Justice in Moscow,* 234–35; and Rand, *Comrade Lawyer,* 13.

136. For an analysis of how often workers challenged their dismissals, see Lampert, "Job Security and the Law in the USSR," 265; and Ger P. van den Berg, "Judicial Settlement," 54.

137. Markovits, "Pursuing One's Rights," 689–761.

138. Hendley, "The Ideals of the *Pravovoe Gosudarstvo,*" 315–36.

139. See Krygier, "Marxism and the Rule of Law," 637–63.

140. See chapter 2 for an expanded analysis of the role played by law under Leninism.

141. Compare Ronen Shamir, "'Landmark Cases' and the Reproduction of Legitimacy: The Case of Israel's High Court of Justice," *Law & Society Review* 24, no. 3 (1990): 781–805.

142. At the time of their enactment, these reforms were designed to foreclose meddling by Party *apparatchiki.* This problem has, of course, been largely made moot by the collapse of the Party in the wake of the abortive putsch of August 1991.

Chapter 6: Economic Incentives, Labor Unions, and Legal Culture

1. See chapter 3 for an expanded discussion of the obligations imposed on management by Soviet labor law.

2. See Albert O. Hirschman, *Exit, Voice and Loyalty: Responses to Decline in Firms, Organizations, and States* (Cambridge, MA: Harvard University Press, 1970), 21–29. For an application of Hirschman's thesis to the American labor scene, see Richard B. Freeman and James L. Medoff, *What Do Unions Do?* (New York: Basic Books, 1984), 7–11.

3. The argument in the United States is complicated by the low percentage of unionized workers (approximately 15 percent). Some contend that the threat of unionization helps to keep management within the law in nonunionized factories, but Freeman and Medoff (*What Do Unions Do?,* 151) are more ambivalent, noting that whether unionism helps nonunion workers "seems to depend on which workers, which firms, and which sectors are studied."

4. See Robert Knegt, "Regulating Dismissal from Employment: Administrative and Judicial Procedures in the Netherlands," *Law & Policy* 11, no. 2 (1989): 175–87; and Ehrhard Blankenburg and Ralf Rogowski, "German Labour Courts and British Industrial Tribunal Systems: A Socio-Legal Comparison of Degrees of Judicialisation," *Journal of Law and Society* 13, no. 1 (1986): 67–87.

5. In hierarchical terms, the general director of the plant stood below the secretary of the Party organization.

6. See Michael Burawoy and Pavel Krotov, "The Soviet Transition from Socialism to Capitalism: Worker Control and Economic Bargaining in the Wood Industry," *American Sociological Review* 57, no. 1 (1992): 19–20, 26–28.

7. Adam Smith, *The Wealth of Nations* (New York: Penguin Books, 1986).

8. See Peter L. Berger, *The Capitalist Revolution: Fifty Propositions about Prosperity, Equality, and Liberty* (New York: Basic Books, 1986), 15–31.

9. James Willard Hurst, *Law and Markets in United States History: Different Modes of Bargaining Among Interests* (Madison: University of Wisconsin Press, 1982), 67.

10. Who holds the upper hand varies among firms and within firms depending on the workers' level of qualification and the transferability of their skills, among other factors. See, generally, Oliver E. Williamson, *The Economic Institutions of Capitalism: Firms, Markets, Relational Contracting* (New York: Free Press, 1985), 206–72.

11. See Robert A. Kagan and John T. Scholz, "The 'Criminology of the Corporation' and Regulatory Enforcement Strategies," in *Enforcing Regulation,* eds. Keith Hawkins and John M. Thomas (Boston: Kluwer-Nijhoff, 1984), 77.

12. Ibid., 70–72, 80–83. See also Williamson, *The Economic Institutions of Capitalism,* 43–67.

13. See Robert J. Flanagan, *Labor Relations and the Litigation Explosion* (Washington, D.C.: Brookings Institution, 1987).

14. See Ed A. Hewett, *Reforming the Soviet Economy: Equality Versus Efficiency* (Washington, D.C.: Brookings Institution, 1988), 1–4.

15. See, generally, Merle Fainsod, *How Russia is Ruled,* 2d ed. (Cambridge, MA: Harvard University Press, 1963).

16. The personnel schedule *(shtatnoe raspisanie),* which was generated at the enterprise level and vetted at the ministerial level, detailed the positions and the wage levels permitted by the plan. As I discussed in chapters 3 and 4, layoffs had to be reflected in this document, and, if they were not, this constituted definitive proof of a sham layoff. One measure of the increased autonomy granted to enterprise management in the late 1980s was the fact that managers were permitted to change the personnel schedule on their own authority.

17. For example, Berliner, *Factory and Manager in the USSR;* David Granick, *Management of the Industrial Firm in the USSR* (New York: Columbia University Press, 1954); and Granick, *The Red Executive.*

18. Western economists who studied the Soviet economy long ago concluded that the practice of hoarding labor was widespread among Soviet enterprises. For example, Joseph S. Berliner, *The Innovation Decision in Soviet Industry* (Cambridge, MA: MIT Press, 1976), 165–69; and Philip Hanson, "The Serendipitous Soviet Achievement of Full Employment: Labour Shortage and Labour Hoarding in the Soviet Economy," in *Labour and Employment in the USSR,* ed. David Lane (Brighton, United Kingdom: Wheatsheaf Books, 1986), 85–86. With the increased candor permitted by the policy of *glasnost',* their Soviet counterparts

also began to acknowledge the practice. For example, I. I. Gladkii, "Intensivnoi ekonomike—effektivnuiu zaniatost'," 3; and Kotliar, "Nuzhno li nam polnaia zaniatost'," 2.

19. As with production, capital investment was dictated by the plan. The investment policy of the Soviet Union, which tended to favor massive new construction projects over the capital renovation of the existing industrial base, meant that the predominance of manual labor persisted for longer in the Soviet context (outside of the cosseted defense industry) than in the West. Moreover, the technology necessary to mechanize the production line was often unavailable in the Soviet Union, which raised the thorny question of hard currency reserves, to which enterprise management had no access. See, generally, David A. Dyker, *The Process of Investment in the Soviet Union* (Cambridge: Cambridge University Press, 1983); and Tamas Bauer, "Investment Cycles in Planned Economies," *Acta Oeconomica* 21, no. 3 (1978): 243–60.

20. For a cogent analysis of the unintended consequences of this practice of "storming," see Joseph S. Berliner, *Soviet Industry from Stalin to Gorbachev: Essays on Management and Innovation* (Ithaca: Cornell University Press, 1988), 49–52.

21. Berliner, *Soviet Industry from Stalin to Gorbachev*, 27.

22. See Medvedev, *Let History Judge*, 111–28; and Lewin, *The Making of the Soviet System*, 232, 241–43.

23. Berliner, *Soviet Industry*, 27.

24. Janos Kornai, *The Economics of Shortage* (Amsterdam: North Holland, 1980); and Janos Kornai, *The Socialist System: The Political Economy of Communism* (Princeton: Princeton University Press, 1992), 140–45.

25. See Kostakov, "Zaniatost': defitsit ili izbytok?" 78–79; and Iakovets, "Trudovoi potentsial obshchestva," 43–44.

26. A good example is Andropov's campaign to increase labor discipline, initiated soon after he became general secretary of the Communist Party in 1982. See Zhores A. Medvedev, *Andropov* (New York: W. W. Norton, 1983), 127–34.

27. See *Pravda*, 19 January 1988, 1–2, for the text of the joint decree announcing this campaign. See, generally, "Problemy ratsional'nogo i ekonomnogo," 36–52.

Gorbachev was not the first Soviet leader to initiate reforms designed to rationalize the workforce. Previous efforts, such as the Brezhnev-era Shchekino experiment, were unsuccessful. See Bob Arnot, "Soviet Labour Productivity and the Failure of the Shchekino Experiment," *Critique*, no. 15 (1982): 31–56; and Peter Rutland, "The Shchekino Method and the Struggle to Raise Labour Productivity in Soviet Industry," *Soviet Studies* 38, no. 2 (1984): 345–65.

28. See *Ekonomika i zhizn'*, no. 2 (1991): 14–15, for the text of the decree.

29. See Hendley, "Does Law Matter in the Soviet Economic Reform Process?" 131–34.

30. I am referring here to the overall balance of power in the Soviet economic system, which undeniably favored the central planners and ministerial officials,

who determined the parameters of success. My previous characterizations of enterprise managers as powerful referred to their position vis-à-vis workers.

31. These reforms are best known for reinstituting the traditional sector-based industrial ministries and rescinding a number of other Khrushchev-era administrative reforms. See, generally, Abraham Katz, *The Politics of Economic Reform in the Soviet Union* (New York: Praeger Publishers, 1972); Karl W. Ryavec, *Implementation of Soviet Economic Reforms: Political, Organizational, and Social Process* (New York: Praeger Publishers, 1975).

32. *Sobranie postanovlenii pravitel'stva SSSR,* nos. 19–20, item 155 (1965).

33. Olympiad S. Ioffe, "Law and Economy in the USSR," *Harvard Law Review* 95, no. 7 (1982): 1606.

34. Compare Macaulay, "Non-Contractual Relations in Business," 55–67.

35. G. Kulagin, "Ob"edinenie, predpriiatie i ministerstvo," *Kommunist,* no. 3 (1966): 87. See also Katz, *The Politics of Economic Reform,* 158–74; and Ryavec, *Implementation of Soviet Economic Reforms,* 80.

36. See, generally, Hewett, *Reforming the Soviet Economy,* 303–60; and Aslund, *Gorbachev's Struggle for Economic Reform.*

37. Goods produced pursuant to *goszakazy* were subject to price controls, but the state was obligated to provide the necessary inputs. As to production in excess of these *goszakazy,* enterprise management was free to negotiate with potential purchasers over the price. The resulting "contractual prices" *(dogovornye tseny)* were inevitably higher than the prices set by the state *(gosudarstvennye tseny),* but the responsibility for obtaining the required inputs rested solely on enterprise management. For an account of how Soviet managers at one Moscow enterprise responded to these conditions, see Burawoy and Hendley, "Between Perestroika and Privatization," 371–402.

38. "O gosudarstvennom prepriiatii (ob"edinenii)," *Vedomosti SSSR,* no. 26, item 385 (1987). Like its predecessor, this law also attempted to give enterprise management some recourse against ministerial arbitrariness. Although the procedural mechanism was more clearly articulated, it was rarely used because managers were reluctant to risk the ire of ministerial officials.

39. See Paul R. Gregory, "The Impact of Perestroika on the Soviet Planned Economy: Results of a Survey of Moscow Economic Officials," *Soviet Studies* 43, no. 5 (1991): 859–73.

40. See Luryi, "The Scientific-Technical Revolution and Soviet Labor Legislation," 213.

41. See Peter Hauslohner, "Gorbachev's Social Contract," *Soviet Economy* 3, no. 1 (1987): 54–87.

42. The existence of the "second economy" in the Soviet Union contributed to the persistence of inequality in living standards despite egalitarian wage policies. See Gregory Grossman, "The 'Second Economy' in the USSR," *Problems of Communism* 26, no. 5 (1977): 25–40.

43. Mstislav Molodtsov, "Benefits in Addition to Wages and Salaries in the USSR," *Comparative Labor Law* 3, no. 2 (1980): 149–55. As I discuss in this chapter, these functions were typically delegated to the enterprise trade union committee.

44. For example, at an aircraft manufacturing plant in Saratov that was part of the cosseted Soviet military-industrial complex, workers routinely waited 25 years for housing of the legally-mandated square meterage. See Hendley, "Legal Development and Privatization," 134. See also Elizabeth Teague, "The Absentee Vote: Worker Discontent and Labor Productivity in the Soviet Union," *Workers Under Communism,* no. 2 (1982): 23.

45. See Ann Helgenson, "Geographical Mobility—Its Implications for Employment," in *Labour and Employment in the USSR,* ed. David Lane (Brighton, United Kingdom: Wheatsheaf Books, 1986), 145–50.

46. This created a thriving market in sham (but illegal) marriages, particularly with permanent residents of Moscow and other large urban centers.

47. Obtaining permission to move to a sparsely populated region that suffered from a chronic shortage of workers, such as the northern regions of Russia or certain remote areas of Siberia, was rarely a problem.

48. See David Granick, *Job Rights in the Soviet Union: Their Consequences* (Cambridge: Cambridge University Press, 1987), 31–33.

49. See David Granick, "Labor Markets in the USSR," *Occasional Paper of the Kennan Institute for Advanced Russian Studies,* no. 78 (1979): 5–8. The Stalinist labor laws that made it a criminal offense to quit had been rescinded soon after Stalin's death in 1953. See Nove, *Economic History of the U.S.S.R.,* 261–64.

50. This, of course, raises the question of why Soviet workers were unwilling to mobilize the law to serve their interests. This question will be addressed in the fourth part of this chapter.

51. For a variety of interpretations of the development of American unions, see Derek C. Bok, "Reflections on the Distinctive Character of American Labor Laws," *Harvard Law Review* 84, no. 6 (1971): 1394–463; Joel Rogers, "Divide and Conquer: Further 'Reflections on the Distinctive Character of American Labor Laws,'" *Wisconsin Law Review,* no. 1 (1990): 1–147; and William E. Forbath, "The Shaping of the American Labor Movement," *Harvard Law Review* 102, no. 6 (1989): 1109–256.

52. For examples of successful cross-cultural comparisons of, respectively, the development and decline of unions and the underlying legal structures, see Lowell Turner, *Democracy at Work: Changing World Markets and the Future of Labor Unions* (Ithaca: Cornell University Press, 1991); and Clyde W. Summers, "Worker Participation in the U.S. and West Germany: A Comparative Study from an American Perspective," *American Journal of Comparative Law* 28, no. 3 (1980): 367–92.

53. See Flanagan, *Labor Relations and the Litigation Explosion.*

54. See David E. Feller, "A General Theory of the Collective Bargaining Agreement," *California Law Review* 61, no. 3 (1973): 663–855.

55. For an overview of American labor law, see Weiler, *Governing the Workplace;* and Robert A. Gorman, *Basic Text on Labor Law: Unionization and Collective Bargaining* (St. Paul: West Publishing, 1976).

56. A number of American labor law scholars have argued that the law, particularly in forbidding unauthorized wildcat strikes during the terms of collective bargaining agreements that contain arbitration clauses, merely perpetuates the existing power relationships. For example, James B. Atleson, *Values and Assumptions*

in American Labor Law (Amherst: University of Massachusetts Press, 1983); and Katherine Van Wezel Stone, "The Post-War Paradigm in American Labor Law," *Yale Law Journal* 90, no. 7 (1981): 1509–80.

57. Whether this right is meaningful in practice is open to question. Compare Feller, "A General Theory," 852–56, with Michael J. Goldberg, "The Duty of Fair Representation: What the Courts Do in Fact," *Buffalo Law Review* 34, no. 1 (1985): 91–159.

58. The reasons for low union participation and the contributory role of the legal structure have been much debated. For example, Leo Troy, "The Rise and Fall of American Trade Unions: The Labor Movement from FDR to RR," in *Unions in Transition: Entering the Second Century,* ed. Seymour Martin Lipset (San Francisco: Institute for Contemporary Studies Press, 1986), 77–109; and Rogers, "Divide and Conquer," 47–59.

59. See Weiler, *Governing the Workplace,* 11–20; and Freeman and Medoff, *What Do Unions Do?*

60. See Kathleen A. Thelen, *Union of Parts: Labor Politics in Postwar Germany* (Ithaca: Cornell University Press, 1991), 48–60; and Robert A. Kagan, "How Much Does Law Matter? Labor Law, Competition, and Waterfront Labor Relations in Rotterdam and U.S. Ports," *Law & Society Review* 24, no. 1 (1990): 35–60. Compare Charles F. Sabel, "The Internal Politics of Trade Unions," in *Organizing Interests in Western Europe: Pluralism, Corporatism, and the Transformation of Politics,* ed. Suzanne D. Berger (Cambridge: Cambridge University Press, 1981), 209–44.

61. See Peter J. Katzenstein, *Small States in World Markets: Industrial Policy in Europe* (Ithaca: Cornell University Press, 1985). Compare Joseph L. Badaracco, *Loading the Dice: A Five-Country Study of Vinyl Chloride Regulation* (Boston: Harvard Business School Press, 1985).

62. See Thelen, *Union of Parts,* 42–48.

63. Recent data indicate that 98 percent of the workforce belonged to the union. Walter D. Connor, *The Accidental Proletariat: Workers, Politics, and Crisis in Gorbachev's Russia* (Princeton: Princeton University Press, 1991), 200.

64. Trade unions were the only Soviet social organization for which dues were automatically deducted from workers' pay. Dues for the Communist Party were not paid in this way.

65. Leaders of the alternative independent trade unions stressed this as the principal reason for their difficulty in building a constituency among workers ("Al'ternativnye profsoiuzy: vozmozhnosti i real'nost'" [roundtable], *Sotsialisticheskoe issledovanie,* no. 2 [1990]: 84).

66. Profkomy also decided who would be permitted to go on enterprise-sponsored trips *(putevki)* within the Soviet Union or Eastern Europe. It also made loans to workers who found themselves short from time to time.

67. See Isaac Deutscher, *Soviet Trade Unions: Their Place in Soviet Labour Policy* (London: Royal Institute of International Affairs, 1950), 42–52; and Blair A. Ruble, "Industrial Trade Unions in the USSR," in *Trade Unions in Communist*

States, eds. Alex Pravda and Blair A. Ruble (Boston: Allen & Unwin, 1986), 24–25.

68. See A. V. Vasil'ev, "Sotsial'nye funktsii sovetskikh profsoiuzov i ikh zakonodatel'noe zakreplenie: problemy i resheniia," *Sovetskoe gosudarstvo i pravo*, no. 5 (1990): 87.

69. Ruble, "Industrial Trade Unions," 25. West European unions have successfully walked this tightrope by preserving their identity as *workers'* representatives and by insisting that the gains from increased productivity be equitably shared and used to improve working conditions.

70. See *Trud*, 6–9 September 1989.

71. L. V. Nikitinskii, "Pravovaia inspektsiia truda: priroda i pravootnoshenie," *Sovetskoe gosudarstvo i pravo*, no. 9 (1980): 125–30.

72. See Burawoy and Hendley, "Between Perestroika and Privatization," 372–77.

73. The data indicated that 68 percent were top-level managers and 28 percent were engineers or mid-level managers *(inzhenerno-tekhnicheskie rabotniki)* (Vasil'ev, "Sotsial'nye funktsii sovetskikh," 88).

74. Approximately half of workers surveyed appraised the authority of the union as average, while one third considered it low ("Al'ternativnye profsoiuzy," *Sotsialisticheskoe issledovanie*, no. 2 [1990]: 90–91).

75. See chapter 3 for a detailed discussion of the procedure for resolving disputes within Soviet enterprises.

76. In the United States, collective bargaining agreements are often quite lengthy and detailed and are printed up in small booklets that many workers keep in their pockets for quick reference.

77. See Blair A. Ruble, "Factory Unions and Workers' Rights," in *Industrial Labor in the U.S.S.R.*, eds. Arcadius Kahan and Blair A. Ruble (New York: Pergamon, 1979), 68–69.

78. See M. Eisler, "O sootvetstvii kollektivnykh dogovorov zakonodatel'stvu o trude," *Sovetskoe pravo*, no. 6 (1980): 430–37.

79. The law was changed in 1992. It now imposes upon management a duty to bargain in good faith and provides remedies if it fails to do so. Although the new law is promising, conversations with labor activists in Moscow in September 1992 indicate that it has not had much impact on management behavior. For the text of the new law, see *Rossiiskaia gazeta*, 28 April 1992. See, generally, Kathryn Hendley, "Preliminary Framework for Labor Contracts," *Survey of East European Law* 3, no. 4 (1992): 5–6.

80. M. V. Baglai, "Perestroika i profsoiuzy," *Kommunist*, no. 12 (1987): 80–90.

81. Livshits, "Trudovoe zakonodatel'stvo," 53.

82. See E. Klopov and L. Gordon, "Rabochee dvizhenie: novyi etap," *Narodnyi deputat*, no. 7 (1990): 47–53; and Peter Rutland, "Labor Unrest and Movements in 1989 and 1990," *Soviet Economy* 6, no. 3 (1990): 345–84.

83. See *Trud*, 6–9 September 1989.

84. For example, *Trud*, 15 November 1990, 1 (Gorbachev meets with delegates

to 1990 trade union congress); and "Ryzhkov Addresses Trade Union Congress," *FBIS,* SU/0906 (October 27, 1990): B5–B9.

85. See Kagan and Scholz, "The 'Criminology of the Corporation,'" 67–95; and Williamson, *The Economic Institutions of Capitalism,* 68–84.

86. See Black, "Mobilization of Law," 126–29.

87. Witness the creation of the National Labor Relations Board in the United States in the 1930s as an alternative to the ordinary trial courts, which had proved themselves friends of management by stifling union organization for decades through the power of injunctions. See James A. Gross, *The Making of the National Labor Relations Board* (Albany: State University of New York Press, 1974). See, generally, William E. Forbath, *Law and the Shaping of the American Labor Movement* (Cambridge, MA: Harvard University Press, 1991).

88. The danger that lawyers will act as gatekeepers, discouraging certain types of claims for financial or substantive reasons, is discussed in the second part of chapter 5. See, generally, Trubek, Sarat, Felstiner, Kritzer, and Grossman, "Costs of Ordinary Litigation," 72–123.

89. The claim that getting rid of perennially drunk workers was virtually impossible was patently not true. In my review of the records of a Moscow trial court between 1982 and 1989, I found that the court did not require medical evidence of intoxication but routinely accepted the word of coworkers or supervisors regarding telltale signs in the worker's behavior or the presence of alcohol on his or her breath.

90. See Black, "Mobilization of Law," 134.

91. See Ehrhard Blankenburg and Ralf Rogowski, "German Labour Courts and the British Industrial Tribunal Systems: A Socio-Legal Comparison of Degrees of Judicialisation," *Journal of Law and Society* 13, no. 1 (1986): 74–81.

92. Article 36, Russian Labor Code. Compare this to Germany, where a worker has a 60 percent chance of obtaining a lump sum settlement by going to court, making reinstatement irrelevant in most cases (Blankenburg and Rogowski, "German Labour Courts," 80).

93. Ger van den Berg, "Judicial Settlement of Individual Labor Disputes in the Soviet Union," *Review of Socialist Law* 11, no. 2 (1983): 47–73.

94. See Black, "Mobilization of Law," 132.

Chapter 7: Summary and Speculations

1. See chapter 2 for an extended discussion of the rule of law.

2. Nonet and Selznick, *Law and Society in Transition,* 58.

3. The contours of this autonomous sphere depend to some extent on the underlying legal culture. As a general matter, judges in countries with a common law legal tradition have greater flexibility in interpreting the written law than do their counterparts in countries with civil law legal traditions.

4. V. I. Lenin, "State and Revolution," in *The Lenin Anthology,* ed. Robert C. Tucker (New York: W. W. Norton, 1975), 314–15, 369–84. See Jane Burbank, "Lenin and the Law," *Slavic Review* 54, no. 1 (1995): 23–44.

5. See, generally, Beirne and Sharlet, "Toward a General Theory of Law and Marxism," 17–44.

6. See *Justice in the U.S.S.R.*, 13–65.

7. Sharlet, "Stalinism and Soviet Legal Culture," 168–78.

8. See Kaminskaya, *Final Judgment.*

9. See Shelley, "Soviet Courts as Vehicles," 163–86.

10. The limited statistical data available on mobilization of law in the labor realm in the Soviet Union supports my thesis that relatively few workers had recourse to the law. See Ger P. van den Berg, "Judicial Settlement of Individual Labor Disputes in the Soviet Union," *Review of Socialist Law* 9, no. 2 (1983): 125–64.

11. See, generally, Alec Nove, *The Soviet Economic System* (London: Allen & Unwin, 1977).

12. See Mancur Olson, "The Hidden Path to a Successful Economy," in *The Emergence of Market Economies in Eastern Europe,* eds. Christopher Clague and Gordon C. Rausser (Cambridge, MA: Blackwell Publishers, 1992), 55–75.

13. See Berliner, *Factory and Manager in the USSR.*

14. See, generally, Ruble, "Industrial Trade Unions in the USSR," 23–47.

15. The Soviet constitutions adopted in 1936 and 1977 both stated unequivocally that the judiciary was independent and should rely solely on the law in rendering decisions.

16. See, generally, Ginsburgs, "Soviet Judicial Elite," 293–311; and Quigley, "Law Reform and the Soviet Courts," 59–75.

17. See Barry, "Quest for Judicial Independence," 257–75.

18. For example, Diego Gambetta, ed., *Trust: Making and Breaking Cooperative Relations* (New York: Blackwell Publishers, 1988); and Richard Rose, "Post-communism and the Problem of Trust," *Journal of Democracy* 5, no. 3 (1994): 18–29.

19. David Stark ("Path Dependence and Privatization Strategies," 48–54) has argued that historical legacies cannot be ignored in the economic reform process, that market-based economic reforms cannot be effected merely by applying technocratic rules with no consideration for existing institutional arrangements and culture. His notion of "path dependence" is also relevant to any analysis of legal reform.

20. See, generally, Fuller, *Morality of Law;* and Selznick, *Law, Society, and Industrial Justice.*

21. See Tyler, *Why People Obey the Law.*

22. See Nonet and Selznick, *Law and Society in Transition,* 58.

23. Fuller, *Morality of Law,* 33–94.

24. See Summers, "Effective Remedies for Employment Rights," 457–546.

25. Markovits, "Pursuing One's Rights," 689–761.

26. Ibid., 751.

27. A group of Western economists has argued that the level of monopolization of the Russian economy is substantially less than had been assumed. While their data are persuasive, what they tell us about enterprise behavior is less clear. My

interviews with enterprise managers reveal that they continue to believe that a majority (70 to 80 percent) of their suppliers are monopolists, and these beliefs inform their behavior. Even following the breakup of the Soviet Union, information flows continue to be severely constrained. See Annette N. Brown, Barry W. Ickes, and Randi Ryterman, "The Myth of the Monopoly: A New View of Industrial Structure in Russia" (1993, photocopy).

28. Weber, *Max Weber on Law*. See also Reinhard Bendix, *Max Weber: An Intellectual Portrait* (Berkeley and Los Angeles: University of California Press, 1977), 385–415; Alan Hunt, *The Sociological Movement in Law* (Philadelphia: Temple University Press, 1978), 93–133; Anthony T. Kronman, *Max Weber* (Stanford: Stanford University Press, 1983); and David M. Trubek, "Max Weber on Law and the Rise of Capitalism," *Wisconsin Law Review*, no. 3 (1972): 720–53.

29. See, generally, Berman, *Law and Revolution*.

30. In his *Law in Modern Society*, Unger builds on the Weberian framework to provide additional insights into the process of rationalization.

31. See Lev, "Judicial Authority and the Struggle for an Indonesian Rechtsstaat," 37–42.

32. See Gennady M. Danilenko, "International Law and the Future of Rechtsstaat in Russia," in *Law and Democracy in the New Russia*, eds. Bruce L. R. Smith and Gennady M. Danilenko (Washington, D.C.: Brookings Institution, 1993).

33. For an analysis of the extent to which the Soviet bureaucracy was in fact a Weberian bureaucracy, see Jan Pakulski, "Bureaucracy and the Soviet System," *Studies in Comparative Communism* 19, no. 1 (1986): 3–24.

34. Given the slow development of market institutions (such as spot markets), Soviet-style behavior such as hoarding may persist in the short run.

35. This is also a point that Unger emphasizes in *Law in Modern Society* (74).

36. See Maxim Boyko, Andrei Shleifer, and Robert W. Vishny, "Privatizing Russia," *Brookings Papers on Economic Activity* no. 2 (1993): 179–90.

37. See Mary McAuley, "Politics, Economics, and Elite Realignment in Russia: A Regional Perspective," *Soviet Economy* 8, no. 1 (1992): 46–88; and Gail W. Lapidus, "From Democratization to Disintegration: The Impact of Perestroika on the National Question," in *From Union to Commonwealth*, eds. Gail W. Lapidus and Victor Zaslavsky with Philip Goldman (Cambridge: Cambridge University Press, 1992), 45–70.

38. The debate over economic reform is beyond the scope of this chapter. See, generally, Josef C. Brada, "The Transformation from Communism to Capitalism: How Far? How Fast?" *Post-Soviet Affairs* 9, no. 2 (1993): 87–110; and Peter Murrell, "What Is Shock Therapy? What Did It Do in Poland and Russia," *Post-Soviet Affairs* 9, no. 2 (1993): 111–40.

39. See Boris Yeltsin, *The Struggle for Russia*, trans. Catherine A. Fitzpatrick (New York: Times Books, 1994).

40. For example, Steve Erlanger, "From This Boss's Seat, Yeltsin Appears Small," *New York Times*, 8 January 1993, A4 (reporting on the "boss" of Ivanovo, a town 150 miles northeast of Moscow); and Serge Schmemann, "New Leaders of

Ancient City Try to Lead Russia to Reform," *The New York Times,* 9 August 1992, 1, 6 (reporting on developments in Nizhny Novgorod [formerly Gorky]).

41. See Stephen Handelman, "Inside Russia's Gangster Economy," *New York Times Magazine,* 24 January 1993, 12–15. See, generally, Diego Gambetta, *The Sicilian Mafia: The Business of Private Protection* (Cambridge, MA: Harvard University Press, 1993).

42. Bribery is not a new phenomenon in Russia. It existed and even flourished during the Soviet period. See Simis, *USSR: The Corrupt Society.* But the sort of corruption among governmental officials that has emerged in the post-Soviet period tends to be more brazen and reflects less fear of being caught and of the potential consequences. See Celestine Bohlen, "Corruption Grows Greedy in Russia," *New York Times,* 14 March 1992, 4.

43. See Jim Leitzel, Clifford Gaddy, and Michael Alexeev, "Mafiosi and Matrioshki: Organized Crime and Russian Reform," *The Brookings Review* 13, no. 1 (1995): 26–29.

44. See Chalmers Johnson, *MITI and the Japanese Miracle: The Growth of Industrial Policy, 1925–1975* (Stanford: Stanford University Press, 1982); Robert Wade, *Governing the Market: Economic Theory and the Role of Government in East Asian Industrialization* (Princeton: Princeton University Press, 1990), 305–24; and John Zysman, *Governments, Markets, and Growth: Financial Systems and the Politics of Industrial Change* (Ithaca: Cornell University Press, 1983), 285–320.

45. Johnson, *MITI and the Japanese Miracle,* 315.

46. See R. H. Coase, *The Firm the Market and the Law* (Chicago: University of Chicago Press, 1988), 7–9.

47. See Karin Chaudry, "The Myths of the Market and the Common History of Late Developers," *Politics & Society* 21, no. 3 (1993): 258–66.

Selected Bibliography

Books and Articles in English

Abel, Richard L. "Capitalism and the Rule of Law: Precondition or Contradiction?" *Law & Social Inquiry* 15, no. 4 (1990): 685–97.

Ajani, Gianmaria. "The Soviet Experience with Codification: Theoretical and Comparative Perspectives." In *The Soviet* Sobranie *of Laws: Problems of Codification and Non-Publication,* edited by Richard M. Buxbaum and Kathryn Hendley, 275–97. Berkeley: International and Area Studies, University of California, 1991.

Aleksandrov, N. G. *Soviet Labour Law.* Delhi, India: University Book House, 1961.

Armstrong, George M. "The Evolution of the Concept of Fault and Impossibility of Performance in the Soviet Law of Contracts Between Enterprises." *Review of Socialist Law* 7, no. 4 (1981): 387–405.

———. *The Soviet Law of Property.* The Hague, the Netherlands: Martinus Nijhoff, 1983.

Arnot, Bob. "Soviet Labour Productivity and the Failure of the Shchekino Experiment." *Critique,* no. 15 (1982): 31–56.

Ash, Timothy Garton. *The Uses of Adversity: Essays on the Fate of Central Europe.* New York: Random House, 1989.

Aslund, Anders. *Gorbachev's Struggle for Economic Reform: The Soviet Reform Process, 1985–88.* Ithaca: Cornell University Press, 1991.

Atiyah, P. S., and Robert S. Summers. *Form and Substance in Anglo-American Law: A Comparative Study of Legal Reasoning, Legal Theory, and Legal Institutions.* Oxford: Oxford University Press, 1987.

Atleson, James B. *Values and Assumptions in American Labor Law.* Amherst: University of Massachusetts Press, 1983.

Badaracco, Joseph L. *Loading the Dice: A Five-Country Study of Vinyl Chloride Regulation.* Boston: Harvard Business School Press, 1985.

Ball, Alan M. *Russia's Last Capitalists: The NEPmen, 1921–1929.* Berkeley and Los Angeles: University of California Press, 1987.

Barry, Donald D. "The USSR Supreme Court: Recent Developments." *Soviet Studies* 20, no. 4 (1969): 505–27.

———. "The Soviet Union." In *Governmental Tort Liability,* edited by Donald D. Barry, 21–78. Leyden, the Netherlands: A. W. Sijthoff, 1970.

———. "Compensation for Damages Caused by the Acts of Soviet Criminal Justice Organs: The 1981 Legislation." *Review of Socialist Law* 8, no. 4 (1982): 331–40.

———. "The Quest for Judicial Independence: Soviet Courts in a *Pravovoe Gosudarstvo.*" In *Toward the "Rule of Law" in Russia? Political and Legal Reform in the Transition Period,* edited by Donald D. Barry, 257–75. Armonk, NY: M. E. Sharpe, 1992.

Bauer, Tamas. "Investment Cycles in Planned Economies." *Acta Oeconomica* 21, no. 3 (1978): 243–60.

Becker, Theodore L. *Comparative Judicial Politics: The Political Functioning of Courts.* Lanham, MD: University Press of America, 1987.

Beirne, Piers, and Robert Sharlet. "Toward a General Theory of Law and Marxism: E. B. Pashukanis." In *Revolution in Law: Contributions to the Development of Soviet Legal Theory, 1917–1938,* edited by Piers Beirne, 17–44. Armonk, NY: M. E. Sharpe, 1990.

Beissinger, Mark R. "The Party and the Rule of Law." *Columbia Journal of Transnational Law* 28, no. 1 (1990): 41–58.

Bendix, Reinhard. *Max Weber: An Intellectual Portrait.* Berkeley and Los Angeles: University of California Press, 1977.

Berger, Peter L. *The Capitalist Revolution: Fifty Propositions about Prosperity, Equality, and Liberty.* New York: Basic Books, 1986.

Berliner, Joseph S. *Factory and Manager in the USSR.* Cambridge, MA: Harvard University Press, 1957.

———. *The Innovation Decision in Soviet Industry.* Cambridge, MA: MIT Press, 1976.

———. *Soviet Industry from Stalin to Gorbachev: Essays on Management and Innovation.* Ithaca: Cornell University Press, 1988.

Berman, Harold J. *Justice in the U.S.S.R.: An Interpretation of Soviet Law.* Rev. ed. Cambridge, MA: Harvard University Press, 1963.

———. *Law and Revolution: The Formation of the Western Legal Tradition.* Cambridge, MA: Harvard University Press, 1983.

———. "What Makes 'Socialist Law' Socialist?" *Problems of Communism* 20, no. 5 (September-October 1977): 24–30.

———. "The Rule of Law and the Law-Based State *(Rechtsstaat).*" *The Harriman Institute Forum* 4, no. 5 (1991).

Black, Donald J. *The Behavior of Law.* New York: Academic Press, 1976.

———. "The Mobilization of Law." *The Journal of Legal Studies* 2, no. 1 (1973): 125–50.

Blankenburg, Ehrhard, and Ralf Rogowski. "German Labour Courts and British Industrial Tribunal System: A Socio-Legal Comparison of Degrees of Judicialisation." *Journal of Law and Society* 13, no. 1 (1986): 67–92.

Bok, Derek C. "Reflections on the Distinctive Character of American Labor Laws." *Harvard Law Review* 84, no. 6 (1971): 1394–463.

———. "A Flawed System." *Harvard Magazine* 85, no. 3 (May-June 1983, 38, 40–45, 70–71.

Bork, Robert H. *The Tempting of America: The Political Seduction of the Law.* New York: Free Press, 1990.

Boyko, Maxim, Andrei Shleifer, and Robert W. Vishny. "Privatizing Russia." *Brookings Papers on Economic Activities,* no. 2 (1993): 139–92.

Brada, Josef C. "The Transformation from Communism to Capitalism: How Far? How Fast?" *Post-Soviet Affairs* 9, no. 2 (1993): 87–110.

Breslauer, George W. "Evaluating Gorbachev as Leader." *Soviet Economy* 5, no. 4 (1989): 299–340.

———. "In Defense of Sovietology." *Post-Soviet Affairs* 8, no. 3 (1992): 197–238.

Brown, Annette N., Barry W. Ickes, and Randi Ryterman. "The Myth of Monopoly: A New View of Industrial Structure in Russia." 1993. Photocopy.

Brzezinski, Zbigniew K. *The Soviet Bloc: Unity and Conflict.* Rev. ed. Cambridge, MA: Harvard University Press, 1967.

Bunce, Valerie. "Should Transitologists Be Grounded?" *Slavic Studies* 54, no. 1 (1995): 111–27.

Burawoy, Michael. "The End of Sovietology and the Renaissance of Modernization Theory." *Contemporary Sociology* 21, no. 6 (1992): 774–85.

———, and Kathryn Hendley. "Between Perestroika and Privatization: Divided Strategies and Political Crisis in a Soviet Enterprise." *Soviet Studies* 44, no. 3 (1992): 371–402.

———, and Pavel Krotov. "The Soviet Transition From Socialism to Capitalism: Worker Control and Economic Bargaining in the Wood Industry." *American Sociological Review* 57, no. 1 (1992): 16–38.

Burbank, Jane. "Lenin and the Law." *Slavic Review* 54, no. 1 (1995): 23–44.

Burrage, Michael. "*Advokatura:* In Search of Professionalism and Pluralism in Moscow and Leningrad." *Law & Social Inquiry* 15, no. 3 (1990): 433–78.

Butler, William E. *Soviet Law.* London: Butterworths, 1983.

———. "Toward a *Svod zakonov* in the USSR." In *Codification in the Communist World,* edited by Donald D. Barry, F. J. M. Feldbrugge, and Dominik Lasok, 89–111. Leiden, the Netherlands: A. W. Sijthoff, 1975.

Cahn, Edmond N. *The Sense of Injustice: An Anthropocentric View of Law.* New York: New York University Press, 1949.

Cappelletti, Mauro. *The Judicial Process in Comparative Perspective.* Oxford: Clarendon Press, 1989.

Carbon, Susan B. "Judicial Retention Elections: Are They Serving Their Intended Purpose?" *Judicature* 64, no. 5 (1980): 210–33.

Cardozo, Benjamin N. *The Nature of the Judicial Process.* New Haven: Yale University Press, 1921.

Chaudry, Karin. "The Myths of the Market and the Common History of Late Developers." *Politics & Society* 21, no. 3 (1993): 245–66.

Chayes, Abram. "The Role of the Judge in Public Law Litigation." *Harvard Law Review* 89, no. 7 (1976): 1281–316.

Chukovskaya, Lydia. *Sofia Petrovna.* Translated by Aline Werth. Evanston, IL: Northwestern University Press, 1967.

Clark, John, and Aaron Wildavsky. *The Moral Collapse of Communism: Poland as a Cautionary Tale.* San Francisco: Institute for Contemporary Studies Press, 1990.

Coase, R. H. *The Firm the Market and the Law.* Chicago: University of Chicago Press, 1988.

Cohen, Leonard J. "Judicial Elites in Yugoslavia: The Professionalization of Political Justice." *Review of Socialist Law* 11, no. 4 (1985): 313–44.

Collins, Hugh. *Marxism and Law.* Oxford: Oxford University Press, 1982.

Connor, Walter D. *The Accidental Proletariat: Workers, Politics, and Crisis in Gorbachev's Russia.* Princeton: Princeton University Press, 1991.

Conquest, Robert. *The Great Terror: A Reassessment.* New York: Oxford University Press, 1990.

Dahl, Robert A. *Polyarchy: Participation and Opposition.* New Haven: Yale University Press, 1971.

Damaska, Mirjan R., *The Faces of Justice and State Authority: A Comparative Approach to the Legal Process.* New Haven: Yale University Press, 1986.

Danilenko, Gennady M. "International Law and the Future of the Rechtsstaat in Russia." In *Law and Democracy in the New Russia,* edited by Bruce L. R. Smith and Gennady M. Dannilenko, 96–106. Washington, D.C.: Brookings Institution, 1993.

Davies, Joseph E. *Mission to Moscow.* New York: Simon & Schuster, 1941.

Dawson, John P. *The Oracles of the Law.* Ann Arbor: University of Michigan Press, 1969.

Deutscher, Isaac. *Soviet Trade Unions: Their Place in Soviet Labour Policy.* London: Royal Institute of International Affairs, 1950.

———. *Stalin: A Political Biography.* 2d ed. New York: Oxford University Press, 1966.

Di Palma, Giuseppe. *To Craft Democracies: An Essay on Democratic Transitions.* Berkeley and Los Angeles: University of California Press, 1990.

Djilas, Milovan. *The New Class: An Analysis of the Communist System.* New York: Praeger, 1957.

Doder, Dusko, and Louise Branson. *Gorbachev: Heretic in the Kremlin.* New York: Viking Penguin, 1990.

Draper, Theodore. "Who Killed Soviet Communism?" *New York Review of Books* 39, no. 11 (June 11, 1992): 7–14.

Dworkin, Ronald. *Law's Empire.* Cambridge, MA: Harvard University Press, 1986.

Dyker, David A. *The Process of Investment in the Soviet Union.* Cambridge: Cambridge University Press, 1983.

Eckhoff, Torstein. "Impartiality, Separation of Powers, and Judicial Independence." *Scandinavian Studies in Law* 9 (1965): 9–48.

Ehrmann, Henry W. *Comparative Legal Cultures.* Englewood Cliffs, NJ: Prentice-Hall, 1976.

Ely, John Hart. *Democracy and Distrust: A Theory of Judicial Review.* Cambridge, MA: Harvard University Press, 1980.

Fainsod, Merle. *How Russia Is Ruled.* 2d ed. Cambridge, MA: Harvard University Press, 1963.

Feifer, George. *Justice in Moscow.* New York: Simon and Schuster, 1964.

Feller, David E. "A General Theory of the Collective Bargaining Agreement." *California Law Review* 61, no. 3 (1973): 663–855.

Felstiner, William L. F., Richard L. Abel, and Austin Sarat. "The Emergence and Transformation of Disputes: Naming, Blaming, Claiming . . ." *Law & Society Review* 15, nos. 3–4 (1980–81): 631–54.

Flanagan, Robert J. *Labor Relations and the Litigation Explosion.* Washington, D.C.: Brookings Institution, 1987.

Forbath, William E. "The Shaping of the American Labor Movement." *Harvard Law Review* 102, no. 6 (1989), 1109–256.

———. *Law and the Shaping of the American Labor Movement.* Cambridge, MA: Harvard University Press, 1991.

Forsyth, Christopher. "The South African Judiciary in Time of Crisis." In *The Role of Courts in Society,* edited by Shimon Shetreet, 25–35. Dordrecht, the Netherlands: Martinus Nijhoff, 1988.

Foster, Frances H. "Procedure as a Guarantee of Democracy: The Legacy of the Perestroika Parliament." *Vanderbilt Journal of Transnational Law* 26, no. 1 (1993): 1–109.

Freeman, Richard B., and James L. Medoff. *What Do Unions Do?* New York: Basic Books, 1984.

Friedman, Lawrence M. *Total Justice.* New York: Russell Sage Foundation, 1985.

Fuller, Lon L. *The Morality of Law.* Rev. ed. New Haven: Yale University Press, 1969.

Galanter, Marc. "Reading the Landscape of Disputes: What We Know and Don't Know (and Think We Know) About Our Allegedly Contentious and Litigious Society." *UCLA Law Review* 31, no. 1 (1983): 4–71.

———. "Why the 'Haves' Come Out Ahead: Speculations on the Limits of Legal Change." *Law & Society Review* 9, no. 1 (1974): 95–160.

Gambetta, Diego. *The Sicilian Mafia: The Business of Private Protection.* Cambridge, MA: Harvard University Press, 1993.

———, ed. *Trust: Making and Breaking Cooperative Relations.* New York: Blackwell Publishers, 1988.

Getty, J. Arch. *Origins of the Great Purges: The Soviet Communist Party Reconsidered, 1933–1938.* New York: Cambridge University Press, 1985.

Ginsburgs, George. *The Citizenship Law of the USSR.* Boston: Martinus Nijhoff, 1983.

———. "The Soviet Judicial Elite: Is It?" *Review of Socialist Law* 11, no. 4 (1985): 293–311.

Ginzburg, Evgeniia. *Journey into the Whirlwind.* Translated by Paul Stevenson and Max Hayward. New York: Harcourt, Brace & World, 1967.

Glazer, Myron P., and Penina M. Glazer. *The Whistleblowers: Exposing Corruption in Government and Industry.* New York: Basic Books, 1989.

Glazyrin, V., V. Nikitinskii, N. Maksimova, and A. Yarno. *Soviet Employee's*

Rights in Law. Translated by James Riordan. Moscow: Progress Publishers, 1987.

Goldberg, Michael J. "The Duty of Fair Representation: What the Courts Do in Fact." *Buffalo Law Review* 34, no. 1 (1985): 89–171.

Goldman, Sheldon. "Carter's Judicial Appointments: A Lasting Legacy." *Judicature* 64, no. 8 (1981): 344–55.

———. "Reagan's Judicial Legacy: Completing the Puzzle and Summing Up," *Judicature* 72, no. 8 (1989): 318–30.

———. "The Bush Imprint on the Judiciary: Carrying on a Tradition." *Judicature* 74, no. 6 (1991): 294–306.

Gorbanevskaia, Natalia. *Red Square at Noon.* Translated by Alexander Lieven. London: Andre Deutsch, 1972.

Gorman, Robert A. *Basic Text on Labor Law: Unionization and Collective Bargaining.* St. Paul: West Publishing, 1976.

Granick, David. *Management of the Industrial Firm in the USSR.* New York: Columbia University Press, 1954.

———. *The Red Executive: A Study of the Organization Man in Russian Industry.* Garden City, NY: Doubleday, 1960.

———. *Job Rights in the Soviet Union: Their Consequences.* Cambridge: Cambridge University Press, 1987.

———. "Labor Markets in the USSR." *Occasional Paper of the Kennan Institute for Advanced Russian Studies,* no. 78, 1979.

Graziadei, Michele, and Ugo Mattei. "Judicial Responsibility in Italy: A New Statute." *American Journal of Comparative Law* 38, no. 1 (1990): 103–26.

Gregory, Paul R. "The Impact of Perestroika on the Soviet Planned Economy: Results of a Survey of Moscow Economic Officials." *Soviet Studies* 43, no. 5 (1991): 859–73.

———, and Robert C. Stuart. *Soviet Economic Structure and Performance.* 2d ed. New York: Harper & Row, 1981.

Grodin, Joseph R. *In Pursuit of Justice: Reflections of a State Supreme Court Justice.* Berkeley and Los Angeles: University of California Press, 1989.

Gross, James A. *The Making of the National Labor Relations Board.* Albany: State University of New York Press, 1974.

Grossman, Gregory. "The 'Second Economy' in the USSR." *Problems of Communism* 26, no. 5 (1977): 25–40.

Grossman, Joel B., Herbert M. Kritzer, Kristin Bumiller, and Stephen McDougal. "Measuring the Pace of Civil Litigation in Federal and State Trial Courts." *Judicature* 65, no. 2 (1981): 86–113.

Habscheid, Walther J. "Election, Status and Responsibility of the Judiciary in Switzerland." In *The Role of Courts in Society,* edited by Shimon Shetreet, 127–41. Dordrecht, the Netherlands: Martinus Nijhoff, 1988.

Hanson, Philip. "The Serendipitous Soviet Achievement of Full Employment: Labour Shortage and Labour Hoarding in the Soviet Economy." In *Labour and Employment in the USSR,* edited by David Lane, 83–111. Brighton, United Kingdom: Wheatsheaf Books, 1986.

———. "Property Rights in the New Phase of Reforms." In *Milestones in Glasnost and Perestroyka,* edited by Ed A. Hewett and Victor H. Winston, 415–40. Washington, D.C.: Brookings Institution, 1991.

Hasnas, John. "The Myth of the Rule of Law." *Wisconsin Law Review,* no. 1 (1995): 199–233.

Hauslohner, Peter A. "Managing the Soviet Labor Market: Politics and Policymaking under Brezhnev." Ph.D. diss., University of Michigan, 1984.

———. "Gorbachev's Social Contract." *Soviet Economy* 3, no. 1 (1987): 54–87.

Hazard, John N. *Settling Disputes in Soviet Society: The Formative Years of Legal Institutions.* New York: Columbia University Press, 1960.

———. *The Soviet System of Government.* 3d ed. Chicago: University of Chicago Press, 1964.

———. "Is Russian Case Law Becoming Significant as a Source of Law?" *Parker School Journal of East European Law* 1, no. 1 (1994): 23–46.

Helgenson, Ann. "Geographical Mobility—Its Implications for Employment." In *Labour and Employment in the USSR,* edited by David Lane, 145–75. Brighton, United Kingdom: Wheatsheaf Books, 1986.

Henderson, Jane. "Law of the USSR: On the Status of Judges in the USSR." *Review of Socialist Law* 16, no. 3 (1990): 305–38.

Hendley, Kathryn. "Does Law Matter in the Soviet Economic Reform Process? A Case Study of the Law Governing Internal Transfers." *Review of Central and East European Law* 18, no. 2 (1992): 101–34.

———. "The Ideals of the *Pravovoe Gosudarstvo* and the Soviet Workplace: A Case Study of Layoffs." In *Toward the "Rule of Law" in Russia? Political and Legal Reform in the Transition Period,* edited by Donald D. Barry, 315–36. Armonk, NY: M. E. Sharpe, 1992.

———. "Legal Development and Privatization in Russia: A Case Study." *Soviet Economy* 8, no. 2 (1992): 130–57.

———. "Preliminary Framework for Labor Contracts." *Survey of East European Law* 3, no. 4 (1992): 5–6.

———. "The Spillover Effects of Privatization on Russian Legal Culture." *Transnational Law & Contemporary Problems* 5, no. 1 (1995): 33–64.

Hewett, Ed A. *Reforming the Soviet Economy: Equality Versus Efficiency.* Washington, D.C.: Brookings Institution, 1988.

Hirschman, Albert O. *Exit, Voice and Loyalty: Responses to Decline in Firms, Organizations, and States.* Cambridge, MA: Harvard University Press, 1970.

Hoebel, E. Adamson. *The Law of Primitive Man: A Study in Comparative Legal Dynamics.* Cambridge, MA: Harvard University Press, 1954.

Holmes, Oliver Wendell. *The Common Law.* Boston: Little, Brown, 1923.

Hough, Jerry F. "Understanding Gorbachev: The Importance of Politics." *Soviet Economy* 5, no. 4 (1989): 89–109.

Howard, Charles G., and Robert S. Summers. *Law: Its Nature, Functions, and Limits.* Englewood Cliffs, NJ: Prentice-Hall, 1965.

Hunt, Alan. *The Sociological Movement in Law.* Philadelphia: Temple University Press, 1978.

Hurst, James Willard. *Law and Markets in United States History: Different Modes of Bargaining among Interests.* Madison: University of Wisconsin Press, 1982.

Huskey, Eugene. "Between Citizen and State: The Soviet Bar (Advokatura) under Gorbachev." *Columbia Journal of Transnational Law* 28, no. 1 (1990): 95–116.

———. "Government Rulemaking as a Brake on Perestroika." *Law & Social Inquiry* 15, no. 3 (1990): 419–32.

———. "From Legal Nihilism to *Pravovoe Gosudarstvo:* Soviet Legal Development." In *Toward the "Rule of Law" in the Russia? Political and Legal Reform in the Transition Period,* edited by Donald D. Barry, 23–42. Armonk, NY: M. E. Sharpe, 1992.

Ioffe, Olympiad S. *Soviet Law and Soviet Reality.* Dordrecht, the Netherlands: Martinus Nijhoff, 1985.

———. "Law and Economy in the USSR." *Harvard Law Review* 95, no.7 (1982): 1591–625.

———, and Peter B. Maggs. *Soviet Law in Theory and Practice.* New York: Oceana Publications, 1983.

Ivanov, S. "Labor Law in Socialist Countries: Three Issues of General Theory." *Comparative Labor Law Journal* 11, no. 1 (1989): 81–90.

Jackson, Donald W., and James W. Riddlesperger Jr. "Money and Politics in Judicial Elections: The 1988 Election of the Chief Justice of the Texas Supreme Court." *Judicature* 74, no. 4 (1991): 184–89.

Jacoby, Sanford M. "The Duration of Indefinite Employment Contracts in the United States and England: An Historical Analysis." *Comparative Labor Law* 5, no. 1 (1982): 85–128.

Johnson, Chalmers. *MITI and the Japanese Miracle: The Growth of Industrial Policy, 1925–1975.* Stanford: Stanford University Press, 1982.

Jones, Anthony, and William Moskoff. *Ko-ops: The Rebirth of Entrepreneurship in the Soviet Union.* Bloomington: Indiana University Press, 1991.

Jowitt, Kenneth. *New World Disorder: The Leninist Extinction.* Berkeley and Los Angeles: University of California Press, 1992.

———. "Soviet Neotraditionalism: The Political Corruption of a Leninist Regime." *Soviet Studies* 35, no. 3 (1983): 275–97.

Juviler, Peter. "Secret Justice and Personal Rights." In *The Soviet* Sobranie *of Laws: Problems of Codification and Non-Publication,* edited by Richard M. Buxbaum and Kathryn Hendley, 156–72. Berkeley: International and Area Studies, University of California, 1991.

Kagan, Robert A. *Regulatory Justice: Implementing a Wage-Price Freeze.* New York: Russell Sage Foundation, 1978.

———. "How Much Does Law Matter? Labor Law, Competition, and Waterfront Labor Relations in Rotterdam and U.S. Ports." *Law & Society Review* 24, no. 1 (1990): 35–69.

———, Bobby D. Infelise, and Robert R. Detlefsen. "American State Supreme Court Justices, 1900–1970." *American Bar Foundation Research Journal,* no. 2 (1984): 371–408.

———, and John T. Scholz. "The 'Criminology of the Corporation' and Regulatory Enforcement Strategies." In *Enforcing Regulation,* edited by Keith Hawkins and John M. Thomas, 67–95. Boston: Kluwer-Nijhoff, 1984.

Kaiser, Robert G. *Why Gorbachev Happened: His Triumphs, His Failure, and His Fall.* New York: Simon and Schuster, 1991.

Kaminskaya, Dina. *Final Judgment: My Life as a Soviet Defense Attorney.* Translated by Michael Glenny. New York: Simon and Schuster, 1982.

Katz, Abraham. *The Politics of Economic Reform in the Soviet Union.* New York: Praeger, 1972.

Katzenstein, Peter J. *Small States in World Markets: Industrial Policy in Europe.* Ithaca: Cornell University Press, 1985.

Kelsen, Hans. *Pure Theory of Law.* Translated by Max Knight. Berkeley and Los Angeles: University of California Press, 1967.

Kiernan, Brendan, and Joseph Aistrup. "The 1989 Elections to the Congress of People's Deputies in Moscow." *Soviet Studies* 43, no. 6 (1991): 1049–64.

Klose, Kevin. *Russia and the Russians: Inside the Closed Society.* New York: W. W. Norton, 1984.

Knegt, Robert. "Regulating Dismissal from Employment: Administrative and Judicial Procedures in the Netherlands." *Law & Policy* 11, no. 2 (1989): 175–87.

Kommers, Donald P. "The Federal Constitutional Court in the West German Political System." In *Frontiers of Judicial Research,* edited by Joel B. Grossman and Joseph Tanenhaus, 73–132. New York: John Wiley and Sons, 1969.

Kornai, Janos. *Economics of Shortage.* Amsterdam: North Holland, 1980.

———. *Socialist System: The Political Economy of Communism.* Princeton: Princeton University Press, 1992.

Kroll, Heidi. "Breach of Contract in the Soviet Economy." *Journal of Legal Studies* 16, no. 1 (1987): 119–48.

Kronman, Anthony T. *Max Weber.* Stanford: Stanford University Press, 1983.

Krygier, Martin. "Marxism, Communism, and Narcissism." *Law & Social Inquiry* 15, no. 4 (1990): 707–30.

———. "Marxism and the Rule of Law: Reflections after the Collapse of Communism," *Law & Social Inquiry* 15, no. 4 (1990): 633–63.

———. "A Morality Tale." *The National Interest,* no. 23 (1991): 96–100.

Kurland, Philip B. "The Constitution and the Tenure of Federal Judges: Some Notes from History." *University of Chicago Law Review* 36, no. 3 (1969): 665–98.

Lafon, Jacqueline Lucienne. "The Judicial Career in France: Theory and Practice under the Fifth Republic." *Judicature* 75, no. 2 (1991): 97–106.

Lampert, Nicholas. *Whistleblowing in the Soviet Union: Complaints and Abuses Under State Socialism.* London: Macmillan, 1985.

———. "Job Security and the Law in the USSR." In *Labour and Employment in the USSR,* edited by David Lane, 256–77. Brighton, United Kingdom: Wheatsheaf Books, 1986.

Lapidus, Gail W. "From Democratization to Disintegration: The Impact of Perestroika on the National Question." In *From Union to Commonwealth,* edited by Gail W. Lapidus and Victor Zaslavsky with Philip Goldman, 45–70. Cambridge: Cambridge University Press, 1992.

Leitzel, Jim, Clifford Gaddy, and Michael Alexseev. "Mafiosi and Matrioshki: Organized Crime and Russian Reform." *The Brookings Review* 13, no. 1 (1995): 26–29.

Levitsky, Serge L. *Copyright, Defamation, and Privacy in Soviet Civil Law.* Alphen aan den Rijn, the Netherlands: Sijthoff & Noordhoff, 1979.

Lev, Daniel S. "Judicial Authority and the Struggle for an Indonesian Rechtsstaat." *Law & Society Review* 13, no. 1 (1978): 37–71.

Lewin, Moshe. *Russian Peasants and Soviet Power: A Study of Collectivization.* Translated by Irene Nove. New York: W. W. Norton, 1975.

———. *The Making of the Soviet System: Essays in the Social History of Interwar Russia.* New York: Pantheon Books, 1985.

———. *The Gorbachev Phenomenon: A Historical Interpretation.* Berkeley: University of California Press, 1988.

Lipson, Leon. "Socialist Legality: The Road Uphill." In *Russia under Khrushchev,* edited by Abraham Brumberg, 444–69. New York: Frederick A. Praeger, 1962.

Litvinov, Pavel, comp.. *The Trial of the Four: A Collection of Materials on the Case of Galanskov, Ginzburg, Dobrovolsky, and Lashkova (1967–68).* Translated by Janis Sapiets, Hilary Sternberg, and Daniel Weissbort. New York: Viking Press, 1972.

Livshits, R. Z., and V. I. Nikitinskii. *An Outline of Soviet Labour Law.* Moscow: Progress Publishers, 1977.

Loeber, Dietrich Andre. "Statutes of the Agencies of State Administration in the Soviet Union—An Unexplored Area of Codification." In *Codification in the Communist World,* edited by Donald D. Barry, F. J. M. Feldbrugge, and Dominik Lasok, 221–38. Leyden, the Netherlands: A. W. Sijthoff, 1975.

Luryi, Yuri. "The Scientific-Technical Revolution and Soviet Labor Legislation." In *Soviet and East European Law and the Scientific-Technical Revolution,* edited by Gordon B. Smith, Peter B. Maggs, and George Ginsburgs, 213–39. New York: Pergamon, 1981.

Macaulay, Stewart. "Non-Contractual Relations in Business: A Preliminary Study." *American Sociological Review* 28, no. 1 (1963): 55–67.

Malia, Martin. "A New Russian Revolution?" *New York Review of Books* 38, no. 3 (July 18, 1991): 29–31.

Malle, Silvana. *Economic Planning in the Soviet Union: Continuity and Change.* London: Macmillan, 1990.

Markovits, Inga. "Pursuing One's Rights under Socialism." *Stanford Law Review* 38, no. 3 (1986): 689–761.

———. "Law and *Glasnost':* Some Thoughts About the Future of Judicial Review Under Socialism." *Law & Society Review* 23, no. 3 (1989): 399–447.

———. "Last Days." *California Law Review* 80, no. 1 (1992): 55–129.

Mason, Anthony F. "Judicial Independence and the Separation of Powers—Some

Problems Old and New." *University of British Columbia Law Review* 24, no. 2 (1990): 345–59.

Massell, Gregory J. *The Surrogate Proletariat: Moslem Women and Revolutionary Strategies in Soviet Central Asia.* Princeton: Princeton University Press, 1974.

McAuley, Mary. *Labour Disputes in Soviet Russia, 1957–65.* Oxford: Clarendon Press, 1969.

———. "Politics, Economics, and Elite Realignment in Russia: A Regional Perspective." *Soviet Economy* 8, no. 1 (1992): 46–88.

Medvedev, Roy A. *Let History Judge: The Origins and Consequences of Stalinism.* Translated by Colleen Taylor. New York: Alfred A. Knopf, 1972.

Medvedev, Zhores A. *Andropov.* New York: W. W. Norton, 1983.

———. *Gorbachev.* New York: W. W. Norton, 1986.

Merryman, John Henry. *The Civil Law Tradition: An Introduction to the Legal Systems of Western Europe and Latin America.* 2d ed. Stanford: Stanford University Press, 1985.

Miller, Richard E., and Austin Sarat. "Grievances, Claims, and Disputes: Assessing the Adversary Culture." *Law & Society Review* 15, nos. 3–4 (1980–81): 525–65.

Molodtsov, Mstislav. "Benefits in Addition to Wages and Salaries in the USSR." *Comparative Labor Law* 3, no. 2 (1980): 149–55.

Morrison, Fred L. "The Swiss Federal Court: Judicial Decision Making and Recruitment." In *Frontiers of Judicial Research,* edited by Joel B. Grossman and Joseph Tanenhaus, 133–62. New York: John Wiley and Sons, 1969.

Muller, Ingo. *Hitler's Justice: The Courts of the Third Reich.* Translated by Deborah Lucas Schneider. Cambridge, MA: Harvard University Press, 1991.

Muniz-Arguelles, Luis, and Migdalia Fraticelli-Torres. "Selection and Training of Judges in Spain, France, West Germany and England." *Boston College International and Comparative Law Review* 8, no. 1 (1985): 1–37.

Murrell, Peter. "What Is Shock Therapy? What Did It Do in Poland and Russia?" *Post-Soviet Affairs* 9, no. 2 (1993): 111–40.

Neumann, Franz. *The Rule of Law: Political Theory and the Legal System in Modern Society.* Dover, NH: Berg Publishers, 1986.

Newcity, Michael A. *Taxation in the Soviet Union.* New York: Praeger, 1986.

Nonet, Philippe, and Philip Selznick. *Law and Society in Transition: Toward Responsive Law.* New York: Octagon Books, 1978.

Nove, Alec. *An Economic History of the U.S.S.R.* New York: Penguin Books, 1969.

———. *The Soviet Economic System.* London: Allen & Unwin, 1977.

Oda, Hiroshi. "Judicial Review of Administration in the USSR." In *The Impact of Perestroika on Soviet Law,* edited by Albert J. Schmidt, 157–73. Boston: Martinus Nijhoff, 1990.

O'Donnell, Guillermo, Philippe C. Schmitter, and Laurence Whitehead, eds. *Transitions from Authoritarian Rule: Prospects for Democracy.* Baltimore: Johns Hopkins University Press, 1986.

Olson, Mancur. "The Hidden Path to a Successful Economy." In *The Emergence of Market Economies in Eastern Europe,* edited by Christopher Clague and Gordon C. Rausser, 55–75. Cambridge, MA: Blackwell Publishers, 1992.

Osakwe, Christopher. "An Examination of the Modern Soviet Law of Torts." *Tulane Law Review* 84, no. 1 (1979): 1–79.

Pakulski, Jan. "Bureaucracy and the Soviet System." *Studies in Comparative Communism* 19, no. 1 (1986): 3–24.

Plucknett, Theodore F. T. "The Place of the Legal Profession in the History of English Law." *Law Quarterly Review* 48, no. 191 (1932): 328–40.

Pomorski, Stanislaw. "State Arbitrazh in the U.S.S.R.: Development, Functions, Organization." *Rutgers-Camden Law Journal* 9, no. 1 (1977): 61–116.

———. "The Future of the State Enterprise and the 'Restructuring' of the National Economy in the USSR." *Tulane Law Review* 61, no. 6 (1987): 1383–95.

Pravda, Alex, and Blair A. Ruble. "Communist Trade Unions: Varieties of Dualism." In *Trade Unions in Communist States,* edited by Alex Pravda and Blair A. Ruble, 1–21. Boston: Allen & Unwin, 1986.

Quigley, John. "Socialist Law and the Civil Law Tradition." *American Journal of Comparative Law* 37, no. 4 (fall 1989): 781–808.

———. "Law Reform and the Soviet Courts." *Columbia Journal of Transnational Law* 28, no. 1 (1990): 59–75.

Rand, Robert. *Comrade Lawyer.* Boulder, CO: Westview Press, 1991.

Raz, Joseph. "The Rule of Law and Its Virtue." In *The Authority of Law: Essays on Law and Morality,* 210–29. Oxford: Clarendon Press, 1979.

———. "The Purity of the Pure Theory." In *Essays on Kelsen,* edited by Richard Tur and William Twining, 79–97. Oxford: Clarendon Press, 1986.

Reddaway, Peter. "The End of the Empire." *New York Review of Books* 38, no. 18 (November 7, 1991): 53–59.

Remnick, David. *Lenin's Tomb: The Last Days of the Soviet Empire.* New York: Random House, 1993.

Resnik, Judith. "Managerial Judges." *Harvard Law Review* 96, no. 2 (1976): 376–448.

Rheinstein, Max. "Who Watches the Watchmen?" In *Interpretations of Modern Legal Philosophies: Essays in Honor of Roscoe Pound,* edited by Paul Sayre, 589–610. New York: Oxford University Press, 1947.

Rogers, Joel. "Divide and Conquer: Further 'Reflections on the Distinctive Character of American Labor Laws.'" *Wisconsin Law Review,* no. 1 (1990): 1–147.

Rose, Richard. "Postcommunism and the Problem of Trust." *Journal of Democracy* 5, no. 3 (1994): 18–29.

Rubenstein, Joshua. *Soviet Dissidents: Their Struggle for Human Rights.* Boston: Beacon Press, 1980.

Rubin, Ed. "Law and Legislation in the Administrative State." *Columbia Law Review* 89, no. 2 (1989): 369–427.

Ruble, Blair A. "Full Employment Legislation in the USSR." *Comparative Labor Law* 2, no. 3 (fall 1977): 176–85.

———. "The Soviet-American Comparison: A High-Risk Venture." *Comparative Labor Law* 2, no. 4 (winter 1977): 247–59.

———. "Factory Unions and Workers' Rights." In *Industrial Labor in the U.S.S.R.*, edited by Arcadius Kahan and Blair A. Ruble, 59–84. New York: Pergamon. 1979.

———. "Industrial Trade Unions in the USSR." In *Trade Unions in Communist States,* edited by Alex Pravda and Blair A. Ruble, 23–52. Boston: Allen & Unwin, 1986.

Rudden, Bernard. "The Role of the Courts and Judicial Style under the Soviet Civil Codes." In *Codification in the Communist World,* edited by Donald D. Barry, F. J. M. Feldbrugge, and Dominik Lasok, 317–31. Leiden, the Netherlands: A. W. Sijthoff, 1975.

Rutland, Peter. "The Shchekino Method and the Struggle to Raise Labour Productivity in Soviet Industry." *Soviet Studies* 38, no. 2 (1984): 345–65.

———. "Productivity Campaigns in Soviet Industry." In *Labour and Employment in the USSR,* edited by David Lane, 191–208. Brighton, United Kingdom: Wheatsheaf Books, 1986.

———. "Labor Unrest and Movements in 1989 and 1990." *Soviet Economy* 6, no. 3 (1990): 345–84.

Ryavec, Karl W. *Implementation of Soviet Economic Reforms: Political, Organizational, and Social Process.* New York: Praeger, 1975.

Sabel, Charles F. "The Internal Politics of Trade Unions." In *Organizing Interests in Western Europe: Pluralism, Corporatism, and the Transformation of Politics,* edited by Suzanne D. Berger, 209–44. Cambridge: Cambridge University Press, 1981.

Sacco, Rodolfo. "The Romanist Substratum in the Civil Law of the Socialist Countries." *Review of Socialist Law* 14, no. 1 (1988): 65–86.

Sakharov, Andrei. *Memoirs.* Translated by Richard Lourie. New York: Vintage Books, 1992.

Satter, Robert. *Doing Justice: A Trial Judge at Work.* New York: Simon & Schuster, 1990.

Savitskii, V. M. "Aspects of Judicial Reform in the USSR." *Coexistence,* no. 28 (1991): 119–31.

Schmitter, Philippe C., and Terry Lynn Karl. "The Conceptual Travels of Transitologists and Consolidologists: How Far East Should They Attempt To Go?" *Slavic Review* 53, no. 1 (1994): 173–85.

Schwarz, Solomon M. *Labor in the Soviet Union.* New York: Praeger, 1952.

Selznick, Philip. *Law, Society, and Industrial Justice.* New York: Russell Sage Foundation, 1969.

Shamir, Ronen. "'Landmark Cases' and the Reproduction of Legitimacy: The Case of Israel's High Court of Justice." *Law & Society Review* 24, no. 3 (1990): 781–805.

Sharlet, Robert. *Soviet Constitutional Crisis: From De-Stalinization to Disintegration.* Armonk, NY: M. E. Sharpe, 1992.

———. "Pashukanis and the Rise of Soviet Marxist Jurisprudence, 1924–1930." *Soviet Union* 1, no. 2 (1974): 103–21.

———. "Stalinism and Soviet Legal Culture." In *Stalinism: Essays in Historical Interpretation,* edited by Robert C. Tucker, 155–79. New York: W. W. Norton, 1977.

———. "Pashukanis and the Withering Away of the Law in the USSR." In *Cultural Revolution in Russia, 1928–1931,* edited by Sheila Fitzpatrick, 169–88. Bloomington: Indiana University Press, 1984.

Shapiro, Leonard. *The Communist Party of the Soviet Union.* 2d ed. New York: Vintage Books, 1971.

Shapiro, Martin M. *Courts: A Comparative and Political Analysis.* Chicago: University of Chicago Press, 1981.

Shelley, Louise I. *Lawyers in Soviet Work Life.* New Brunswick: Rutgers University Press, 1984.

———. "Soviet Courts as Vehicles for Political Maneuver." *Soviet Union* 13, no. 2 (1986): 163–86.

———. "The Political Function of Soviet Courts: A Model for One-Party States." *Review of Socialist Law* 13, no. 3 (1987): 263–83.

Shetreet, Shimon. "Judicial Independence: New Conceptual Dimensions and Contemporary Challenges." In *Judicial Independence: The Contemporary Debate,* edited by Shimon Shetreet and Jules Deschenes, 590–681. Dordrecht, the Netherlands: Martinus Nijhoff Publishers, 1985.

Shklar, Judith N. *The Faces of Injustice.* New Haven: Yale University Press, 1990.

Simis, Konstantin M. *USSR: The Corrupt Society.* Translated by Jacqueline Edwards and Mitchell Schneider. New York: Simon and Schuster, 1982.

Simorot, Z. K. "Trade Union Protection of Labour Rights in Cases of Dismissal." In *Comparative Labour Law,* edited by W. E. Butler, B. A. Hepple, and Alan C. Neal, 87–91. Hants, United Kingdom: Gower Publishing, 1987.

Slider, Darrell. "The Brigade System in Soviet Industry: An Effort to Restructure the Labor Force." *Soviet Studies* 29, no. 3 (1987): 388–405.

Smith, Adam. *The Wealth of Nations.* New York: Penguin Books, 1986.

Smith, Gordon B. *The Soviet Procuracy and the Supervision of Administration.* Alphen aan den Rijn, the Netherlands: Sijthoff & Noordhoff, 1978.

Smith, Steve D. "Reductionism in Legal Thought." *Columbia Law Review* 91, no. 1 (1991): 68–109.

Sobchak, Anatoly. *For a New Russia.* New York: Free Press, 1992.

Solomon, Peter H., Jr. "The U.S.S.R. Supreme Court: History, Role, and Future Prospects." *American Journal of Comparative Law* 38, no. 1 (winter 1990): 127–42.

Solzhenitsyn, Aleksandr I. *The Gulag Archipelago: 1918–1956, I–II.* Translated by Thomas P. Whitney. New York: Harper & Row, 1973.

Stark, David. "Path Dependence and Privatization Strategies in East Central Europe." *Eastern European Politics and Societies* 6, no. 1 (1992): 17–54.

Stone, Katherine Van Wezel. "The Post-War Paradigm in American Labor Law." *Yale Law Journal* 90, no. 7 (1981): 1509–80.

Summers, Clyde W. "Worker Participation in the U.S. and West Germany: A Comparative Study from an American Perspective." *American Journal of Comparative Law* 28, no. 3 (1980): 367–92.

———. "Effective Remedies for Employment Rights: Preliminary Guidelines and Proposals." *University of Pennsylvania Law Review* 141, no. 2 (1992): 457–546.

Talbott, Strobe, trans. and ed., *Khrushchev Remembers.* Boston: Little, Brown, 1970.

Teague, Elizabeth, "The Absentee Vote: Worker Discontent and Labor Productivity in the Soviet Union." *Workers Under Communism,* no. 2 (1982), 22–26.

Thelen, Kathleen A. *Union of Parts: Labor Politics in Postwar Germany.* Ithaca: Cornell University Press, 1991.

Toharia, Jose J. "Judicial Independence in an Authoritarian Regime: The Case of Contemporary Spain." *Law & Society Review* 9, no. 3 (1975): 475–96.

Tribe, Laurence H. *American Constitutional Law.* 2d ed. Mineola, NY: Foundation Press, 1985.

Troy, Leo. "The Rise and Fall of American Trade Unions: The Labor Movement from FDR to RR." In *Unions in Transition: Entering the Second Century,* edited by Seymour Martin Lipset, 77–109. San Francisco: Institute for Contemporary Studies Press, 1986.

Trubek, David M. "Max Weber on Law and the Rise of Capitalism." *Wisconsin Law Review,* no. 3 (1972): 720–53.

———, Austin Sarat, William L. F. Felstiner, Herbert M. Kritzer, and Joel B. Grossman. "The Costs of Ordinary Litigation." *UCLA Law Review* 31, no. 1 (1983): 72–123.

Tucker, Robert C. *Stalin in Power: The Revolution from Above, 1928–1941.* New York: W. W. Norton, 1990.

———. "Stalin, Bukharin, and History as Conspiracy." In *The Soviet Political Mind: Stalinism and Post-Stalin Change.* New York: W.W. Norton & Company, 1971.

———, ed. *The Lenin Anthology.* New York: W. W. Norton, 1975.

Turner, Lowell. *Democracy at Work: Changing World Markets and the Future of Labor Unions.* Ithaca: Cornell University Press, 1991.

Tyler, Tom R. *Why People Obey the Law.* New Haven: Yale University Press, 1990.

Ulam, Adam B. *Stalin: The Man and His Era.* New York: Viking Press, 1973.

Ulc, Otto. *The Judge in a Communist State: A View From Within.* Columbus: Ohio University Press, 1972.

Unger, Roberto Mangabeira. *Law in Modern Society: Toward a Criticism of Social Theory.* New York: Free Press, 1976.

Vaksberg, Arkady. *Stalin's Prosecutor: The Life of Andrei Vyshinsky.* Translated by Jan Butler. New York: Grove Weidenfeld, 1991.

van den Berg, Ger P. "Judicial Settlement of Individual Labor Disputes in the Soviet Union." *Review of Socialist Law* 9, no. 2 (1983): 125–64.

———. "Soviet Labor Laws in the Collection of USSR Laws." In *The Soviet Sobranie of Laws: Problems of Codification and Publication,* edited by Richard

M. Buxbaum and Kathryn Hendley, 68–101. Berkeley: International and Area Studies, University of California, 1991.

van Koppen, Peter J. "The Dutch Supreme Court and Parliament: Political Decisionmaking versus Nonpolitical Appointments." *Law & Society Review* 24, no. 3 (1990): 745–80.

Viola, Lynn. "The Campaign To Eliminate the Kulak as a Class, Winter 1929–1930: A Reevaluation of the Legislation." *Slavic Review* 45, no. 3 (1986): 503–24.

von Mehren, Arthur. "The Judicial Process: A Comparative Analysis." *American Journal of Comparative Law* 5, no. 2 (1956): 197–228.

Voslenskii, Michael S. *Nomenklatura.* Translated by Eric Mosbacher. Garden City, NJ: Doubleday, 1984.

Wade, Robert. *Governing the Market: Economic Theory and the Role of Government in East Asian Industrialization.* Princeton: Princeton University Press, 1990.

Watson, Alan. *The Making of the Civil Law.* Cambridge, MA: Harvard University Press, 1981.

Weber, Max. *Max Weber on Law in Economy and Society.* Edited by Max Rheinstein. Cambridge, MA: Harvard University Press, 1967.

Weiler, Paul C. *Governing the Workplace: The Future of Labor and Employment Law.* Cambridge, MA: Harvard University Press, 1990.

Williamson, Oliver E. *The Economic Institutions of Capitalism: Firms, Markets, Relational Contracting.* New York: Free Press, 1985.

Wold, John T., and John H. Culver. "The Defeat of the California Justices: The Campaign, the Electorate, and the Issue of Judicial Accountability." *Judicature* 70, no. 6 (1987): 348–55.

Yeltsin, Boris. *Against the Grain.* Translated by Michael Glenny. New York: Summit Books, 1990.

———. *The Struggle for Russia.* Translated by Catherine A. Fitzpatrick. New York: Times Books, 1994.

Zall, Terri A. "Unfair Dismissal in the United States and the United Kingdom: A Procedural Comparison of Remedies." *Comparative Labor Law Journal* 9, no. 3 (1988): 433–49.

Zysman, John. *Governments, Markets, and Growth: Financial Systems and the Politics of Industrial Change.* Ithaca: Cornell University Press, 1983.

Books and Articles in Russian

Antonova, O. "Upravlenie protsessom vysvobozhdeniia i pereraspredeleniia rabochei sily v GDR." *Sotsialisticheskii trud,* no. 1 (1988): 129–35.

Baglai, M. V. "Perestroika i profsoiuzy." *Kommunist,* no. 12 (1987): 80–90.

———. "Pravovoe gosudarstvo: ot idei k praktike." *Kommunist,* no. 6 (1989): 38–47.

Baturin, Iu. M., and R. Z. Livshits, *Sotsialisticheskoe pravovoe gosudarstvo: ot ideiu k osuchshestvleniiu.* Moscow: Nauka, 1989.

Blazhevich, S. "Sluzhba trudoustroistva v novykh usloviiakh: Problemy, perspektivy, razvitiia." *Sotsialisticheskii trud,* no. 12 (1988): 27–29.

Bugrov, L. Iu. *Sovetskoe zakonodatel'stvo o perevodakh na druguiu rabotu.* Krasnoiarsk: Izdatel'stvo krasnoiarskogo universiteta, 1987.

———. "Perestroika i razvitie sovetskogo zakonodatel'stva o perevodakh na druguiu rabotu." *Sovetskoe gosudarstvo i pravo,* no. 12 (1988): 38–46.

Egorov, V. V. "K razvitiiu prava na trud v sovetskom zakonodatel'stve." *Sovetskoe gosudarstvo i pravo,* no. 10 (1980): 81–85.

Eisler, M. "O sootvetstvii kollektivnykh dogovorov zakonodatel'stvu o trude." *Sovetskoe pravo,* no. 6 (1980): 430–37.

Ershov, V. "Rassmotrenie sporov, sviazannykh s perevodami na druguiu rabotu." *Sovetskaia iustitsiia,* no. 12 (1989): 21–22.

Fatuev, A., and E. Chezhina. "Stat'ia 25 KZoT RSFSR: problemy i suzhdeniia." *Sotsialisticheskii trud,* no. 7 (1990): 84–93.

Gavrilina, A. K. "Rassmotrenie sudebnymi organami sporov, sviazannykh s premeneniem norm ob oplate vynuzhdennogo progula." In *Komentarii sudebnoi praktike za 1978 god,* edited by E. V. Voldyreva and A. I. Pergament, 31–40. Moscow: Iuridicheskaia literatura, 1979.

Germanov, E. "Vmeste s profkomom i STK." *Sotsialisticheskii trud,* no. 12 (1988): 70–74.

Gladkii, I. I. "Intensivnoi ekonomike—effektivnuiu zaniatost'." *Sotsialisticheskii trud,* no. 5 (1988): 3–9.

Glazyrin, V. V. "Effektivnost' primeneniia pravovykh sredstv ukrepleniia trudovoi distsipliny." *Problemy sovershesnstvovaniia sovetskogo zakonodatel'stva,* no. 28 (1984): 107–19.

Gliantsev, V. "Spornye voprosy rassmotreniia del, sviazannykh s perevodom i peremeshcheniem rabotnikov." *Sovetskaia iustitsiia,* no. 18 (1989): 5–7.

Golovanova, E. A. *Prekrashchenie trudovogo dogovora.* Moscow: Iuridicheskaia literatura, 1966.

———. *Perevody rabochikh i sluzhashchikh na druguiu rabotu.* Moscow: Iuridicheskaia literatura, 1986.

———. "Formulirovka prichiny uvol'neniia." *Sovetskaia iustitsiia,* no. 7 (1989): 26–27.

Gorelko, N. "Obespechenie zaniatosti vysvobozhdaemykh rabotnikov." *Sovetskaia iustitsiia,* no. 20 (1989): 19–21.

Grebenkin, E. "Rastorzhenie trudovogo dogovora po initsiative administratsii." *Sovetskaia iustitsiia,* no. 21 (1989): 21.

Iakovets, Iu. "Trudovoi potentsial obshchestva: tendentsii i perspektivy." *Sotsialisticheskii trud,* no. 8 (1988): 43–50.

Ioffe, O. S. *Sovetskoe grazhdanskoe pravo.* 3 volumes. Leningrad: Izdatel'stvo Leningradskogo Universiteta, 1958–65.

Ivanov, S. A. "Krizis sovetskogo trudovogo prava." *Sovetskoe gosudarstvo i pravo,* no. 7 (1990): 39–47.

Khatskevich, M., and L. Moroz. "Sudebnye postanovleniia po delam o vosstanovlenii na rabote." *Sovetskaia iustitsiia,* no. 12 (1990): 9–10.

Kniazev, A. "Razreshenie sudami sporov o vosstanovlenii na rabote (obzor nadzornoi praktiki)." *Sovetskaia iustitsiia,* no. 12 (1983): 10–12.

Kollom, T. "O sudebnoi praktike po delam o vosstanovlenii na rabote." *Sovetskoe pravo,* no. 2 (1980): 107–13.

———. "Sudebnaia praktika po delam o vosstanovlenii na rabotu." *Sovetskoe pravo,* no. 4 (1982): 248–53.

Kolosov, V. K. *Trudovye spory.* Moscow: Profizdat, 1986.

Kommentarii k zakonodatel'stvu o trude. Moscow: Iuridicheskaia literatura, 1976.

Kommentarii k zakonodatel'stvu o trude. Moscow: Iuridicheskaia literatura, 1986.

Kommentarii k zakonodatel'stvu o trude. Moscow: Iuridicheskaia literatura, 1988.

Kostakov, V. G. "Zaniatost': defitsit ili izbytok?" *Kommunist,* no. 2 (1987): 78–89.

———. "Polnaia zaniatost': Kak my ee ponimaet?" *Kommunist,* no. 14 (1987): 16–25.

Kotliar, A. "Nuzhno li nam polnaia zaniatost'." *Pravda,* 21 November 1989, 2.

Kovalev, V., and S. Ryzhov. "Sudebnaia praktika primeneniia zakonodatel'stva o trude (obzor)." *Sovetskaia iustitsiia,* no. 15 (1989): 7–9.

Kozlov, V. D. "Pochemu rabochie ogranichivaiut vyrabotku?" *Sotsiologicheskoe issledovanie,* no. 2 (1990): 50–56.

Krivoi, V. I. "Mesto raboty po sovetskomu trudovomu pravu." *Sovetskoe gosudarstvo i pravo,* no. 11 (1989): 53–61.

Kudriavtsev, V. N., and E. A. Lukasheva. "Sotsialisticheskoe pravovoe gosudarstvo." *Kommunist,* no. 11 (1988): 44–55.

Kulagin, G. "Ob"edinenie, predpriiatie i ministerstvo." *Kommunist,* no. 3 (1966): 82–91.

Laptev, V. V. "Zakon o predpriiatii i kodifikatsiia khoziastvennogo zakonodatel'stva." *Sovetskoe gosudarstvo i pravo,* no. 12 (1987): 67–74.

Livshits, R. Z. *Spravochnik pravovogo inspektora truda.* Moscow: Profizdat, 1979.

———. *Trudovoe zakonodatel'stvo: nastoiashchee i budushchee.* Moscow: Nauka, 1989.

———. "Izmenenie trudovogo dogovora." *Sotsialisticheskii trud,* no. 8 (1988): 55–60.

———. "Pravo i zakon v sotsialisticheskom pravovom gosudarstve." *Sovetskoe gosudarstvo i pravo,* no. 3 (1989): 15–22

———. "Trudovoe zakonodatel'stvo: poisk kontseptsii." *Sovetskoe gosudarstvo i pravo,* no. 7 (1990): 47–56.

———, and N. I. Nikitinskii. "Gde neobkhodimy novye resheniia." *Sotsialisticheskii trud,* no. 3 (1989): 85–101.

———. "Reforma trudovogo zakonodatel'stva: voprosy teorii." *Sotsialisticheskii trud,* no. 1 (1989): 76–89.

Manov, G. N. "Sotsialisticheskoe pravovoe gosudarstvo: problemy i perspektivy," *Sovetskoe gosudarstvo i pravo,* no. 6 (1989): 3–10.

Maslennikov, V. A. "Zakon o trudovykh kollektivakh." *Sovetskoe gosudarstvo i pravo,* no. 12 (1987): 67–74.

Nikitinskii, L. V. "Pravovaia inspektsiia truda: priroda i pravootnoshenie." *Sovetskoe gosudarstvo i pravo,* no. 9 (1980): 125–30.

Nikitinskii, V. I. *Effektivnost' norm trudovogo prava.* Moscow: Iuridicheskaia literatura, 1971.

———. "Pravovye voprosy vysvobozhdeniia izlishnykh rabotnikov." *Sotsialisticheskii trud,* no. 9 (1988): 59–64.

———. "Perestroika fundamenta sistemy zakonodatel'stva o trude." *Sovetskoe gosudarstvo i pravo,* no. 7 (1990): 56–64.

———, and Iu. P. Orlovskii. "Predmet i metod trudovogo prava: izmeneniia v usloviiakh perestroiki." *Sovetskoe gosudarstvo i pravo,* no. 4 (1988): 71–80.

———, and V. Vaipan. "Pravovoe regulirovanie truda v usloviiakh mnogoobraziia form sobstvennosti." *Sotsialisticheskii trud,* no. 1 (1991): 80–88.

Orlo, I., and Kh. Siigur. "Primenenie v sudebnoi praktike zakonodatel'stva, reguliruiushchego trudovoi dogovor." *Sovetskoe pravo,* no. 5 (1988): 333–41.

Orlovskii, Iu. P. "Trudoustroistvo v novykh usloviiakh upravleniia ekonomikoi." *Sotsialisticheskii trud,* no. 1 (1988): 54–60.

Pankin, M. "Novoe v zakonodatel'stve o trude." *Sotsialisticheskii trud,* no. 4 (1988): 64–70.

Pashkov, A. S. "O kontseptsii obnovleniia trudovogo zakonodatel'stva." *Pravovedenie,* no. 2 (1990): 14–25.

Pavlov, A. "Bez soglasiia profkoma." *Sovetskie profsoiuzy,* nos. 1–2 (1990): 56–57.

Petrukhin, I. L. "Pravovoe gosudarstvo i pravosudie." *Sovetskoe gosudarstvo i pravo,* no. 1 (1991): 19–29.

Pleva, V. A. "Perevod na druguiu rabotu pri brigadnoi forme organizatsii truda." *Problemy sotsialisticheskoi zakonnosti,* no. 21 (1988): 67–70.

"Problemy perestroiki zakonodatel'stva o trude." *Sotsialisticheskii trud,* no. 2 (1988): 89–93.

"Problemy ratsional'nogo i ekonomnogo ispol'zovaniia trudovykh resursov" (roundtable). *Sovetskoe gosudarstvo i pravo,* no. 8 (1987): 36–52.

Rylov, V. "Rol' sudebnoi kollegii v povyshenii kachestva rassmotreniia narodnymi sudami trazhdanskikh del." *Sovetskaia iustitsiia,* no. 10 (1990): 11–13.

Shabalina, G. "Spory o vosstanovlenii na rabote (obzor kassatsionnoi i nadzornoi praktiki)." *Sovetskaia iustitsiia,* no. 13 (1990): 19–21.

Shaibekov, K. A. "Pravo sel'skokhoziaistvennogo zemlenopol'zovaniia v SSSR." *Sovetskoe gosudarstvo i pravo,* no. 3 (1977): 50–57.

Shakhov, V. D. "Cootnoshenie poniatii 'trudovoi dogovor' i 'trudovoe pravootnoshenie'." *Sovetskoe gosudarstvo i pravo,* no. 6 (1980): 133–36.

Shcherbakov, V. "Unemployment: Search for Work Abroad" (interview). *Izvestiia,* 13 October 1990. Translated in *BBC Summary of World Broadcasts,* SU/0898, 2 November 1990, A7.

Sheinin, Kh. V. "Rukovodiashchie raz"iasneniia plenuma Verkhovnogo suda SSSR." *Sovetskoe gosudarstvo i pravo,* no. 9 (1980): 70–78.

Shkuro, V. V. "O rasshirenii sudebnoi zashchity trudovykh prav grazhdan." *Sovetskoe gosudarstvo i pravo,* no. 8 (1989): 44–50.

Siigur, Kh. "O trudovom dogovore v usloviiakh intensivnogo razvitiia ekonomiki i polnogo khozrascheta." *Sovetskoe pravo,* no. 4 (1988): 260–62.

Solntsev, M. "Sluzhba trudoustroistva v novykh usloviiakh: Raionnoe zveno." *Sotsialisticheskii trud,* no. 12 (1988): 29–31.

Stavtseva, A. I. "Kommentarii sudebnoi praktiki po trudovym sporam. In *Kommentarii sudebnoi praktiki za 1979 god,* edited by E. V. Voldyreva and A. I. Pergament, 3–35. Moscow: Iuridicheskaia literatura, 1980.

———, and A. K. Gavrilina. "Sudebnaia praktika po trudovym delam." In *Sudebnaia praktika za 1987–88 gg,* 10–35. Moscow: Iuridicheskaia literatura, 1989.

———, and O. S. Khokhriakova. "Sudebnaia praktika po trudovym sporam." In *Kommentarii sudebnoi praktiki za 1984 god,* 3–21. Moscow: Iuridicheskaia literatura, 1985.

Vasil'ev, A. V. "Obshchee sobranie i sovet trudovogo kollektiva: praktika deiatel'nosti i problemy." *Sovetskoe gosudarstvo i pravo,* no. 9 (1989): 59–64.

———. "Sotsial'nye funktsii sovetskikh profsoiuzov i ikh zakonodatel'noe zakreplenie: problemy i resheniia." *Sovetskoe gosudarstvo i pravo,* no. 5 (1990): 86–93.

Volegov, Iu. "Neobkhodimy radikal'nye izmeneniia." *Sotsialisticheskii trud,* no. 8 (1989): 91–96.

Index